More Border Tales

edited by
Bill Gillott & Melanie Lewis

First Issue - 2005

First Edition 2005

Published by
Anchor Print Group Ltd
11 Victoria Street
Syston
Leicester
LE7 2LE

ISBN 0-9549580-0-4

Typeset and Printed by Anchor Print Group Ltd Leicester

FOREWORD

For some years a sequel had been discussed to the now much sought after "Border Tales" compiled by Miss Hester Garnett-Orme, covering the Years 1947 - 1965 of the Southern Border Terrier Club's yearbooks. With the 75th Anniversary of the Southern Border Terrier Club approaching in 2005, what better way to celebrate the anniversary year than to compile this sequel, thereby recording and preserving a permanent record of Border Terriers and their many versatile and varied activities.

As the compilers of this book, at times we were somewhat daunted by the size of the task but, nevertheless, we are both honoured and privileged to be involved in publishing "More Border Tales", the contents of which remain the copyright of the Southern Border Terrier Club, and are articles which have been extracted from the Club Yearbooks covering the period 1966-2000, concluding with an account of Border Terrier 2000, the millennium event, a fitting end to one century and the beginning of another.

Reading through the articles in the Yearbooks was an education and a real pleasure. Thank you to all of the contributors whose efforts are reproduced here and the different magazines for their permission to use the original articles.

Finally, the Southern Border Terrier Club would like to dedicate this book to the memory of Mr R.A. (Bob) Williams (Eignwye) who gave freely of his time to the Club for over half a century.

Bill Gillott and Melanie Lewis

Mr R. A. (Bob) WILLIAMS

I first met Mr Bob Williams back in 1975, when, with my family, I visited his home at Hereford, with a view to purchasing a puppy. A warm welcome awaited us with Bob and his wife Betty. Under his guidance, I selected a puppy, my first show dog, who became Ch Eignwye Wheatear.

From the time we met, we all enjoyed a firm friendship. Bob, who I can only describe as a real "Country Gentleman", was also a very 'gentle man'. He loved his garden, where he nurtured his many plants - it was a sight to behold. He had a very select kennel of Borders, also some Griffons and Yorkshire Terriers. It was with great pride that he showed us his Racing Pigeons, with many a prize bird in his ownership. An English Springer Spaniel, who accompanied him whilst out shooting, completed the Eignwye family.

Bob remained loyal to the Southern Border Terrier Club, serving on the committee for over half a century. He was for many years Chairman of the Club, followed by its President, and at the time of his death, in October 2003, was their Patron.

As a Judge, his services were much sought after, officiating at many of the Breed Club Championship Shows, Crufts and Internationally. A clever and knowledgeable breeder, he owned and/or bred the beautiful Ch Eignwye Enchantress, Ch Eignwye Daletyne Santara, Ch Eignwye Tweed, my own Ch Eignwye Wheatear and Ch Eignwye What's What. The influential stud dog Solway Cawfields Duke also resided at Eignwye. Countless other Borders he bred won top honours and indeed some were the foundation stock for some of our well-known kennels.

Bob had the superb gift of knowing exactly how to present his dogs, always neat in outline, whilst still retaining a very natural tweedy finish to the jacket - a skill that was envied by many of us.

When I was appointed the Secretary of the Southern Border Terrier Club, Bob teasingly told the members at the A.G.M. "She has all the right credentials, and like her predecessor, Mrs Frances Wagstaff, she also obtained her first show Border from me" - almost as though it was a pre-requisite to hold the position of Office!!

Breeders and Judges of Bob's calibre are few and far between, he has played his part in setting a high standard for our breed. May we go forward richer for having enjoyed his friendship and the knowledge he has imparted with us. This book is dedicated to Bob in recognition of his faithfulness and loyalty to the Southern Border Terrier Club - a fitting tribute to one who has given so much to the Club and to the Border Terrier. He is greatly missed.

Melanie Lewis
Hon. Secretary

History of the Foundation of the Southern Border Terrier Club

On going through old records of the club, we find that the Southern Counties Border Terrier Club was founded in 1930. The founder members were A. D. Farmer, Esq., of Thame, Oxon., who died in 1934, and our late chairman, J. J. Pawson, Esq., of Hartley Wintney, Berks., who died in 1965. Twenty-one members were enrolled that summer, and the title was registered with the Kennel Club on October 20th, 1930. After the war the club became, as it is known, "The Southern Border Terrier Club."

Needs of a Terrier

"You want for this country a terrier that can run with hounds, or, better still, that can follow up and run behind hounds - the sort that hunts a cover or darts away on a fox's line is useless. If he can be taught and trained to keep back with the second horseman so much the better. You want one that won't tire, but is forward to come up handy when he's wanted, and will 'go in' right up to the fox below ground and will speak to him before he tries to tackle him. Jock here is great at this, he goes in like a bolt from a bow, and squeezes right up to the beggar without loss of time, and gives him notice to quit. If he can't get right up to him he will lie up and bark till he is hoarse, and this always lets one know where he is, and saves time if digging is required. He has the valuable habit of coming out then, and waiting and watching to see if his orders are going to be obeyed, for nothing makes a fox more likely and more anxious to bolt, if he has anything left in him at all, than, after having been well sworn at, to find his attacking enemy retire in silence. Then, if his orders are not obeyed, Jock goes in again with even more determination. How he manages I don't know. I think he only says and looks, "cut along out of this or I'll murder you !' Anyhow, his threats are nearly always promptly acted on, and the fox, feeling far safer above ground though pursued by the pack, than being niggled at and tormented by a little demon in the darkness below ground, once more faces the daylight and often gives a good chase, thanks to dauntless little Jock."

"Yes," said Bill, "I think it's the most tremendous piece of pluck ever exhibited or possible to dream of. Think of it. To crawl up a long pitch dark tight hole leading into the earth's bowels, and often filled with ice-cold water, and to boldly attack his unseen foe; a foe his equal in weight, possibly superior in power of punishment, equally savage, and most probably occupying a better position for repelling attack than he does. 'Pon my word, it's equal to a man stalking a wounded tiger on foot !"

Hound and Horn in Jedforest by T. Scott Anderson

Mr. Scott Anderson was Master and hunted the Jedforest pack from 1892-1903. The country lies in Roxburghshire and adjoins the countries of the Duke of Buccleuch's, the Border, the College Valley and the Niddesdale, and lies in the heart of the country from which the Border Terrier originated.

Reflections

My visit to Britain was prompted by a desire to meet friends I have corresponded with for a number of years; to meet as many Border Terrier breeders and to see as many dogs as possible. Being somewhat of a sentimentalist, I wanted to start out in the area where the breed originated and to see the rugged beauty of the Border country. This was all accomplished with the help of good friends who gave so generously of their time and their cars to drive me about.

I was really thrilled by the warm reception I received and the days passed all too quickly. The hospitality of the people who allowed me to see their dogs at all odd hours of the day and evening, regardless of convenience, was especially appreciated. In many instances I was able to see parents or close relatives of a number of the dogs that have been exported to America, and this in itself was very interesting. The temptation to visit ancient landmarks and world-famous castles and museums was great, but the purpose of my trip concerned Border Terriers in particular and a fairly straight course was managed with only two sight-seeing tours in Edinburgh and London that did not include Borders.

For some time I have felt concerned after reading the British judges' critiques and the columnists' reports expressing their own and their readers' opinions on the increasing size of exhibits, also frequent mention of the danger of losing the real otter head. Reading at one time that the breed has improved through the years then at another time reading that we are failing on this or that point can be alarming, and I wanted to see for myself.

When one considers that we are fortunate to get ten Borders together for a show, one can imagine how impressed I was to see that many in ONE class at the Northern Border Terrier Club Limited Show at Morpeth and again at the Southern Border Terrier Club Championship Show at W.E.L.K.S. Since five or six of the ones I had the pleasure of seeing at home or in the ring have since completed their championships with others well on the way, it was my privilege to be exposed to top quality in the breed.

In general, I was VERY pleased with the Borders and especially with the bitches, for there did not seem to be the noticeable variation in size as there was in the dogs. In fact, it seemed that with few exceptions, dogs that would come close to the Standard of the breed were in the minority, with the majority of males well up to size. I did not see any 131b. dogs or 11 lb. bitches and wonder if these would not be just too small for today's requirements. I thought the heads were very lovely and am not worried about them and there were no more faults in conformation than one finds in any breed.

It is a difficult question to answer when one is asked how the dogs in America compare to those in Britain. Without Borders having been exported from Britain there wouldn't be any in America and since there are still so few of them (76 individual registrations in 1966), for every good dog one may see in the breed in America, there will be five or six in Britain. We do not have the opportunity to use as many different studs as we might like and in general, our dogs are smaller than many I saw in Britain.

American Borders are a reflection of their British breeding, but whether we go forward or fall backward depends on the way we use the bloodlines that have come to us. It has been our good fortune to work hand in hand with the breeders in Britain and for the American Club to gain much valued information and guidance from the British clubs. It is my belief and conviction that we should continue to work together for the best interest of the breed. Realising that dogs may vary from year to year, depending on the combination of bloodlines, it would seem that both the British and American breeders must consider what is best for the future of the breed, particularly in regard to size, which must not get out of hand.

As I look back on the wonderful weeks spent with Border Terriers and the people who made me feel so much at home, I am positive that no-one could have had a more perfect holiday.

Marjory L. Van der Veer

The Colour Question

Having been asked to write something about the coat colour of the Border, I must admit that the following ideas are purely conjecture gleaned from the experience with my own dogs.

Is it, I wonder, generally realised how utterly complex the question of coat colour is in dogs? Nearly every breed inherits its colour in a different way. In some breeds black is dominant to red and in others it is the reverse. Borders come in the agouti, or speckled range of colours and it seems that there used to be a dilution factor which prevented the solid colours.

We know that Borders, Dandies and Bedlingtons all came from the same strains of rough terriers owned by the tinkers, gipsys and tin-miners who travelled all over the North, and even to Ireland, in the eighteenth century and that these terriers were red, wheaten, liver (yellow) or brindle colours. In the early Kennel Club registrations of Borders various colours are given, red, yellow, dun, brindle, wheaten, saddle back and even "mouse" colour! Why is it then that the show Borders of today seem to be becoming a uniform grizzle colour, and the real old saddle backs have become black and tan?

It seems a great pity that all the various old colours should be allowed to die out. Possibly the colours given in the standard of the breed are not explicit enough, or, again, we may have lost some colours because the judges at shows don't like the pale colours ; they don't "catch the eye" and so people started to breed from "nice rich colours." It is also said that the grizzles have tidy coats and don't need much attention, but there seems to be no connection in the genetic inheritance of colour and length of coat. Is it not more likely that people just happened to get a few good coated grizzles which appealed to the judges and so with inter-breeding this colour has become general?

I have had some very light wheatens with excellent skin and short, hard coats. One of my first was a half-sister to Ch. Jedworth Bunty, and both were light coloured with dark ears and eyes and had the best of coats. This bitch's puppies were all light coloured - two had liver noses and I think would probably be called "mouse" colour in the old days. They never had any brindle puppies and were very hard and game. Another light red I had threw the real old saddle backs - dark saddle and wheaten legs - not the tan we get today. These all had grey or silver hairs in the dark saddle. There were also one or two real brindles about, almost striped with dark bands on a red coat, giving a most peculiar effect.

I think many working terriers in the North are still of a nice clear red colour and some huntsmen prefer the blue and tans - or saddle backs, which is a better description of the colour - I have one now which is a clear wheaten and her skin and coat are particularly good. Her sire is a Devon Hunt terrier. Unfortunately her mouth is wrong, so she should not be bred from.

So far as I know no authentic attempt has been made to determine the mode of inheritance of colour in Borders, Bedlingtons or Dandies and so I will very tentatively give my ideas. I think that our old light colours must carry a dilution factor for red and black, possibly the same as that which appears in the old liver coloured Bedlington (which also had liver coloured noses) and that by allowing these light colours to die out we are losing the factor and are allowing the black hairs to become dominant. Blue and tan to blue and tan matings carried on for several generations will become more and more dark until they are really black and tan with black predominating. If some clear light reds or wheatens were bred together for a few generations and then mated to a blue and tan of the old type we might, I think, get back some of the old colours.

It would be amusing to show a "mousey" one with a liver nose, which our standard says "is not a serious fault" and call it a "new colour.' Such a one might breed some very attractive colours.

by Hester Garnett-Orme

Tree-climbing Terriers

While walking recently, with two of my Border Terriers, they struck a line on the path and dashed into a thick patch of brambles and bracken, in the centre of which stood a thorn tree, about 14ft. high and very dense.

A furious hunt ensued round and round the thick patch, until I saw a black animal with a tail climbing the main stem of the thorn. Thinking it was a cat, and having an intense dislike of the terriers chasing and killing one of them, I waded into the undergrowth to try and get them away.

To my astonishment the "cat" was the blue Border, climbing the tree, while her daughter, already *in* the top-most branches, was yelping furiously at a grey squirrel, which had taken refuge in a neighbouring and taller tree.

The younger bitch eventually half scrambled and half fell to the ground of her own accord; but I had a difficult job to rescue her poor old mother, who was stuck in the tree-top, afraid to move in any direction.

I would be interested to know if any of your readers have had a similar experience with dogs?

Dorothy Clarke (Mrs.)
"Horse and Hound"

Some Dogs of my Life

I have been asked to write something! The subject must be dogs. I can only write of my own. Strange as it may seem, I became the very proud owner of a Spaniel - a very small liver coloured bitch called Bill when I was 8 or 9 years old.

When I left school my father gave me a Terrier called Dick. He came from Hunt Kennels and was nearer the true type of Parson Jack Russell's terrier than any that flourish under his name today, he was well up on the leg, broken coated and a bit bigger than the average Border. He was game and tough and went to ground, he used to get up a drain, I suppose it was 8 or 9 inches and quite long and always got out with the greatest of ease. He died at Christmas 1933 aged about 14. I had, over the years, known several Borders and decided to have one. I got him from some Hunt Kennels, he was born in September 1933 and 6 months old. He was by Ch. Dinger and was red wheaten. I registered him as Mischievous Mike. He was said to have been to ground with his dam - he was much too young. He caught a few rabbits and rats, and would sit patiently at a rat hole all day. I once showed him at an A.V. Show and he was placed 3rd in Maiden in a big class which thrilled me! He got ill in the Autumn of 1938, and after 7 weeks struggle, died at Christmas! I am fairly certain he had "Hard Pad", then hardly known.

I always wanted to breed dogs, but met with parental disapproval. I decided to ride over it. Since then I have had quite a few and bred quite a lot, but will only dwell on the few outstanding characters. I bought a dog pup from the late Mrs. Lawrie, he was by Ch. Wedale Jock and red. I registered him "Buster Brown." I had a bitch from Mrs. Mulcaster "Portholme Beatrice" (Sally) also red. Then the war started. We had an old Labrador bitch, retired for some seasons owing to my father giving up shooting owing to ill health. She and my two Borders caught on average three rabbits a week! Buster was also a ratter and much in demand at thrashing time. I bred two or three litters during the war, one accidental as somebody left a door open and Buster got out!

I kept a bitch pup, she turned out the smallest Border I've ever seen - "Coundon Bridget." She was a great character; she used to go to ground and drew rabbits nearly as big as herself. She loved to ride in my bicycle basket and had all the shopping stuffed around, under and on top of her, just a little face popping out. She died rather tragically at four years old in 1946 an awful loss.

I then bought "Coundon Stella" from Mrs. Mulcaster in 1947. I mated her to Deerstone Dauntless and she had six pups. I kept one, Minnie of Coundon, she was well known as I showed her a lot. She was a character and very game, but no use as a brood bitch; she lived to be nearly 15.

I bought "Ravensdowne Roxena" (Zoe) bred by Miss Fair, from Mrs. Twist, she was six months old and Mrs. Twist had only had her for four months, yet Zoe has never forgotten her. She usually sees her once a year at the Club Show at Boddington and chatters and sings to her, and in 1966 she won the Veterans class, handled by Mrs.

Twist. Now Zoe is "The goose that laid the golden eggs". So many good ones go back to her today, including Hanleycastle Russ and Farmway Red Robin. By Ch. Billy Boy she had Ch Winstonhall Coundon Tim and my Ch. Coundon Trudy out of one litter.

I have always been two minded about dew claws and the Tim/Trudy litter were left on. She is a terrific hunter and digger, and will tackle anything. She has never torn a claw, they are small and neatly set close to her "wrists." The nails never get overgrown. I see her use them to clean herself. They also serve as tooth picks when she gets gummed up with soil. She is a great character and always loved the younger pups Zoe had and looked after them better than Zoe; if they fought she parted them and scolded them! But when "Troena" her daughter had her first family, she was bitterly offended and would have nothing to do with her or the pups for seven weeks. When they were playing in the winter sunshine, Trudy sat with her back to them and I knew she was longing to "give in." She suddenly went up to Troena, got her by the scruff and much to my joy they started to play. Troena, who was obviously hurt by Trudy's offhandedness, was overjoyed and they madly raced round and round the garden. Then Trudy turned her attention to her grandchildren and from then on took over complete management of them - so all was well.

The dogs are allowed to sit on the sofa which is covered with a big dog blanket. Trudy has her corner. One evening recently Troena was on the sofa and Trudy on the floor started barking and looked towards the window. Troena looked puzzled, and as she always copies Trudy, started to bark too. It was pouring with rain and I could not imagine that there was anyone in the garden. Trudy then went to the garden door and barked, this got Troena off the sofa. Trudy quickly jumped on, made her little mark in her corner and settled down for the evening. Troena had not been in her corner, but was in the way, so she was lured off by a ruse! Who says dogs can't reason?

E. A. Turrall

Wynalone Border Terriers

I suppose I am one of the oldest Border Terrier breeders, as I had my first Border Terrier at the end of the First World War, and have never been without them since that time.

In those days my interest was in the working side rather than show. I did all the breeding and training of the terriers for the Cambridgeshire Hunt.

I had a strong team of old-fashioned smooth fox terriers and one day Mr. Mayor, of Cambridge, asked me if I would take two of his Borders and get them entered to ground so that he could show in the working classes. They were two of the best - game and keen to work. I soon got working certificates for them from the Master, Mr. Douglas Croesman, and that is how I got my first Border pup. Mr. Mayor gave me a little three-months-old bitch, Piddy, and she practically lived in my pocket and always slept on my bed. She never left me and when old enough enjoyed hunting as much as I did and ran all day with me. One day she bolted four foxes out of a long drain. I did not keep count of the many foxes and otters she bolted, but if an earth or drain held she lost no time in bolting it.

When the cubbing season ended and I rode, Piddy was carried in the bag by the second horseman. She was always in great demand for fox or other hunting because she never wasted time and was always ready to go.

When the Second World War broke out I was down in the Gloucestershire country and Col. Turner, the Master, always sent for her to bolt foxes. She was 11 years old then and still so game, poor little lady. They put her to ground to bolt a fox, but there was a badger there and my Piddy was killed. I have never worked another since that day; but I have kept my interest in these game little terriers, breeding an odd litter and showing occasionally (not very successfully!), but I enjoy the show, seeing the terriers and meeting their sporting owners. I am now reduced to two old bitches and one puppy that I hope to show in 1968.

M. M. Comerford

Border Terriers in Holland

It seems already a long time ago that I started with my first Border Terrier bitch, "Urtica's Letty," a daughter from Raisgill Rego x Glenluffin Red Queen, the only two Borders here in Holland, imported by Mrs. Langhout. I was very enthusiastic about her, especially about her temperament; always active, playing with the tennis ball, friendly with people and children. But I had to be careful when she was too eager to take away something another Cocker bitch already had, it was a fight.She was a very good mother. I once had two litters, one from Letty and one from Dinah, our black Cocker Spaniel. I had to let Dinah out for 5 minutes and when I returned to let her in Letty was sitting between the Cocker puppies and acting as if they were her puppies. She simply jumped over the underdoor into the nursery. I believe she preferred to have all the Cocker and Border babies together in her box. I imported for her a very good Border dog, and English champion, Golden Imperialist, from Mr. Leatt ("Sandy" reached the age of 14 years) and this couple gave me four litters. I made Golden Imperialist an Int. Champ. and between his daughters, three became champions. We bought another English Champion, Braw Boy ("Macky") and made him an Int. Champ. too. From this son of Ch. Billy Boy I bred only one litter with my Ch. Tassel's Red Queen.

Macky was a very attractive Border and I was very sad when I lost him after two years through a kidney disease. As at first I did not take his illness too serious, I sold all the puppies from that litter and am lucky to have a granddaughter from him now; a young bitch from Braw Boy's daughter and Winstonhall Dunkie. But returning to Braw Boy, when he died I needed another dog for the bitches of Golden Imperialist, and as we loved Braw Boy's type and temperament, I decided to take a Billy Boy line. I saw in Our Dogs the winning dog in those days, Ch. Winstonhall Coundon

Tim, was a son of Billy Boy, and I wrote to Miss Long. She had two litters and I bought three young dogs of 10 weeks old. Two of them went undershot, and I was happy that "Dunkie," the best in type, had a good mouth. So I decided to keep him and he really is a very good stud dog; he inherits his type, his red colour and gave us several typical Borders. I even mated him with good success to some of his daughters. But as I wanted some new blood I went with Tassel's Red Ginny (W. Dunkie x T. Red. Queen) to an English imported dog in Germany Ch. Tedhars Traveller (Knavesmire Kopper x Harranby Radar) from Herr H. Wohl. This mating gave me one bitch and one dog and you already guess what will happen? I am keeping this dog, who now is one year, and I have every hope that I will breed good typical Borders from him.

In the meantime friends of mine in Belgium imported a good dog from Mr. Hall, "Deerstone Decisive," so if necessary I can go to Belgium for a mating as I have two dogs now.

We are not using our Borders for work, as some people in England love to. They have to be companions and some people like them because they are so active, friendly with people and not yet "overbred" as some terrier breeds are nowadays. Most of our Borders are at their best outside in the country, and they are doing very well with our Spaniels, maybe as both breeds love hunting. They are ideal for sportsmanlike people.

A H Wetzel de Raad

Are Show Winners Too In-bred?

From time to time, suggestions have been made that the more successful show dogs were "too in-bred." This belief has been voiced on and off for many years, but it appears to be becoming increasingly widely held, especially among people who have never made a study of the facts.

To consider this proposition, which has been presented as a serious charge against show dogs, and particularly against big winners at leading shows, we must first determine what "in-breeding" means.

The term has a specific biological meaning, but is not well defined in the majority of lay dictionaries. Originally, it was probably an abbreviation of the more explicit term "incest breeding," which offended Victorian susceptibilities.

The different systems of breeding pedigree animals are concisely set out in Professor Crew's well known work, *Animal Genetics-An Introduction to the Science of Animal Breeding,* on page 273, where he states: "In in-breeding, the closest types of breeding possible are practised, sire to daughter, dam to son, brother to sister; in line breeding, the matings are between individuals within one line of descent, excluding those which constitute in-breeding." On later pages, Professor Crew makes it clear that line breeding involves repeated matings within the same family. He defines what he calls "out-breeding" as "that system of mating in which the individuals concerned are unrelated." An out-bred dog is often referred to as an outcross.

Professor Crew and other geneticists agree in emphasising the harm that can come from in-breeding among unsuitable animals. He stresses the absolute necessity of "vigorous selection" among the offspring of closely related parents.

There can be no doubt that at the beginning of this century (and earlier) in-breeding as defined by Professor Crew was widely practised. Most of our breeds of dogs - and many of our farm animals - were created in this way, and amazing examples of the degree of pre-potency achieved by very close in-breeding have been preserved.

It is important to realise that in-breeding as defined above is seldom practised today. It cannot be said that no dog breeders ever practise in-breeding, but the facts show that the majority of the successful ones do not do so. The winners at modern dog shows are generally not in-bred or even line bred with Professor Crew's definitions. I believe it is most important to all concerned that these facts should be recognised.

If misleading propaganda had the effect of persuading less experienced breeders that in-breeding alone was the secret of success in the show ring, there is a real danger that these less experienced breeders might tend to mate closely-related dogs in the hope of finding a short cut to success. This would be a retrograde step from every point of view. Only the most experienced breeders are qualified to make the strict selection necessary when choosing parents for close breeding, and novice breeders would hardly be able to identify the less-sound puppies which would certainly result from close breeding with unsuitable parents.

If unsound puppies, bred on these lines were passed on to the public, this could only result in dissatisfaction, as their unsoundness became more evident, in misery for the unfortunate puppies concerned and in complaints about pedigree dogs.

It is important, therefore, to ascertain to what extent it is true that leading show winners are in-bred; when the first attack of Cruft's winners was made three years ago in a leading Sunday paper, I had a random sample of the principal winners checked, to see whether or not they were in-bred or line bred as defined at the beginning of this article. Ironically, the only principal winner who came near the definition of in-breeding or line breeding was not exhibited in the show classes but was among the Obedience Champions.

To give a complete picture I have now studied the three-generation pedigree of every group winner at the last three Cruft's Shows. In 1965, there were five group winners, of which four were complete out-crosses; no name appeared twice among the fourteen ancestors shown in the three-generation pedigree. The fifth had one name who appeared twice - his paternal grandmother had the same sire as his maternal grandmother. This cannot be described as in-breeding in any sense of the word, and is not even line breeding within the meaning of Professor Crew's definition as developed in his subsequent paragraphs on the subject.

In 1966 there were six group winners of which, again, four were bred from completely unrelated parents, as defined above. Of the other two, one had a great-grandfather on his sire's side who also appeared as a great-grandfather on his dam's side. The sixth was the only group winner in any of the three years which came within Professor Crew's definition of line breeding as explained in his book. It was not within his definition of in-breeding, but none the less this one group winner was closely bred as opposed to all the other winners of groups.

In the 1967 show, of the six group winners, four again were complete out-crosses, with no name appearing twice on a three-generation pedigree; of the other two, one had a paternal grandmother who also appeared as a maternal grandmother. The sixth, which was bred in Canada, had two great-grandparents each of whom appeared on both sides of the pedigree.

One of the group winners in 1966, an out-cross, was also a group winner and Best in Show in 1967, so that the total number of dogs who won groups in the three years were sixteen. Of these, one was within Professor Crew's definition of line breeding, four were bred from parents who were cousins, going back to the fourth generation, and eleven were absolute and complete outcrosses. There was not one case of in-breeding.

So much for the more successful dogs shown at Cruft's in the last three years. These dogs won Best in Show awards up and down the country, and I have no doubt that examination of the pedigrees of other leading winners would show a similar result.

I appreciate that mere facts will never overcome prejudice and that ill-informed critics will never cease to decry show dogs as "in-bred," often without having any knowledge either of the meaning of the term "in-bred" or of the pedigrees of the dogs concerned. In my view, it is just as impossible to tell whether or not a dog is in-bred by examining him without having seen his pedigree, as it is to tell whether a stud dog would suit your favourite bitch by examining his pedigree without having seen the dog in the flesh.

> *"You know his outward appearance, very true; but that is a minor point, after all. It is character that is all important, in dogs as in men."*
>
> Alexandre Dumas

By Colonel Sir Richard Glyn, Bart., OBE, TD, DL, MP.

Reprinted by kind permission of the author and of the Editor of the Kennel Gazette.

On Keilder-side the wind blaws wide;
There sounds nae hunting horn
That rings sae sweet as the winds that beat
Round banks where Tyne is born.

From Jacobite's Exile - A. C. Swinburne

Why No Book For Judges?

In reply to Mrs. F. Marchant's article in Dog World, February 14, 1969, headed "Why no book to instruct judges?

If Mrs. Marchant or any novice person wishes to become a canine judge, they cannot learn from a book; in fact, such a book would be too difficult to write. Breeds and movement vary greatly.

First and foremost one must have an eye for the work and a great love of dogs. The first step he or she must take is to read all breed standards carefully, not once, but many times. Then go to all types of shows, pick out the breeds you are interested in and watch an experienced judge. Quite often well known all rounder judges refresh their memory by reading the standards of the breeds they are to judge.

Make notes on each dog while it is being examined, and mark how you would place them. Make a note how the judge places each one. If a judge has not too many breeds to go over that day, tell the judge when he has completed the breed you are interested in, that you are a novice wishing to learn, and ask him or her why he placed his winners in that order. Most judges will be willing to spare you a few minutes of their time. If it's terriers you are interested in, then watch all types of terriers, and the same for other groups.

Some societies run Novice Judging Competitions. Enquire if there is one in your area.

B. S. T. Holmes

Henry has a brush with the vicar

... and so a Special Award joins the Terrier Show Rosettes on the wall

The last of the working terrier shows was approaching, and my refusal to include my dog Henry in my team for the final contest had evoked severe criticism from the family.

Earlier in the summer I had shown Henry once, but his total anti-social behaviour on this occasion had precluded him from further competition. Incidentally, it had also resulted in his becoming the subject of a paternity order filed by the owner on behalf of a bull terrier bitch which had been entered in the comic-dog section of that particular show.

Actually Henry is a good sort of working terrier, but one who believes in living his life to the full. However, when a letter appeared in "Horse and Hound" from Mr. Vernon Bartlett setting out a questionnaire regarding the type of terrier required by the late Parson Jack Russell, it was forcibly pointed out to me that Henry physically scored 10 out of 10.

WHAT'S ONE WILD OAT?

"Why let personal prejudice intrude? Why should Henry's one wild oat blot his showing career? Why ....? etc., etc." These were the questions I had to contend with.

I omitted to disclose that Henry's one wild oat had resulted in a rich harvest of four and a half couple of the oddest-looking puppies, but I was out-numbered and finally agreed that he should travel with the team. There was also a lucky let out in the schedule.

Following the show there was terrier racing and I figured that Henry would be far better suited to the rough-and-tumble of the racecourse than the dressage of the show ring. This, in the words of the pop groups, was Henry's scene.

So, collecting the dog from the airing cupboard, where he had been drying out after a morning's water-rat hunting, I loaded him in the Land Rover with the bitches Spice, Spick and Sting and set off on our way to the show.

The Tober Tor Working Terrier Show and Races were run on behalf of the vicar, who needed a new roof for his church, and as I arrived there was every indication that the response had been excellent. For the first time, however, I was unable to raise much enthusiasm for the showing classes, throughout which I was picturing myself in the winner's enclosure with Henry later in the afternoon.

SOME CHAMPION.

Impatiently I watched the championship being awarded to a terrier which I knew had never been deeper below ground than the bedclothes, and then hurried to the car to collect my runner.

Henry was just finishing the last of my sandwiches and looked in no condition to walk, let alone race, and the dreadful thought crossed my mind that I might be warned off for entering a non-trier. But then I remembered that he was pretty fit, having been excercised with the hunters prior to cubhunting, and with any luck he might be sick before his race.

Now terrier racing in the far west is still in its infancy - effective but a little primitive. The terriers are boxed in a set of traps the front of which is opened by pulling a lever. The quarry is a set of foxes' brushes fastened to a nylon cord which is wound up on a tyreless rim attached to the spinner of a tractor some 100 yards away.

The start is in two phases. The official shouts "Take it away, Bert," whereupon the tractor driver engages his gear, followed by "Let 'em go, Fred," and terriers are released. If all goes well the brushes are propelled tractorwards, finally disappearing beneath a tarpaulin.

Henry and I watched the first two races from the sidelines, and I was delighted to see he was showing an intelligent interest in the proceedings, straining at his lead to be off, and when his turn came he entered the traps like an old stager.

Before each race the brushes are waved in front of the traps whilst the owners exhort their terriers to produce their best. I must admit that my "Hitch 'im, Henry" sounded a bit weak compared to the other blood-curdling inducements, but I was encouraged by the glint in the dog's eye which seemed to say, "I'll hitch something, don't you worry."

Bert then took it away and Fred let 'em go. What followed is a little vague.

The Vicar, who was a bit deaf, had not heard the instructions to Bert and Fred. Viewing a possible purchaser for one of his raffle tickets on the opposite side of the track, he had crossed to collect from his victim right in front of the flying brushes, catching up the cord in his trouser leg. Fortunately the string snapped, but not before it had grassed the Vicar, leaving him attached to the brushes like a fallen Davy Crockett.

FLYING START.

Meanwhile my favourite was away to a flier and pulling away from his competitors he arrived at the check several lengths clear.

Now a fox with a brush or a Vicar with a brush are all the same to Henry, so he promptly laid hold of his quarry. The parson, realising the significance of his attachment, attempted to sit on it, whereupon Henry, who had now been joined by his companions, set about removing the obstruction.

All at once the track became a seething mass of terriers, brushes and clergy. "Never seen terriers break up a pair of trousers like it," commented one wag, as one by one we retrieved our charges. Henry, I was horrified to see, had a piece of holy shirt in his mouth.

I must say the Vicar took it all in excellent part; neither was he the loser by this impromptu cabaret. We all had a whip round, raffle ticket sales doubled and the bowler who had won the pig put it up for auction.

The proceeds must have been considerable and will, I hope, go a long way towards restoring not only the top half of the church but the lower half of its incumbent.

As I write, I have before me a few cups and rosettes to indicate a fairly successful working terrier show season. Amongst the rosettes pinned on the wall I have been unable to resist the temptation to include a small piece of the tail of a shirt.

Anon

(Reprinted by permission from "Horse and Hound," March 7th, 1969).

Memories

My dearest memories of dogs happen to be of Border Terriers. At 16 years of age my father had Wire Fox Terriers and he said that my education on dogs needed more than he could give me; so to that great "pro" I was sent. I refer to Hilderbrand H. Wilson.

I had not been long with "H.H." when I was sent to the station to collect a "strange terrier," it being sent on from a Mr. Johnson, to trim and handle at C.C. Shows. When I saw my charge I could not think this was to be shown. I only had Airedale, Irish and Fox Terrier coats to handle, but this was a "Border Terrier" - my first Border charge. A few weeks passed and having watched H.H. trim a Border, I soon had my eye, and the first show was close by (I refer to Leeds C.C. for dogs, and the Flower Show, in Roundhay Park). We arrived at the show in real old English sunshine (not the wet stuff we get now) with two Airedales, two Irish, two Smooth Fox and one Wire, and with "It" my Border, which I had grown to love so much. The show went on, and the "boss" came to me and said in his Yorkshire, "Tha'll have to show t' Border." He was to be busy in another ring and his order was you do - or. In I went, rather hot under the collar, with my Border. The judge, Harry Calvert, of "Trevlac" Wire Fox Terrier fame. My charge was brought out with a few more and the rest sent out by this time. I was hot, but hotter still when the judge gave me 1st and C.C. My mind stood still at this, my first C.C. with a Border Terrier. But I soon came to when "H.H." congratulated me on my win and good handling. The name of that dog was "Gay Fine," and he won quite a few C.Cs. before being sold to a Mrs. Rimmer.

We had a few Border Terriers from Mr. Johnson, the owner of "Gay Fine." The next I handled was "Ch.What Fettle," and I say now, if this dog was here today he would still win, he was so good.

But my most treasured memory of a Border is when I bought one for 3d.-yes, a silver 3d. piece; but he won 1 C.C. and 2 Res. C.Cs. (Some price - some dog).

Thompson Coates

Pleasing Results

I have been a great admirer of the Border Terrier for several years now, and in the course of attending many of the larger shows, it has been a pleasure to meet various owners who all seem to have a genuine interest in the breed as a whole.

I had often considered owning a Border but the general impression that I had gathered, was that they were a slow terrier to enter to fox, and when they did enter they were inclined to be rather hard.

The type of terrier that I have always used for work are the now commonly known Jack Russell Terriers, a game sort of terrier that have given me a great deal of satisfaction

In my enthusiasm to go to Border Shows, however, I decided to buy myself a Border, at least I would have an added interest in the terrier world. I approached Mr. Arthur Duxbury and agreed to buy an adult bitch from him. Some weeks later I had her mated to Arthur's fine dog, Ch. Ribbleside Falcliff Trident. I was very pleased indeed with the resulting litter, and my wife and I noticed in the first few weeks the wide comparison of rearing the seemingly sober Border pups, to the more erratic Jack Russells.

Two of the pups are at present doing very well in their respective hunt kennels, and the two that I kept back for myself are also doing well.

Although I hadn't really bothered to try and work the mother (Ribbleside Blue Haze), I let her come with me whenever I went hunting. She was very interested in the first fox that she came in contact with, but was inclined to worry more about the spade flying around her than the fox. After assuring herself that the noise behind her wasn't harmful she entered the earth. I didn't see her again for three hours, and when I had dug up to her, she was firmly locked to the mask of the fox, after this she went to several more foxes before the season's end. Apart from giving her vocal encouragement she proved to be quite a sensible sort who could work an earth unaided.

Out of the two terriers I kept back for myself, the bitch (Deadlock Dust) hasn't shown any immediate interest, but she has got plenty of time to do so. The dog (Deadlock Fox Flint), however, has been going to ground since he was 10 months old and is fast becoming a hard but very efficient working terrier, and I very much hope to show them this year.

I also had a bitch off Mr. Frank Jackson (Clipstone Penny Plain). Again this bitch proved quite easy for me to enter to fox, and was working for me very well indeed at 13 months of age. On another occasion I invited Frank and Jean Jackson to come up to the "Tickham" and if it were possible to bring an unentered dog with them, I would try and enter it to fox for them.

Jean decided to give "Clipstone Barleycorn" (Gem) a chance to work, a chance that she eventually enjoyed very much.

I encouraged Gem to enter an old drain that contained a fox, she entered the drain with extreme caution, not really appreciating what was in store for her. She didn't go up to her fox right away, and I asked Frank to call her out, and I would put a reliable terrier in to show her what was required. I chose for this job a Jack Russell dog that is an excellent worker, and has a wonderful temperament with other terriers. I put Revel in the drain and he lost no time in getting up to the fox and started speaking in his usual deep voice. Gem wasn't long following him in, and after a few minutes she was also speaking to the fox. I called Revel out after a time and tried Gem on her own. She was really keen by now, and went up to her fox, speaking repeatedly. After a while I let Flint into the drain. When it was convenient for us to get near the terriers we found them side by side and doing very well together, until the fox was dealt with.

I then suggested to Frank that we should try her in a natural earth. I let Flint go into an occupied earth with Gem close on his heels, both terriers were working their quarry very well. When we had nearly got to the fox, Flint took a hold of him. Gem also moved in for a hold and seized the fox by the mask; it was at this stage that we considered that enough had been learned by Gem, and we stepped in while she was still very very keen and pulled the terriers away.

The bitch had received one or two minor wounds which were negligible. Both Frank and Jean were pleased with Gem's performance, a feeling that is very understandable really.

Four of these terriers mentioned went to ground to fox virtually right away, and two of these were very young indeed to show such sensible ability and to work their foxes without taking any unnecessary punishment. A tribute indeed to the working instincts of the Border Terrier, and more than enough proof to convince me that they are a worthy terrier to have in any hunt kennels.

E. Bannister ("Terrierman")

What kind of dog is that?

We sit proudly by the travelling cages, displaying what we feel to be the grandest dogs in the whole world, the Border Terrier. Within half an hour a small group usually appear with index finger pointed towards "Deerstone Dent" or "Buckhurst Lark," asking that classic question.

We had been close to the Border Terrier for many years in England, emigrating to Canada in 1956, it was not until 1967 that we felt we were in a position to do what we really had in mind, that was to help popularise the breed in Canada, so we imported "Deerstone Dent" from Mr. Hall, in Yorkshire. He has turned out to be a fine stud dog.

The Border is not well represented at the shows over here, there are so few of them in the country, so we feel we have quite a selling job on our hands, so when these aforementioned groups approach we are highly delighted to explain how and where the Border Terrier was developed, how it has changed so little over the years, its conformation, temperament, and working qualities, plus all other pertinent details.

We have encountered many humorous situations caused by the lack of knowledge of the Border, one good one comes to mind. As members of an obedience club, we meet each week to train our dogs and for many weeks a certain lady with her standard poodle would go to great lengths to ensure that she was not adjacent to my wife and Dent who was being trained at that time. This seemed quite an odd attitude to take but it was dismissed by us as a possible snobbish quirk. Later we had occasion to take the Kennel Club Certificate down to our Club stating that Dent was now a champion. On seeing this, this particular lady must have felt some remorse as she approached to say "I always thought he was a little mongrel" and this accounted for the fact that she always liked to keep at a distance. In the two years that we have been showing we have noticed with great pleasure that more interest seems to be developing for the Border and we hope to play our small part in producing some show quality puppies from time to time. 1969 has been a good year for us, we successfully campaigned Dent and Lark making them both champions. Dent also got his C.D. in obedience and is working on his open. Lark at present is being trained for her C.D.

We successfully applied for and got our kennel name "Redrob", which we feel is a nice twist to Border. We travelled to many shows and met hundreds of nice people, but I think the highlight of our year was our invitation to show at the Border Terrier Club of America's Speciality Show, in Connecticut; we travelled 1,250 miles that weekend and had a wonderful time; we brought home some ribbons, too. The other big event was our first litter, five lovely puppies on August 1st, two dogs and three bitches. All gone to grand homes.

Arthur Bowers

Otter Hunting in 1864

Otter-hunting assumed quite a new phase on the Teviot last Thursday as the meet with Dr. Grant's rare little pack was attended by no less than seventy-six mounted sportsmen, and but for the difficulty of hiring horses the numbers would have been swelled to a hundred. The meet was at half-past three, and the river was so low that the master, on his chestnut "Robin" and in his Garibaldi shirt, hunted his hounds nearly all the time in the centre of the stream. In addition to the horsemen there were upwards of 200 of the Hawick weavers, &c., with whom this is a peculiarly favourite sport.

The drag of the first otter was hit on almost immediately, but he escaped into a large covered drain, from which there was no chance of dislodging him. A second otter, which had not completed its night's fishing, was found soon after, and tallyhoed amid great excitement over the weir. Ringwood was swimming the drag up the pool in such a masterly manner that the master, than whom no fairer hunter exists, declined to lift them and leave the old dog; and the otter, being headed by the footpeople, took to the country, and made a ring through several fields of oats and up a glen. The hounds pressed him so hard that he did not stay long in the river when he reached it again and, taking to the open once more, he gained the Rule River by a short cut, and so to ground on a perfectly hopeless fastness after a very grand burst.

Another drag was touched upon, but the sun came out very warm after nine o'clock, and nothing more could be done. It was a very memorable scene, and one which the old, conventional otter-hunters could hardly realise. "Sandy," the noted little Carlisle huntsman, was there in his scarlet cap and with his brass-tipped pole, and rendered great service. The rivers are dreadfully low, and the otters have made such a complete exodus to the lochs that the Ale on the following day was drawn blank - (July 23 rd, 1864).

Anon

Badgers

I was exercising my Border Terriers one evening last summer just before dusk along the side of a forestry. Suddenly I heard them giving tongue and, looking in that direction, I saw two of my Borders attacking a large badger which had obviously been caught out on top on his evening prowl. My two Borders were quickly joined by the other two and all four proceeded to engage in a running fight with this badger.

Being more than pre-occupied dealing with the attacks of my Borders, I was able to stand up close and witness this brawl. At one stage the badger had all four Borders hanging on to him, but gradually, by administering punishment to each of the Borders in turn, he edged his way back to his sett and retreated down it whilst I held up my terriers with the aid of a thumb stick and suitable rating.

This was the second occasion my Borders have had this experience and both times the badger escaped with nothing worse than a few bites and, presumably, bruises. The Borders stuck gamely to their quarry, but were unable to inflict much punishment and all suffered a fair share of wounds inflicted by the badgers.

Having seen the Essex Foxhounds once mob a badger, which eventually shook itself and wandered off apparently unscathed, I am convinced that a terrier is unlikely to be able to kill a badger on its own unaided.

Major D. T. Ide-Smith

MISS GARNETT-ORME

Hester Garnett-Orme with her Borders
taken by Dr. and Mrs. Pough while on a visit from U.S.A. in 1970.

I have been asked to write an appreciation on behalf of the Club with regard to the late Miss Hester Garnett-Orme.

Miss Orme became President in 1949 after being a member since 1935. For many years she collaborated with Mrs. Twist, Mrs. Symon and Miss Eccles in producing the Year Books. In 1953 Miss Orme published "Border Terrier Champions and Challenge Certificate Winners." This was really an important booklet as it contained all names appearing in a four generation pedigree, arranged alphabetically. It had entailed a great amount of work and was of tremendous use to people who were interested in breeding to blood lines. Another publication "Border Tales" appeared in 1967, mainly compiled from articles from past Year Books 1947-65.

Miss Orme was born in Northamptonshire on August 21st 1905 and her home was at Tam House, near Skipton, until her father left there about 1923. Her father still retained Greenfield Buckden, near Skipton until his death in 1957 and Miss Orme spent part of the summer there each year. When we became friends she usually visited us when at Buckden and I remember a very pleasant evening spent at Greenfield along with her brother and his wife. She was a great help to me in my breeding operations with advice on blood lines and particulars of dogs appearing in old pedigrees. I purchased a four months' pup "Raisgill Radella of Deerstone" which became our house pet and the dam of "Ch. Deerstone Destiny" and "Ch. Deerstone Desirable". Miss Orme first started breeding Borders while living at Hill Lodge, Pangbourne, Berkshire, about 1934 and had quite a large kennel up to the war. During the war she continued with a few dogs to keep her strain going and kept breeding from her own dogs until her death on June 20th 1971. Amongst the winners she bred, perhaps "Ch. Swallowfield Shindy" was the best known. She had always been interested in the working side of the breed and during the latter part of her life concentrated on this and research on the breed. During the war she owned "Ch. What Fettle" and she sent him along with "Raisgill Rasta" for me to show for her at one of the big Skipton shows. "Rasta" won a first and "What Fettle" was best of breed, the judge being Mr. James Garrow. "What Fettle" was then 7 years of age and a great dog of character. Miss Orme, although of a quiet disposition, showed quite a sense of humour with her friends and I valued her help and friendship very highly. She was always ready to assist anyone with advice on breeding problems and will be long remembered with respect and affection by so many of us - the Club has lost a good friend.

Robert Hall

Direction for Show Preparation

The following Directions for Show Preparation have been laid down by Annual General Meetings of the Southern Border Terrier Club:-

"Exhibitors and judges should be reminded that it is not in keeping with the sporting traditions of the breed to have the coat trimmed, or to have the head and tail supported by the handler in the ring. Borders should be shown on a loose lead.

The coat should be of a natural weather-resisting character; old, dead coat may be stripped off by hand when necessary." The use of a razor, or strip comb embodying a razor in the preparation of dogs for show is strongly objected to."

A Day's Work

I have a Border Terrier dog, 15 months old, bred by Miss Eccles at Monxton, which I am fortunate in being able to work with Spooners and West Dartmoor Foxhounds. One morning, recently, we put a fox into a 10 inch cast iron drain-pipe, part of a disused turbine, about 100 yards long and open at both ends. Tarn was put in at the lower end of the pipe and within a few minutes two foxes had bolted. However, the continued marking of the terrier about halfway down the drain, told of yet another occupant. For three hours the battle raged up and down the pipe, as the fox refused to bolt. We could only stand by and hope that the terrier was not being too badly punished. At last, terrier and fox worked up nearly to the top entrance to the pipe and I heard Tarn catch hold. In a few minutes, the fox's brush appeared and we were able to draw out the biggest dog fox I think I have ever seen, with the terrier firmly clamped to his mask. Hounds had been taken home and we would have let the fox go, but he was badly injured about the jaw, and was immediately shot.

Apart from some small grazes, where he had butted his head against the sides of the pipe, Tarn was unmarked. A brave and clever terrier, I think, in his first season's work.

Mrs. D. E. Clarke, Devon

A STROLL

Some Borders were out for a stroll
When they found a most interesting hole,
But with room just for three
Number four could not see
And it bored her she found on the whole.

A. M. Mountain

THE BORDER TERRIER

Whether wheaten, red or saddleback,
Gameness it never does lack,
Tenacity, courage, always alert,
Never gives in, even when hurt.

At the ready to every call,
Is this terrier, to some so small,
Over mountain, over dale,
He can clamber without fail.

His weatherproof coat so tight and rough
Protects him when the job gets tough,
Come hail or snow, or wind, or ice,
He's off to work in a trice.

This terrier is such a gay bold fellow,
Always bright, rarely mellow,
But can you such a terrier order?
Of course you can, just ask for a BORDER.

J. Fagan

Werescote Socks

Socks came from a line of hard working west country terriers. We got him at 8 weeks and he was very early maturing for a Border Terrier and killed his first rat at 6 months old. He rapidly graduated to 'coypu,' but this was a mistake as he was put off for a while. However he recovered his nerve and killed several coypu before they disappeared.

He was shown twice. At Norwich he won 3rd in a puppy class. Elated by this I took him to Southend and showed him in a Border Terrier class, where he was bottom, which was a pity as he liked showing very much.

He was a very good rough shooting dog, really well disciplined, with a quite uncanny knowledge of the range of a gun. He knew it was a waste of time to go out of range and sensibly did not do so. He had a very good nose and once beat a good labrador on a running bird. He did not retrieve but killed anything he got hold of rapidly and then he was totally uninterested in the dead. He also weighed up the competence of the guns. He would not go with our boys until he thought they would shoot something. Later he had the idea that my eldest son shot better than my husband which was rather insulting.

His really great day was at a very good rough shoot in Suffolk, working up the wide hedges and ditches. We were asked to bring a dog and our host was rather surprised at the dog we brought, but he really did work better than all the others in pouring rain in brambley hedges and ditches and my husband shot far more than any one else as a result.

For years the North Norfolk Harriers had wanted to kill a fox. Eventually they ran one to ground and wanted a terrier. Some cairns were brought and were totally uninterested so my husband went home and fetched our Borders as Sankence Spindle was an experienced dog, having regularly worked with the West Norfolk Foxhounds. She was very much too old and had lost one eye but she went down and marked the fox. Socks heard the sounds of battle and was simply raging to go. When she came up, having been badly bitten, he went down and proved himself bold and true. He got hold of this very big fox and drew it from the hole. This is, of course, not correct. A terrier should speak to the fox not fight it.

Incidentally, though Sankence Spindle was badly bitten, as soon as she had cleaned herself of blood she was mad to go again. What bold little dogs they are.

On the river Avon in Hants there were rumours that there were a lot of wild mink about (do a lot of damage) but nothing was really known. So, staying down there we said we would look for a mink. My husband stood on a bridge over a big ditch and the dogs were worked up the ditch towards him. Suddenly a mink appeared, to his surprise, and he shot at but only wounded it. Socks came up, hunted around and marked it in a hollow willow. Eventually he got inside, there was a scurry and the mink got into the water. My daughter fell in also, from excitement. Socks hunted around and marked it in another hollow tree. This had a small opening halfway up. We knocked a hole in the bottom and Socks went in. There was a most awful hissing and growling. like about 10 cats fighting, coming from the tree via the little hole, when suddenly a mixture of black and red fell into the water, which turned out to be Socks and the dead mink.

In addition to being a very good bold dog, he was extremely nice, very faithful and very clever. He immediately recognised my daughter after 2 years in America.

He regularly went out shooting till he was 11 and was really very fit till he became totally blind and deaf and died at the age of 13 years.

Juliet Manners

If You Have Tears.....

My first Border died of hard pad at the age of 5, at least he was so hopelessly ill he was put to sleep. The Labrador bitch, who was his pal at the moment of his decease set up a mournful howl. This was about 6 years ago, but I have never forgotten it and have been under the impression that dogs know instinctively if a companion dies.

Last year my much loved Ch. Coundon Troena, known as "Tracey" suddenly died of a coronary thrombosis. She was full of fun and enjoyed life. She and her adopted daughter known as "Trimmer", really her grand-daughter, were the greatest of pals. It happened late one evening. There was a sudden cry of agony. I went to her, she was dead. Trimmer was in the room and must have been sound asleep. I rushed poor Tracey off to the vets, though I had only a slender hope and no more by the time I got there. I left Trimmer alone. When I got back she obviously didn't know what had happened. They always slept together and she only missed her at very late bedtime. She looked at me as much as to say, "Where is Tracey?" and wouldn't settle. I can't describe how I felt, but I never got over it. She obviously missed her terribly and was sad and lonely for months. Some months later I took her to a Hunt Terrier Show. When I got there I noticed a woman with a Bedlington type terrier, one typical with a roach look, the other in the distance, to me, looked just like Tracey.

When in the ring Trimmer refused to show. I had to drag her around and she was hopeless until suddenly in the mid-distance, she saw the woman with the "Bedlingtons". She suddenly became alert and up on her toes, pulled towards them and showed as she had never shown before! The judge remarked that she had woken up a bit late and placed her 3rd.

I thought I must take her up to those dogs to let her see it wasn't "Mother". But it was very cold, and started to rain and by the time we came out of the ring the woman and dogs had disappeared and so I came away, feeling none the less sad. But every story should have a happy ending and about 2-3 months later I gained a nice puppy, which "Trimmer" adopted straight away. So she is a happy little dog again. But I don't think she has any idea what happened to poor old "Tracey". I suppose it was so sudden, late at night and she was asleep.

E A Turrall

CONGRATULATIONS

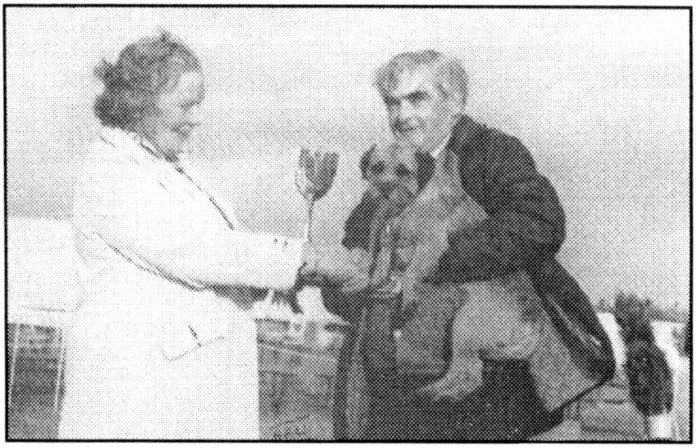

Mr. Ted Hutchinson handling Ch. Step Ahead, making breed history winning his third Terrier Group within 11 days. Above he is seen winning the Terrier Group award at Darlington following the preceding triumphs at Leicester and Birmingham.

Hunting

I've been asked to write an article about hunting, a subject that has many facets. I am not going to try to tell you how to enter your dog, the people that work them don't need me to tell them what to do. To the uninitiated I say, when your opportunity comes, leave it to the expert on the spot. What I do propose to do is try and help those people who want to hunt and don't know how to set about it.

To paraphrase Mrs. Beeton, "First find your hunt!" An invaluable publication is the Horse and Hound year book published annually. I doubt if the public library can help. It costs £1.50 so try and borrow one if you can. It gives a list of all registered hunts in England, Scotland, Wales and Ireland; Fox-hounds, Drag hunts, Harriers. Bassets, Beagles and Otterhounds, the name, and address of the master, secretary of the hunt staff, and sometimes the hon. sec. of the supporter's club, a short description of the country, plough, moorland, etc and the best centres to operate from. If the hunt is inconveniently tucked away in a corner you may need two, sometimes three sections to complete the picture. Having decided upon your hunt you have to make its acquaintance. Watch the local paper for an advertisement of theirs or any other local hunt terrier shows. If you are really clever you will slip into W. H. Smith's on Friday morning and study the advertisement pages in Horse and Hound, a rather pricey weekly paper, and sidle out without buying.

At the show, entries are taken on the field, so arrive in good time. Borders are rather poor relations and usually relegated to one class, Border and Lakeland X, that means any dog that is black, black and tan, or any shade of brown, so they are a very mixed lot. You may be surprised to find the class confined to those holding a working certificate has the worst entry. The great majority of those present have never been hunting and never will be, but they are 'Jack Russells' and this is a Jack Russell show. They get a very good classification, divided sexes, and subdivided again into rough and smooth coats.

The supporters will have a corner somewhere to take subscriptions and enrol new members. You can get a lot of information there. You may get a chance to ask the huntsman if he will consider using your terrier, if he says they only use their own and have plenty, don't be too despondent, hunt regimes change very quickly these days and the new lot may be different. More-over, if by then you are known as a regular follower you will have a much better chance. The show winds up with terrier racing. The dogs go mad with excitement - the noise is terrific. Try and put into one of the later heats and let the dog stand alongside and get an idea of what's going on.

As autumn draws near, ring the supporters club and ask when and where they are starting and can you come out? Cubbing used to be restricted to invitation only at first, no crowds to distract the young entry learning their job, and less chance of damage to standing corn. Nowadays, anyway in the provincial countries, this rule has lapsed and all are welcome. You will get far more fun with a small, unfashionable pack. Fewer followers mean more freedom, and a chance to take your own line if you want to — but don't head the fox, and do remember, as soon as you step off the road you are a guest on somebody's land. Going hunting gives you the privilege of crossing land that at other times you would not be allowed on, so treat it as a rather outsize in gardens, and you won't go far wrong.

Hunting people are mostly a helpful, friendly lot, so don't be shy of asking questions. They will be only too ready to help and put you in the know of things. Expressions may sound rather odd at first. "He's blowing out" doesn't refer to a person or a thing, but means the hounds have drawn blank and are being collected to move off somewhere else. If, as sometimes happens, there is no vantage point to see from, you rely on the huntsman's voice and horn for what is happening, so try and pick up the various calls as soon as possible.

Now we come to you, the dogs, and the car. Put in a spade, you are far more likely to be digging than a fox. If you venture off the road good ground clearance is essential, people will always help to pull you out. We all get stuck sometime or other, but if it happens every day it gets a bit boring. The seats and floor can be covered in old rugs and sacks, but if a wet and muddy dog gets in and has a good shake you can't do much about the roof. A fine morning in early autumn is sheer bliss, but cold wet weather lies ahead, and tough waterproof clothing that will stand up to scrambling through barbed wire fences is essential, not to speak of woods that sprout brambles everywhere, and the almost inpenetrable undergrowth that grows unchecked in half grown forestry plantations. If that's where the fox has gone to ground, and it's the sort of place he usually chooses, the terriers and the tools have to get there somehow. If you want to be a professional, and carry a set of tools, the least you will need will be a long handled hedge slasher, a grubaxe, two or three assorted spades and shovels, and an iron bar with a pointed end.

The dogs need water - they get very thirsty - a bowl, and sponge. Also a tube of soft Penicillin with a long nozzle that will go right down into bites. Some always get their eyes bunged up with mud and sand, Golden eye ointment is better than a dirty paw ! If they shiver, and are obviously in pain, half an *Anadin* tablet or something of that sort often works wonders. First Aid saves a lot of trouble later on. Good coats are essential, they may have to stay tied up for several hours awaiting their turn. A long dead coat gets plastered in mud, holds the wet and they are damp and cold. The old coat gets scraped off underground, the new coat comes very quickly, and the constant massage keeps it in wonderful condition. Shoulders and sides may get rubbed bare and a ruff is left fore and aft - a sort of lion clip. I take it off at the back but leave it around the throat untouched, a good mouthful of hair helps to blunt the foxes bite. They are bound to look a bit patchy at the end of the season. The old time judges realised this and made due allowance.

Some diggers don't like spectators present, not that anything underhand goes on, but silence is needed, and if you get a crowd of people they always start talking and nothing will stop them. Then you have the owner and dog craning over the edge, "'Just to let him see what's going on", and sending a cascade of dirt on to the man working below, sometimes six or eight feet down, and the dog who won't stop barking. By the way, Borders are getting very unpopular. People from other breeds have complained and told me they are left unattended on the benches and bark and shriek from start to finish. The Border bark is even more penetrating than the Cairn, and we used to consider them bad enough. We boast about having a working breed, so we must see it behaves like one.

Winter and spring pups have an advantage, they are old enough to be taken out after Christmas, a long hard day in the cold is too much for a young pup. The one that may be nervous or overawed at first has time to find its feet and the over-exuberant learns not to bark at every horse and hound it sees. By the time cubbing comes round again it's fully mature, the groundwork is done, and it's ready to start work.

It took me two years to get back into the Hursley. I hadn't liked the set up and stopped going out with them. When the present regime took office I went to the terrier show, most annoyingly it clashed with the Beaufort which I always enjoy. I asked if I could come out and would they use my terriers. "Do come !" they said. "I'm sure we shall want them" Did they? No! Occasionally they didn't bring theirs out and depended on mine We never ran to ground those days. At last my chance came. Out Cubbing, we put a fox to ground on the side of an old scrub covered bank. I was there, and the hunt Terriers left in the hound van. "We've sent for ours, but put yours in while we're waiting if you like". It looked a small place, only two holes about a yard apart. Little Willie, Monster to his friends, had seen one fox.

He'd fished it out of a rabbit hole for the local keeper so I chanced my arm and let him go. For the only time in his life he didn't speak. Anxious enquiries from above and I could hear nothing. Ages past, in reality between five and ten minutes, when the loose earth down one hole started moving. I stood up. "Alfie, you'd better come. I think he's drawing it". I looked down. Half the fox's brush was out and more appearing each second. "Alfie quick, it's nearly out". He shot down the bank and we were just in time to grab fox and dog respectively. Then it was "Let's have that big dog of yours Miss. We want this fox ." We'd made it at last, and were really back in again with a vengeance. He has one peculiarity, he nearly always turns the fox over and draws it out on its back. So I say, don't give up hope, the same thing can happen to you one lucky day.

Some dogs, through no fault of their own, a thoughtless slip by the owner, an occurrence among themselves can result in a dog being thought useless. I've had two instances among mine and in each case was lucky in knowing the cause.

Just after the war, when petrol rationing was still in force, the Hambledon were using Borders. Jack Kealey, the huntsman, was very keen on them, and took a little bitch of mine for the season to enter for me. I went out and handed her over at the end of the day. The first time the terrier men took her out hounds caught a fox and she was straining on the lead. Raring to go he thought. She was, but in the wrong direction. We picked her up the next afternoon. A few days later she slipped out of the feed house via a drain hole usually stopped up with half a brick, she dodged around and stayed just out of reach. Then she disappeared and I went over. No one anywhere had seen her. Would she make for home nearly 30 miles away, or would she look for me where we had been hunting that day, about 3 miles away? I drove up the track where I had parked the car that morning, blew the horn, whistled, called and waited. I started to turn the car around. It was a fiddly job so I opened the door for a better view and in she popped. They were very nice and took her back and she settled down but was returned at the end of the season labelled useless. I took her badger digging during the summer. I sat by the hole nursing a quivering jelly in my arms. I always felt she would go if I handled her myself next season, and to the surprise of everyone except myself, she went and turned out very good indeed. Later I sold her to Alec Laurie who thought the world of her.

The next instance was a dog puppy. He hunted rabbits as soon as he could run, it was before "Mixi", and he went down nearly every hole he came to. If you start early and teach them to come out when you call them it's a great help later on. One day - he was about ten months old - they were busy scratching out rats, and the old boss dog took over his hole and told him to get the hell out of it in no uncertain terms. He sat back and took no further interest. He started hunting again, but only on top, when he came to a hole he packed up. I was doing a lot of work for the Hursley at that time and had a pretty free hand. Every time we had a dig we wasted a few minutes trying him before we put in another dog. He was three years old when the miracle happened. A small place in the bank, he went up to it, cocked his ears, sniffed and disappeared in, straight up to his fox and started to give tongue. He'd watched so often that he knew his job from A to Z and we had no further trouble with him except out exercising, when we were back to when we started.

Chatting with Mr. Vigne one day he told me his dogs had endless fun digging for rats under some old buildings, and that a young dog appeared to have lost interest. He hadn't got a boss dog, but a fearsome old bitch ruled the roost so we concluded that her language had been equal to, if not worse than, that of my old dog.

B. M. L. Eccles

Bangle

We had just lost our cat, we think she was run over but never did find out. The house seemed so empty as she had been a great character. After lots of discussion my husband decided that I could have a dog but it had to be a small one.

I went along to see our vet to tell her that we thought our cat had met with an accident and to ask her advice about what breed of dog might suit us.

She thought for a moment and then said "What about a Border Terrier, your cat was such a character, I think this breed might appeal to you." Well I must be honest and admit that I had never heard of Border Terriers, so her advice was to get a picture book of dogs and to sort through and to go back for another chat.

We did better than that as the following weekend the Birmingham dog show was being held at Stoneleigh. After finding out which day the Border Terriers would be there we set off to see them. At once we fell in love with them and decided we must have one.

We found the Border people very helpful and willing to answer all our questions. It was spring and we had a holiday booked for August so thought we should wait until September to have our puppy. We collected "Beaconfleet Bangle" from Gloucestershire the first week in September.

I put her name down for training at Sutton Coldfield dog training club and we started in January, she was then six months old. I was convinced that we would be winning all the competitions after a few months. But Bangle had other ideas. She barked all the way through every training session for months and it became obvious that competitive obedience was not for us. We decided to join the "Good Citizens" class which is to train dogs to be a well behaved family pet. We got on well in this class and passed our progress test with 97 out of 100 marks, 90 being the pass mark. We won the cup for the highest marks and qualified for the medallion test to be held the following week, which we passed with the same marks. The test consisted of heel work on and off lead, road work (walking on pavement without pulling on lead ignoring other dogs, sitting at kerbs etc., one minute sit stay, and a recall). This meant promotion to the Advanced Citizens class, who train in Sutton Park among all kinds of distractions; i.e. people, cars, other dogs, children and horses and Bangle can't resist chasing horses. The progress tests are held every six months and again I was convinced that we would win the cup, but Bangle again had other ideas and we failed that test and the following test. A few weeks later it was announced that a medallion test was being arranged for the advanced class, this was quite a stiff test consisting of roadwork, heelwork on and off lead, recall through other dogs and people, a five minute sit stay with handler out of sight of dog and a road crossing i.e. stopping the dog at the kerb when she is running towards the handler from the opposite side of road. This is all done in the park on a Sunday afternoon.

Bangle seemed to know that getting this medallion was important to me and she behaved beautifully and we got our medallion, and the following progress test we won the progress cup awarded to the dog making the most progress from the last test, and we won the rose bowl for the highest marks.

It has taken us three years but we are now at the top of the Advanced Citizens class and we have enjoyed every minute of it.

Bangle is quite a character and we have hours of fun with her, she really is tough and full of fun and just right for us.

Mrs. D. Atkins

Border Terrier Sailors

When we went to live aboard "Lone Wanderer"' a 30 foot sloop, with all our worldly possessions plus four active Borders, I wondered how we would survive, let alone manage. However, the dogs fitted themselves in very well and once over the initial strangeness of being confined to a small area they accepted this sensibly and gave no trouble.

Our crew, in order of seniority were:- Spani, aged 15 years, Sprignell Otter 4, Suntan 3 and Kifaru Vixen 1 year. The first 24 hours were a little trying for them - having been well brought up dogs they were loath to mess the deck, but with the aid of much newspaper and sawdust this problem was finally overcome. After this they always used the same spot so we can claim to have the only British registered ship with the Poop deck in front.

Leaving England in October, we had a good deal of bad weather to contend with and, though we carried a fairly comprehensive veterinary kit for the dogs with medicine prescribed for seasickness, nervousness etc. we never had cause to use these. We converted our stern cabin into a dog kennel for bad weather sailing. This also housed our sail bags making it well padded and warm for the dogs. They quickly learned that when the order was given they must go into their cabin immediately. We never lost a dog overboard whilst sailing, but they frequently fell off when we were at anchor and they were playing on the deck. For some reason they would always swim to the rudder and hold on until fished out.

Otter has always been a bit of a lad with the girls and left a trail of broken hearts through France when we passed through the French canals. Later on when sailing down to Gibraltar we would sometimes have to stay overnight in a port we did not care for, waiting for his Lordship's return from his amorous adventures.

Suntan seemed to possess a built-in barometer and could always tell when the weather was about to worsen. She would growl and grunt giving us a warning and enabling us to take the sail down in time. In good weather she would be leaning out from the pulpit spotting dolphins.

In Gibraltar we had to wait nearly three months for engine parts. During the whole of this time the dogs remained in quarantine on the boat, however for exercise we used to take them swimming in the harbour accompanying them in our dinghy. This was the highlight of their day and they would make it last as long as possible. When they had all been fished out ready to be returned to the boat, one would invariably dive off starting the whole business all over again. They were good strong swimmers and became pretty flashy divers as well. Suntan, always the show-off, could swim a few feet under water to come up snorting and looking for applause.

We now own a small-holding in Mallorca and run boarding kennels. The surrounding country is quite beautiful, a Border Terrier's dream, with pine woods and rocky hills abounding in rats and rabbits, the latter being occasionally brought home in a fit of generosity, though always in a half consumed state.

Since living here we have had no time to sail but visit the boat regularly to keep her in order and often sleep on board. The dogs are as much at home there as on land. It is our ambition to one day sail around the world but we would not want to do this without our crew of Borders.

Mrs. J. I. Daykin

Why Borders?

During the year of 1974 from February till December while Marcus Ben and later Little Meg gave us so much fun at shows, many friends and relatives of mine have asked me 'Why Borders ?'

I've always loved animals, horses are a little large, they do throw you, even tread on you, I've experienced both! Cats are great fun, lovely soft purry things and I've even had a pet Canary-bird from Hungary, but dogs are my cup-of-tea.

The first Border I met was before the war, a gentleman called Jed from Glos., no doubt well loved and cared for but very independent and I usually saw him drying-out before the hall fire and oh dear, did he smell !

So thinking back, there was Bruce, a liver and white spaniel and Carlo, my father's shooting dog. Some years later Darkey, a lovely black cocker bitch that always wanted her ears doing. Later Ruffy, a darling Hunt Terrier who adored me more than his owner!

After we were married there was Barley, a golden Labrador usually called Bum as my young son couldn't pronounce Barley. They shared kennels and bones while Dandy, a retired Beagle, looked on or got chased by the cat! Our next was Varmit, another Hunt Terrier and she produced Velvet and Valiant, followed by another litter and then Buster, bred by Pat Smythe.

When Buster's days came sadly to an end we were already living in Northumberland but with the prospect of an overseas posting - no dogs - but wherever I went there were these important little brown people strutting about. Charles in the village and somebody else walking up the main road. People were nice up there, you stopped your car for our four-footed friends so unlike the south. And then there was a litter and so Marcus Havius Freeland came into our lives - a blue blanket for boys - a hot water bottle the first night, not for Marcus, he sat up all handful of fun and howled and howled in the middle of his basket in the middle of the night, seconds later he was cuddled, warm and asleep in bed! Next morning I couldn't think why my head was so hot on waking - Marcus reckoned hair was as good as straw and was very happy thankyou.

From then onwards until we were posted abroad six years later Marcus always went to sleep in my arms and was gently slid into his basket but woe-betide anybody who tried to get too close!

Perhaps that explains 'Why Borders'. I wouldn't be without them, their love for us humans is very great, their companionship is marvellous, people could learn a lot from their dogs if they cared to, I just wouldn't be without my little brown children, Marcus, Ben and Little Meg.

Sonia Freeland

Borders in Kenya

Borders are very thin on the ground in Kenya, there were only three shown at the E.A. Kennel Club Show. Two of these, Kenyan Ch. Farmway Tiger Moth of Kilfarn (bred by Miss Rumsam) and her son Kenyan Ch. Tommy Brock of Kilfarn are owned by Mrs. Stewart. The third was Kenyan Ch. Squirrel of Kilfarn, litter sister to Brock, and bred by Mrs. Stewart's daughter, Mrs. Daykin, who has now left Kenya with her Borders and settled in Mallorca. Borders are not classified at shows in Kenya so have to enter in Any Other Variety Terrier. However these have won their C.Cs. under top English judges and are considered very true to type. Brock and Moth accompany Mrs. Stewart when she is exercising her ponies around the coffee farm and generally manage to get into trouble! One day Brock and Moth got onto an Antbear (Aardvark). Brock being some way behind he was caught and held up on the rope which Mrs. Stewart always carries for such an emergency. Meanwhile Moth had the Antbear by the tail and was rapidly being towed down the hole. Mrs. Stewart managed to pull her off, by her own tail, which was a relief as she could easily have been squashed to death. The Antbear being very heavy and strong they could break a terrier's ribs or back, with one swish of their tail or a blow from their forearm. Apparently this incident was enjoyed by all, including the ponies who know all about hunting and considered this a similar sporting event.

Coats are difficult, owing to the climate. There is no proper winter or cold weather so it is difficult to get enough depth of coat and undercoat. Mrs. Stewart is a devoted Borderite and says she would never be without one, although she is not importing any more owing to the political uncertainty in Kenya.

Size in the Working Terrier

The question of size in the working terrier in general, and the Border Terrier in particular arises wherever Border or terrier enthusiasts gather together with time to talk. This is so today and was one of the very first things I heard discussed when I became interested in working terriers of various types in about 1938. So in this one question "times don't change", and nothing concrete has come out of endless hours of discussion.

The real fact of the matter is that in every country where terriers are used for their real work and indeed in any different County or State of those countries the size of terrier for work is agreed with the particular needs of that region in mind.

But first, to clear up the object of this article, I will lay down clearly some of the various methods required of a working terrier (not including ratting, rabbiting and poaching which are important and interesting in themselves but outside my argument).

In England, where orthodox mounted fox-hunting takes place, the terriers do not run with hounds. They are transported either by car or often on horseback in special bags attached to the saddle of the Terrier-man. When the fox is run to ground, the terriers are put in either to bolt the fox or to bark constantly while keeping the quarry busy until the diggers get down to it when it is dispatched. This differs absolutely from the Fell and Mountain countries where the terrier is NOT carried, but is required either to walk with the Huntsman or the followers, or to run with the horses across country (a hard task indeed) and when put to ground, either to bolt the fox or to kill it underground. Far from being a crime to kill underground, as it would be in orthodox fox-hunting, either method is equally welcome, the prime object being to kill the mountain fox, not so much to hunt it.

For otter-hunting the terrier is NEVER required to kill underground, but must either bolt the otter, or keep speaking so that the diggers can get down direct to the otter and bolt it themselves, or with the aid of the terrier. In badger-digging, now illegal in this country but not in Ireland or overseas, the terrier goes to the badger and must bait it so hard and close that the badger MUST keep facing the terrier and is therefore kept from digging into another tier or gallery or from throwing up a barrier of soil. Indeed it is kept so busy that it does not move away, so the diggers can go directly down to the badger and then 'tail' it. I point out that in this country whatever the work, the terrier is NEVER expected to 'draw' the quarry, though of course I have seen this done occasionally with foxes, although I know that this is expected and tested for in Ireland and Scandinavia. But drawing otter, fox or badger is NOT generally recognised as required in a working terrier in this country at least.

There is one other sort of genuine terrier-work that takes place in parts of Scotland and parts of wilder England and Wales, and that is accompanying a keeper or pest officer armed with a gun, and bolting the quarry out of stony cairns or rocky holes to be killed by the gun, or possibly to be worried underground, which is quite legitimate, as again the object is to kill the fox - no method being barred.

So it will be seen that there are two or three big differences in terrier work even in the British Isles, not to mention chip or woodchucks, coons or other overseas work of which I have no personal experience.

The main differences are : (1) That the terrier may be expected to kill underground in one area, but that this would be unforgivable in others. (2) That there is a vast difference in size between British quarries, i.e. badgers, foxes and otters in their girth and bulk as well as their weight and also in the size of their earths and holts. (3) They may have to get themselves to the earth on foot or may always be transported by a car or horse. I cannot say which of these three differences I consider most important regarding size, because the terrier has to get to the earth before it can be put in, and to carry him is not possible in Fell fox-hunting or otter-hunting; but once at the earth he has to be able to enter it before he can either bolt or kill, and when he does get in, South Country mounted packs want him to bolt the fox so that they have their galloping and jumping which is what they are there for, whereas in the mountains the farmers just want the fox dead. So like the famous horse-shoe that lost the battle because of the loss of a nail, the three differences seem interdependent.

For these reasons the Fell-man will extol the size and strength of the big strong-jawed terrier, often the Patterdale or working Lakeland with a touch of Staffordshire Bull Terrier four or five generations behind it; the South Country hunt looks for narrowness of shoulder, lightish weight, so that it can be carried if necessary, and much more bark than bite; while the keeper and pest officer needs an active lithe sort that can get round inside stony cairns; not forgetting the Irishman who likes to draw the quarry for competitive sport and therefore likes a big heavy terrier yet with slim shoulders and front, such as the Kerry Blue, the Soft-coated Wheaten Terrier, or the Glen of Imaal.

Luckily for us, the Border Terrier, with its mounted fell-foxhound background, bred specifically to hunt the big greyhound foxes of Northumberland, (entirely different from the little red furry "Persian cats" of South Country foxes, so much different that I didn't recognise the first south-country fox I ever saw). The Border as I say is a really splendid compromise, leggy enough and strong enough to run with hounds, narrow through shoulder and rib to enter either fox-holes or otter-holts or narrow cracks in rock faces, or even hollow trees. If within the standard of size required by the Kennel Club Standard, 11.5 to 15 lbs, it may either be carried or is able to walk endless miles to the eventual place where the quarry has gone to ground. Yet it has enough size and substance either to bolt the fox or to kill it underground if required, although it does not usually have the natural ferocity of the working Lakeland with its Staffs Bull cross, always to try to kill rather than to bait or bolt. So we have a wonderful all-rounder, the Standard allowing for plenty of variation. The otter-hunter can choose a Border of 11.5 lbs, the mounted fox-hunter a big 15 lb one.

Perfect, one would think, but what do we show people do? We learn the Standard off by heart, we argue it's merit, but very, very few take the slightest notice of the standard of weight when it comes to breeding or judging or even to talking. They invariably go for the bigger ones, even to preferring those right outside the weight standard. This was actually admitted by the five famous judges at a recent talk-in, one a working terrier man, one an out-and-out Border specialist and expert on the breed, one another experienced specialist from a more mountainous district, one a world-famous all-rounder who is also a Border specialist, and one an equally well-known international all-rounder. This all-embracing panel all agreed when asked that they did not care if a Border was right over the standard size, and that they regarded the Standard as only a guide-line. This public and outspoken declaration by 5 judges was borne out by the fact that the five Champions under their inspection that day were all except one right outside the standard, on the large side, one being the highest size for a dog although it was in fact a bitch, another being just half-a-pound oversize that being a bitch too. The others, all dogs, being way above the topmost standard size, indeed by three lbs in one case. Now these experts gave us the reason why they preferred the Border to be oversize, but remember the five Terriers were all Champions, therefore probably fifteen other judges and maybe many more had preferred them at some time or other and given them C.Cs, in one case giving one of them a C.C. myself. In every one of these cases the judges said quite openly that what mattered much more than size was narrowness of shoulders, fronts and rib, and again re-iterated that in their opinions, the Standard was only a guideline.

I think everyone at this talk-in must have pondered carefully about these findings by an acknowledged panel of experts, both from the working point of view and from the show judges, who were remarkably unanimous in their requirements.

Well, in my hunting days I was the Terrier-boy, and it was my job to get the terriers there when wanted and also to persuade or force them to go to ground. They were not all Borders, but most of them were, the others usually being crossed with working Lakelands. To begin with, a heavy Terrier I found very difficult indeed to carry across a couple of fields, or even lead the pulling, tugging varmints when they knew what they were wanted for. The most difficult Terrier we ever had to put down an awkward place was one of our own Border Champions with extra long legs and a slight inclination to tied-in elbows. This bitch could 'star-fish' those long legs so that she got a prop on each corner of the drain or hole and needed two people to disengage those props, after which she went well. The easiest to deal with was a minute white terrier, the size and shape of a big ferret. This could get anywhere and was exactly like posting a long white envelope, but her legs were so short and she was so small as not to be able to get up the fell to a high earth after a long hunt, and she always had to be carried, usually by me, but I don't think she weighed more than nine lbs, if that.

Our biggest hunt Terrier was a mammoth but extremely good-looking pure bred Border dog, something of a mystery man, called Mist. He was given to the Hunt by Mr. George Grundy a famous otter-hunting man and very knowledgeable. "Mist reputedly came from a famous Northumberland show kennel, but we never had his papers or a clue to who he was, obviously being a throwout because of his enormous size. He was perfectly useless as a "Terrier", because he would never enter anywhere if it touched his sides, so could only get where a hound could go. So he was useless for underground work, only ever bolting one otter and that from a huge culvert that the hounds could not get down too, but he went further than them being a Terrier and not afraid of the dark or depth. But he was a great asset, acting as a bramble-pushing spaniel and chasing otters or foxes in cover and brambles over which the hounds had to jump, whereas he, like the quarry, ran underneath it.

Our best working Terriers, one or two of whom became fables in the Lakeland area, such as Smuts and Quill, were nice shapely Borders, not exaggerated, more or less of standard size in their prime, and able to perform everything the Border is expected to do, to follow horse, man or hound, to be narrow to get into any bolt, drain or earth, to be sensible and bait a badger, fox or otter, to prefer to bolt their quarry, but to kill it if absolutely unable to bolt it, and to be sensible enough never to get marked up or injured. (My husband hated a terrier that got marked up or otherwise hurt) and although keen as mustard, willing to come out as soon as called. With these things in mind as Terrier-boy, other things being equal in beauty and conformation, I myself preferred the Standard size Border, believing the Standard to be exactly right in scope and range of size. Nothing I have heard or seen since those now far off days has caused me to change my mind. The Standard, 11.5 to 15 lbs is correct for any type of work, fox, otter or badger, and don't let's change it for a showman's whim. When judging let us all remember that 11.5 lbs is just as correct and useful for work as 15 lbs, and a darned sight better than the oversized Border weighing 17-18 lbs or even more.

Mary Roslin-Williams

Terriers for Work

Every type or breed of working terrier commands my admiration. I must confess that the old type of Jack Russell terrier 14/ 14 is my first choice of a working terrier. The terrier men and the hunting men of the West country like a terrier to run with hounds all day on the moors, so do the Northern hunting men with their Border Terriers. The colour of coat and type of head of these two are not the same, but apart from this the conformation of the two are as like as two peas in a pod. Some people will say when reading this "Ah ! but the late Reverend's terriers had docked tails" (well they hadn't)! I like to see a Russell or a Border cross with a good huntsman hand hold dock as this can be handy in a quick emergency.

Getting back to Border Terriers they were, and are, still (if working) harder and more punishing when facing their quarry. I saw a photo of the Border Foxhounds just lately with their Border Terriers running with hounds. If the hounds don't kill him above ground, the Border Terrier most surely will under ground, unlike the Jack Russell terrier who will bay and tease Charlie until he bolts.

A Shire pack of hounds dislike their foxes killed under ground, as they are out for a very good gallop. I have worked Borders, Russells, Border/Lakelands and Cairn cross to fox, otter and badger (when it was a very old traditional sport). I have even bolted a man, who was a hermit (or a nut case). He had lived in this particular badger sett for over a year, and the police couldn't find his hide out. He broke into the big local farm houses at night for his meals. It was really something to have a Sergeant and two C.I.D. men in one's digging team! They were as pleased to have him as we were to get shot of him!

Our team of terriers were much respected in three hunting countries. In one dig we accounted for 11 badgers in one large earth. Many old locals came and told us we would never get a find in there as it was a massive place, and the Brocklesby Hunt had lost many a good terrier in there. We didn't lose a terrier that day.

I was once taking my pack of terriers, 4 couple, for a walk one Sunday morning by a tributary of the river Bain. I had let them run through an old disused earth there. I had a couple of 11 month old unentered Russell puppies with me so I let them run through for a chance of getting in the dark. Well all the pack had got in by the time I got there. They were throwing their tongues at something. I thought that a Charlie had taken refuge in the old place, or maybe old Brock. I put my head in one of the holes, it didn't smell of fox or badger. Oh dear, I thought, they must be having a fight, all terriers getting in an earth together. But it didn't quite sound like a fight. I didn't fancy leaving them and crossing the busy main road to go and get a spade in case they came out before I returned and got on the road, so I waited.

All of a sudden there was a rush like a cork out of a bottle, out came a big brown animal rolling down the bank with three terriers hanging on for dear life. It was an otter. When he hit the water I was worried in case he took the hanging terriers with him, but they fell off in the water. The other terriers were running out of the earth and down the side of the bank, some trying to swim after him. They hunted him for about 2 hours before losing him in a big reed bed in the middle of a large lake about 2 miles downstream.

The biggest fox I have had with my terriers weighed 18 lbs, he seemed massive; for this part of the country it was a big one.

Among my hunting trophies I have a pad of the last otter killed in Lincolnshire in the Lincolnshire fortnight of the Bucks and Courtney Tracy Otter Hounds before they were disbanded. I followed the Dartmoor Otterhounds in 1974, they had a few couple of B.C.T.O.H. in their pack. We had good days hunting otter and mink. Having worked terriers for twenty years and by no means an old man yet, I have had many happy hours and many heart breaking hours, but I couldn't be without my four-legged companions.

Jeff Burman

A Long Friendship

When we came home from India in the 1920's we settled in an old Cotswold farmhouse in beautiful unspoilt country. My husband started pig-farming, and I thought it would be fun to breed dogs in a small way, having had a nondescript pack of Long dogs and terriers in the Punjab.

We went up to Cruft's to see what the then modern pedigree terrier was like, and carefully inspected the benches. Borders seemed to be the only ones neither yapping, nor in a state of near hysteria, so Borders it was, and a decision that we never regretted.

There were very few in the South in the 20's, so our first bitch, Wasp, came down from Northumberland, wild and frightened after the long train journey, and took some time to settle down. "A curious mixture of ferocity and timidity" is how the breed was described to us by Mr. Dodd, the owner - if my memory does not play me false - of the famous dog Titlington Tatler, and I have found this to be true of many Borders.

When Wasp was due to have her first litter she disappeared and we had a miserable few days searching for her, fearing she had got stuck down an earth.

One morning we saw her picking her way down the hill with a puppy in her mouth. She deposited it in a corner of the barn, went back up the hill, repeating the journey five times until all the family was safely home. She did this every time she whelped, and we never interfered with her plans, nor did we ever discover her hiding place !

This all happened over 50 years ago, and I have never been without a Border since then. We had a few successes in the show ring, but that has never been the side of my life with Borders that has mattered to me as much as the joy and companionship I have had from them.

All dogs are good companions, and I have owned and loved many different breeds, but these brave little dogs seem to have most of the doggy virtues packed into their sturdy bodies and broad intelligent heads. They can delight us with their sporting side, they can soak up as much affection as we care to lavish on them, and return it with interest. They can also infuriate us when we have to crawl downstairs at 3 a.m. to let them in, apologetic and ingratiating, and plastered with mud. But, how thankful we are to hear that bark under the window, for we have all dreaded the tragedy of no return, and it has happened to most Border owners.

There are comic turns of course, like three who lined up in front of the cat every evening to have their faces washed, looking afterwards as if they had been to the hairdresser for the latest swept-up style. Then there was Coco, an impertinent little blue and tan, who would settle herself on my pillow, if she got the chance, and put on the light over the bed by pulling the cord with her teeth !

Now I have only got one, Mrs. Marchant's Ch. Happy Returns who is spending her middle age with me, and is a delightful companion with a passion for oranges and grapes.

I remember them all, and my long life would have been very much the poorer without my Border friends.

Angela G. Wolley

From Suburbia to Sanity

Thank goodness we became interested in a down-to-earth breed like Borders. Had our fancy been one of the more exotic canines, I doubt whether we could have been accepted as quickly in our new part of the country.

We made our move from mid-Sussex to mid-Wales in 1973, amid much interest from people who thought we were mad to move to a world where motorways, training classes, and pollution were non-existent. However, we have proved it is still possible to reach all the dog shows we want to, and our dogs have been able to enjoy what we think is a much more exciting life.

In this part of Wales, there are only three types of dog considered worth keeping: sheep-dogs, hounds, and terriers. All other dogs are classified as "women's pet-dogs". Dogs are expected to do something to earn their rations, and terriers that do not go to ground are definitely viewed with suspicion and amusement, rather like keeping a sheep-dog that was not interested in sheep! The word soon got round that we kept brown terriers, and many people told us stories of heroic deeds by such terriers. A pair had been kept by the Hunt Kennels, and were very highly thought of. Nowadays, the same kennels has Border Terriers, but they are not so highly regarded since an unfortunate incident earlier this season when a hound grabbed hold of a Border as it came out of the bury. (I would have got rid of the hound rather than the Terrier!)

Fox-hunting is an inherent part of everyday life here, "antis" do not bother us. The country is very beautiful, all hills, and is at its best during the winter months (tourists miss such a lot by coming in the summer). We hunt on foot, resorting to cars when we see hounds disappearing over the furthest hill in full cry. A few horses come out on a Saturday, small, thickset ponies, full of stamina to face steep climbs and rough weather. The pack is pure-bred Welsh Hounds, predominantly white, with fabulous voices that make English Hounds sound like a pack of Beagles. They have great independence that enables them to hunt a line over the mountains without any help from the Huntsman, who is often left well behind. Terriers are frequently required during the day's hunting, occasionally to bolt the fox, but more often to push him into a dead-end and mark him until the diggers reach them. Then is the Huntsman's chance to perform his speciality, pulling the fox alive from the bury with his bare hands!

Foxes must be kept down in this type of sheep-rearing country, with its vast uninhabited areas of hill and forestry. Sometimes there is only one practical way of doing this, with hounds to get the foxes on the move, and with guns to shoot them. We keep our Borders well away from the guns, but one of our dogs belonging to the Huntsman does run with hounds in such a pack, and so far no-one has mistaken her for a fox.

Little more than chance brought us to mid-Wales, but when we discovered there had always been terriers at Pine Tree Cottage since it was built nearly 100 years ago, and that we were surrounded by land farmed by another Mr. and Mrs. Sharp, we felt that the place was meant for us and our Borders.

Marie Sharp

Are Borders Catching?

Are you getting the feeling that people nowadays have been so influenced by anti-dog propaganda that they regard your dog-keeping as an anti-social vice, and your beady-eyed Border companion as a dangerous source of all sorts of health hazards on four legs? Of course the responsible dog owner manages his animals in such a way that, whilst they lead a comfortable and happy life, they are not allowed to annoy or inconvenience other people. He/she does not allow them to stray, worry farm livestock, get involved in road accidents, or habitually relieve themselves on the neighbours' front lawn. He makes sure that the new puppy is brought up to behave as his *owner* wants, and not the other way round.

There are many canine disease conditions which are not transferable to humans, and there are several which may be. The most feared of these is rabies of course, which has attracted much recent publicity because of the rapid spread of the 'sylvatic' or fox-borne form of the disease into western Europe and, of particular concern to us in Great Britain, towards the Channel ports. Rabies is a terrible disease, since its symptoms are horrific, and because once they have appeared there is no hope of recovery, in animals or man. Vaccines for prevention are by no means always effective. In this country we have the tremendous advantage of being an island, and the sea barrier can only legally be crossed by animals which then go into carefully controlled quarantine. The six months 'sentence' is absolutely vital as incubation of the disease can be very long, and anyone who attempts to import animals illegally is extremely irresponsible and selfish. If the disease was ever imported in smuggled animals and became established there is no doubt that our attitudes to all facets of dog-ownership, and indeed to mammals generally, would be drastically changed. Other viral infections of dogs are not known to be transmissable to humans.

Parasitic conditions of dogs have also recently been receiving the attentions of the press, particularly infestation with the roundworm Toxocara Canis. As all Border breeders will be aware, puppies can become infected before birth via the dam, and if not treated in the first few weeks of life, may harbour very large quantities of the worms which will severely retard growth and development. After about eighteen months the roundworms seldom cause clinical problems in the dogs themselves, but adult worms in the animal's intestines produce microscopic and resistant eggs which are passed out with the dog's faeces. It is larvae produced from these eggs which may cause trouble in young children if they are swallowed. The condition is called 'visceral larvae migrans'. It is the larvae wandering in the child's tissue which do the damage. It must be stressed however that the condition is very rare indeed, and though each case reported is a tragedy for the family concerned, the risk is minute compared with other childhood ailments. Naturally the responsible dog-owner should treat his stock regularly for roundworms, which is a simple and inexpensive procedure. On normal hygienic grounds quite apart from any specific disease risk dogs should not be exercised in children's play areas, and children taught about normal cleanliness, but this is surely quite a different matter from the wholesale banning of dogs from large public parks advocated by some.

Tapeworm infections in dogs are a potential source of danger to humans. Several different genera of the parasites are involved, and the adult tapeworms may be harboured in the dog without causing marked clinical signs; when they do produce symptoms these are rather non-specific - a general unthriftiness, poor coat, voracious appetite, possibly enteritis.

Gravid segments may be voided with the faeces or leave the host spontaneously, and actively crawl about the coat, depositing numerous eggs.

In the case of Dipylidium caninum, the intermediate host of the worm is the dog flea, and dogs acquire the infection by ingestion of infected fleas.

In other types infection is by ingestion of uncooked offal of intermediate hosts, for example, sheep and rabbit. Where segments are seen on the dog or in its faeces appropriate treatment should be given, to rid the dog both of the tapeworm and fleas. Echinococcus is perhaps the most dangerous genus as far as man is concerned, and in countries such as New Zealand where this is a particular problem, owing to the large population of sheep (the normal intermediate host), regular treatment is required by law.

Other parasites of the dog are fairly host-specific, but dog fleas and sarcoptic mange mites may cause transistory irritation in humans. Obviously this disappears when the dog is treated.

Some bacterial infections may be transmitted from dogs to man, particularly infections of the digestive tract and throat. The most notorious of these is Salmonella (a cause of 'food-poisoning') which is a notifiable disease, and usually occurs in dogs which are in contact with infected farm animals. To prevent such infections being transmitted prompt disposal of dog vomit and faeces should always be practised, together with careful segregation of feeding utensils.

Leptospirosis may be contracted by man, but this is not a very common infection, and is a classic case of prevention being better than a cure. All dogs should be inoculated against the disease, and boosted annually.

One important fungal disease must be mentioned. Ringworm is a fairly common skin condition in the dog, characterised by patchy loss of hair. It can be transmitted to humans, and is usually seen as circular lesions on exposed skin, often the wrists. Treatment is straightforward once the disease is correctly diagnosed.

Is dog-keeping so hair-raising ? Not if owners manage their animals in a sensible way, observing simple rules of hygiene in the housing, feeding and handling of their dogs, and making sure their children are brought up to do so too. Medical and Veterinary research has identified many disease agents, but in addition, has enabled us to make prevention and treatment of diseases more effective.

Elaine M. Davey, M.A.. Vet.M.B., M.R.C.V.S.

Hunting with Borders

On May 1st, 1975, Captain Wallace brought the Heythrop bitches to hunt on Dartmoor, as the guests of Spooners and West Dartmoor Foxhounds.Knowing that foxes are hard to find at this time of year, I put my Border Terrier dog, Tarn and my little three quarters Border dog, Topper on a couple, and set off to try and keep as close to hounds as possible. Many acres of moorland and bog were drawn blank, until hounds marked in the big rocks of 'Little Wistman's Wood'. Topper was put in, and a fox quickly bolted, only to cross the West Dart river and go to ground in the rocks of 'Beardown Tor'. Topper had by now located another fox and was hard at work and I could not leave the rocks, though frantic signals were being made from 'Bear Down Tor' for another terrier. With some misgivings, I gave Tarn to a competent-looking pair of foot followers who had by now arrived, and they took him over. He quickly re-bolted the fox, which immediately returned to the rocks of 'Wistman's Wood'. However, Tarn had by now bolted a second fox, and a few notes on Captain Wallace's horn sent the bitches racing back to him. He laid them on the second fox who provided a short, fast hunt and a kill in the open on Archerton farm. By now, Topper had bolted his second fox and condescended to leave the rocks and be put on his lead, and I was happy to see Tarn coming over the hill, still in charge of his new fricnds, who said he had been as good as gold, and no trouble to pick up after bolting his foxes.

Hounds were then taken to the big forestry at 'Bear Down' from which a good fox went away and gave a fast five mile point, saving his brush in the big covers at 'Fernworthy'. Captain Wallace said it was the best day this season in the West Country, and I had a wonderful day with the terriers, so everybody went home happy.

Mrs D E Clarke

Ch Hobbykirk Destiny retrieving to hand and showing the versatility of Borders

Border Craft

The air trembled with heat and even the crickets were too exhausted to sing. My husband and I lay, prostrate, under a tree while our six-year old Border Terrier, Poppy, lounged in the shade of the wall, her head between her paws, quietly dreaming twitchy dog dreams.

Suddenly, the peace was shattered as our American weekend guest, Ben, enthused into view. "What a marvellous day", he crowed, "I must walk in the forest, breathe in the country's goodness and communicate with nature". We sighed with relief as we had been dreading another afternoon of culture-vulturing round Burgundy. However, we did have some twinges of conscience when our friend gaily went on to announce his decision to take man's best friend with him so that she might help him glory in the beauties of the earth. Poppy looked doubtful as he scooped her out from her cool nest, but her instinctive good manners saved the day and she allowed herself to be spirited away. The hours passed and my husband and I continued to flop about the garden half-heartedly, our brains addled by the August sun. Then came the cool of the evening and with it the return of our mental faculties. To our horror we realised that our guest and Poppy had by then been absent nearly four hours and no happy barking heralded their immediate return. We steadied our shattered nerves with a tot of whiskey and sat down to wait. After what seemed like hours, a bedraggled, crestfallen American shuffled into view holding our beloved dog in his arms. We ran to meet him and listened to his story.

To begin with everything had gone very well. Our guest had spotted buzzards, kites and a couple of booted eagles and felt most exhilarated. Poppy dug out voles and harvest mice and ran around happily. However, Ben eventually decided that he had had enough of the forest and brought Poppy out onto the sun-scorched open plain totally devoid of all cover and shade. After about an hour he was brought up short by an agonised scream from Poppy who was rolling on the ground in pain. A great dog lover, he rushed to her side and carefully examined her pads, legs and body. He could find nothing. He placed her on the ground again and again she collapsed. Suddenly he panicked. What if she had been bitten by an adder? Her melting brown eyes looked up at him trustingly. With gentle words of encouragement he picked up the little dog and carefully cradling her in his arms, started the long walk home.

While Ben talked we subjected Poppy to a thorough examination. Nothing could we find. She did look terribly sorry for herself, but I thought I detected something more than that in her demeanour and decided that immediate action should be taken. I rushed into the kitchen and found a large, juicy marrow bone which I threw across the lawn . . . In one bound Poppy was out of the astonished American's arms and running, like a healthy racehorse, to retrieve her bone. After a preliminary gnaw she picked it up, tail a-wagging and sauntered back to the shade of her wall while we, laughing fit to burst, led the fuming Ben into the house for a drink.

Kate Chevalier

Temperament Does Matter

The three main purposes for which Border Terriers are bred are as companions and family pets, for work and for show.

By reason of their personalities very few Borders are looked upon as pure working utensils to be put away when not required, like the spade and sack which accompany them in their job. Neither do the show dogs, as yet, live in cages or glass palaces so that their breed points are preserved, to be shown off only in the show ring.

When off-duty most working Borders and show Borders are simply companions.

The object of owning any dog, or ten or even twenty, is that it should give pleasure and fun to its owner, and should not be a nuisance, a liability or any sort of danger, or cause anxiety.

There are now present in our breed two kinds of bad temperament which may be inter-related the one to the other. These two character faults are shyness and aggression. Either of these spoil the character of the dog and the pleasure of owning it. Both should be faced up to realistically and stamped out while there are still plenty of true to character Borders about.

First there are the shy and timid cowards. This is hereditary in more cases than not. They will be excused by their owners saying that they do not see enough men, women, children, other dogs, that a blackboard fell on them at their first show, that the judge was rough with them, that they were bitten at the ringside and so on.

The normal twentieth century life of a dog is noisy - be it with traffic, low-flying aircraft, crowds. trains or in the country, farm sounds and the loud noises of nature. There once was a Border frightened by the full-throated song of a blackbird. That Border was not bred from.

A normal dog will react the first time it meets or hears the unexpected. If the temperament is correct the dog will make the mental adjustment to deal with the problem next time without fear.

The nervous dog will just manage to keep control of its nerves until it meets the unexpected. It then will let terror take hold and will frighten itself even further by listening for strange noises, and by golly it will hear them in the normal everyday sounds of this world.

One symptom of a nervous dog is to be terrified of children. The normal reaction of any dog is to dote on them with some latent instinct of long ago, a liking for young animals.

A chronically shy or nervous dog will often make a super one-man-dog type pet although they will avoid contact with other humans apart from their chosen one-man. This apart, it is unfair to inflict these dogs upon the public as they are always an anxiety and not much pleasure to own. They most certainly should not be bred from.

At the other end of the scale comes the aggressive dog. Maybe he develops this as a defence against his nerves. The normal dog is the one to breed for, not the extremes of temperament.

There have always been the odd bad-tempered Borders shown but in the last few years there has been a notable increase in the numbers of these and it is now not unusual to see Borders behaving badly in the ring and around the show, on the benches and even going so far as to bite the judges or bystanders.

For work it seems hardly necessary to say that timidity, hand-shyness, aggression, unnecessary noise of the guarding instinct are nothing short of useless. Just try catching a hand-shy terrier after the fox has bolted or try to pick up a much-needed item of equipment that is being guarded by an over-zealous terrier, or try and separate two fighting terriers to put one of them to ground and you will soon realize that they are not worth their dinners.

Judges can help by penalising bad temperament and sending savage dogs out of the ring. No judge should run the risk of being bitten by an ill-mannered exhibit - why should they? A dog bite is extremely painful. Vicious dogs are not eligible for exhibition under K.C. rules, so the show management can help by refusing the entries of proven vicious dogs.

Breeders must face facts. Borders have, or used to have, a good reputation for breed character and temperament. Don't make excuses for bad temperament. Study the pedigree instead and don't repeat the mistake.

The greatest champions in the world are still just dogs. If they fail as just dogs from Monday to Friday what is the value of their weekend glory?

Anne Roslin-Williams

Letter to Mrs. Felicity Merchant

Dear Wench,

I hear you need an article for the Year Book, so to make you a Happy Girl I will Step Ahead without Warrant from you and write a little non-sense because on this Happy Day I am in Fighting Fettle.

I always was a bit of a Hunty Gowk, filled with Mustard and Fine Fury whenever I see hounds. I feel Wistful to think that the Anti-brigade are trying to stop hunting. Indeed I work like a Beaver to keep the sport going and am always willing to give an Xmas Box to any huntsman who is a Manly Boy or a Fine Fella.

My Destiny is to continue hunting right up to my Final Flutter. The Wizardry and the Magic is to rise up in the Early Morn, waking from a Beautiful Dream, (er, where was I?) Oh yes, I then drink my Coffee which I brew in my Kopper pot. I then Don my Red Glamorous coat, which is Not So Dusty, step into my Regal Rusty Rolls Royce, and with a Northern Gleam in my eye, set off to capture a Mask and Brush from the Foxlair, or the Todearth, in the Nettle bed or the Bracken, although I prefer to hunt a dog fox rather than a Vixen or a Badger. I am afraid I often get shouts of "Late Again" when I arrive, because I often am a Late Arrival.

In Summertime I dress like a Raggamuffin, a Tramp or a Gypsy, in case I should be mistaken for a Beautiful Spy or even a Bint Superior. Clad in my Fully Fashioned stockings and my Tweedie skirt, I put on my Green Briar and some Ready Money into my pocket, pack my basket with a Muffin, a Cream Bun smeared with Cetchup and Nutmeg, a Brussel Sprout and some Dark Chocolate, plus some Whisky, some Sherry Ripe and a Brandy and Soda (Napoleon Brandy of course), Dubonnet mixed with Bitter Lemon is refreshing too. I do not wear my Amethyst Solitaire, my Blue Bracelet or my Blue Gem, or indeed any other Gewgaw in case I should lose a Pearl of great Price or other jewel to the Border Raider or any other Rascal, thieves being always at work.

By 10.30 a.m. I am Wide Awake ready to start off in the Misty Dawn to hunt "Tarka" (or Klein Otti as the Continentals call him) in that Matchless pool called Otterpot, which is not on the Red Tweed, but on that Ace of rivers, the Lune, even though the April Mist, a Blue Haze, is down and it is the season of the Primrose and the Honeysuckle.

Now, is hunting cruel? Nature herself is raw, and we say little about cruelty when the Barn Owl (or should I say the Tawny Owl, to be fair) swoops down in Full Flight at The Cuckoo, a Humming Bird in Fine Feathers, or even a Starling. Likewise humans have a hunting instinct. We read how in history Red Kingpin, Robert the Bruce rescued the Border Queen from Hanleycastle. And of course the Fabulous Gay Gordon and that Bonny Scot, Rob Roy (my Northern Hero) with the help of the Princess Susan saved Lady Lucinda and Lucky Lucy from the hands of that Shady Knight and Smuggler, the Bad Sinbad.

Dauntless Jimmy Tripp, a famous Northern Piper and a Brave Soldier was a bit of a Handy Andy too. Remember how he cleared the jump called Macsleap, dressed as a Minstrel, to visit his Fancy Girl? He always was a bit of a Dandy-How he loved to wear a Marigold in his Batchelors Button-hole when dressed in Mufti. Unfortunately he was Shot in the Dark one Misty Dawn by a Waggoner.

But Half-a-Mo, I am a bit of a Wistielass and a Lucky Lass too and the Realisation comes to me that I must stop my Quest for Future Fame with this Flippant article. I see I have got in a Tangle and used some Labrador names, so please forgive me as a Final Honour.

I wish you all a Happy Dawn on Christmas Day. Don't forget to sing a Carol and to pull the Wishbone with your Merryman, and drink some Wassail too, Why Not Mulligatawny and Mock Turtle soup are good at Xmastide too.

Montime is now up (Fancy my French?) so I bid you a Fond Farewell and a Happy Dawn on Yan Jan too (No, that is not Yak Bob day, that comes in Summertime) When Then? May Time, I think.

Yours with many Happy Returns to the Year Book
from that Yorkshire Lass,

Mary Roslin-Williams
(Not a Countess yet, only an Aristocrat and a Joker)

How I Became Hooked (On Borders)

Way back in the 1920's when I was but a Hobble-De-Hoi (neither a man nor a boy) I was general dogsbody on a farm situated at the foot of the sand dunes near Chapel Point on the Lincolnshire coast.

Owing to this farm land being very criss-crossed by dykes and drains, it was non-hunting country. During the winter months it was usual to find the old Vos (fox) taking up residence under the scrub bushes which thrive on these sand dunes.

Old Vos seemed to know he would be able to dine off mallard and early lamb. Amongst my various jobs around the farm I was expected to rear a few mallard, feed partridges on the autumn stubble, keep a sharp lookout for the flocks of wild geese, and, most important, know when and where Vos had taken up residence, and account for him before he had taken too many mallard or young lambs. To account for him needed me to have a strong terrier or two, capable of entering and either bolting or holding until I could dig down and despatch Vos with a short muzzle gun. A frequent visitor to the farm both professionally and sporting was the local vet Capt. John Shaw. He had moved down from the north and was a right sporting man, loving a partridge shoot or a Sunday morning dig at the foxes.

On one of these visits I had to ask the Captain to check up on one of my old war scarred terriers whose age was beating him. Old Faithfull was ordered retirement.

Capt. Shaw at once promised the next time he went North he would bring back a red terrier. True to his word in 1930 he brought from Tyneside a strong 10 month old reddish brown terrier with a broad flat skull, about 14 inches high with a good mouth, strong muzzle, a coat like pinwire over a snug undercoat good enough to stand the bitter east winds for which our coast is noted. Best of all he had a devilish twinkle in his small dark eye. The Capt. assured me he had brought the first Border Terrier to Lincolnshire.

I called my new pride and joy Geordie. A couple of months later, out one day for a look around the dunes Geordie stopped and sniffed at a hole in the sand bank. A couple more sniffs and he was gone down nearly out of sight. By the time I had broke gun and run some 400 yards to collect a spade expecting a dig, fox and Geordie were out of the hole rolling on the sand and holding fast on to each other barely letting go to catch breath. I stood helpless not able to shoot or strike for fear of injuring my dog. After about ten minutes which seemed like ten hours Geordie got Vos by the throat and made a finish. The head of this fox was mounted and is still a prized family possession.

Came the war years and I was drafted into town, and thought it unfair to change Geordie's way of life. So he was left on the farm and retired as the army had taken over the sand dunes on defence. He died a peaceful death in 1942 (God rest his soul). After this I vowed I would have another Border when hostilities ceased.

In the late 1940s I purchased another Border from Mrs. Scargill (Lindumwold) and since then I have never been without at least three Go-To-Grounders at any one time.

Syd Grantham

Daniel Foxhill Fraser

Daniel was meant for me, of that I am convinced. He was born in Scotland and I live in Vancouver, British Columbia. The story of our meeting is more than a coincidence.

I am a Border Terrier devotee. My first was born here. I had Danny Boy for seven years. His untimely death was caused by his hatred of cats. Then I acquired Jo-Jo (aged two years) from Mr. Veitch of Sutton Valence, Kent. Jo-Jo was a quiet, angelic dog who never barked at anything or even looked at cats. He was country bred, but quickly he adapted himself to my way of life. He was my constant companion for ten years. He knew exactly how to behave under any circumstances. When he was seven, he injured a hind leg. In the vet's office he could walk on four legs, but for me he used only three. Then he developed a kidney ailment.

One Sunday afternoon last June, I took Jo-Jo to a friend's house for tea. As we were getting out of the car, a man with his wife and a little girl went by. In an unmistakable male Scottish accent, I heard these words, "Ach! A Border Terrier. I haven't seen a Border since I left Scotland. My father breeds Borders there. He knows all the breeders in the country." He patted Jo-Jo and remarked upon his beautifully shaped head. I said, "This little dog isn't very well today. I'm going to England. I may need another Border and I can't get one here. Please could I have your name and phone number?" I shall never know why I uttered this odd request for never before have I asked a stranger for his name! Imagine my amazement when half an hour later, Jo-Jo had a stroke. He lived for a week. I was overcome with grief when he had to be put to sleep for he had been a faithful friend.

Suddenly, I recalled the name of Mr. Willan from Scotland. I phoned him. I was leaving for England in ten days so Mr. Willan suggested that I should give him my first address in Sussex and he would write to his father, who in turn would write to tell me where a puppy was available.

My friend in Sussex knew Jo-Jo. When I telephoned her to tell her of my flight arrival time as she was meeting me, I mentioned Jo-Jo's death and the fact that I wanted another Border. Upon my arrival at Gatwick, she remarked, "I'm sorry, but I can't help you to get your Border. I fear you'll have to give up the idea."

"I'm not going back to Canada without one", I replied.

As we were driving towards Rye, she said, "I didn't know you knew anyone in Scotland. There is a letter from Scotland for you."

"My Border Terrier is in that letter", I said and proceeded to tell her of my encounter with Mr. Willan Junior in Vancouver.

The letter explained that Mr. Willan Senior hadn't any puppies but his friends, the Millers at Eddleston, had four beauties ten weeks old. He gave me their phone number. Immediately I called to Scotland. I was invited to meet Daniel (their chosen name, which I didn't change for reasons you will note) and to stay for a few days to see how we got along. I gave the Millers my next address at Exeter so that they could write and tell me how to get to their house.

Half an hour after my arrival at Exeter, my cousin rushed into the garden where I was sipping tea and said, "There's a call for you from Scotland. Hurry up!" I hadn't told her of my quest for Daniel. Mr. Miller explained that he and his wife were coming south to Pershore for an all Border Terrier show at Corse. They would be at the Manor House Hotel, Pershore on Friday (it was then Monday). Would I like to join them Friday night, go to the show Saturday morning and then drive 325 miles north with them to Eddleston? I acepted with alacrity as I had never seen more than six Borders at the same. time. When I told my cousin of my arrangement, she made the trip to Pershore a frightening experience - a train trip to Gloucester, an overnight stay, a coach trip, a taxi, etc., and that with all my luggage! Then she added, "I have relatives in Pershore. I'll phone them and invite myself for the night. I'll come home from my office early and drive you to Pershore." Thus it happened that I reached Daniel in the way I have just described.

We arrived in Eddleston at 1.00 a.m. ! Daniel I had to see immediately. I knew then that he was meant for me. Each morning he would be waiting for me outside the back door. Whenever I called, he would leave his friends and come to me. I recognized a super abundance of intelligence in him even at the tender age of eleven weeks. I bought a tartan collar and leash for him in Edinburgh. Usually puppies resist collars and leashes, but not Daniel. He walked sedately around the garden wearing his new clothes and with nary a tug nor a pull. We became firm friends in those days I spent with him.

Two weeks later, I arrived home to Vancouver International Airport and the following night at 9.00 p.m. Daniel came from Prestwick. He had with him a certificate to say there was no rabies in Scotland and another saying he had a clean bill of health. The airport vet cleared him immediately. As soon as he saw me, he jumped from his cage into my arms. He took no notice of my friend who drove us home, but washed my face over and over again. He went crazy with joy when we finally reached home at 10:00 p.m. Although he was given a very special bed in my room, he decided he would rather sleep on my pillow. He refuses to sleep anywhere else. He waits until I have put the light out over my head and then very carefully he jumps on the bed and takes possession of the top three-quarters of my pillow!

Daniel's life changed completely when he came to Canada. Instead of a delightful Scottish country home with many doggie companions, he found himself living in a house on a city street. He does have a "dog-proof" garden with fruit trees and a lawn, but the front door is taboo unless he is on the leash, for cars constantly go up and down the street.

Then, one day, I took him to school, for I am a teacher of 22 eight year old boys in a private school. He discovered that school rooms have rules! At the age of four months, he learned to sit in a box with his old shoe and a toy bone. There he had to stay from 8.30 a.m. until 10.45 a.m. By this time he was of course house trained. The boys learned that if they touched or played with Daniel during teaching time, Daniel was sent to the car. Consequently, when this happened for the first time, it didn't happen again. Once in a while he goes to the classroom door and asks to go out. The child whose work is finished takes him for a walk. A different boy "walks" him from 10.45-11.05 a.m. and from 12.15-12.45p.m. he sits in the car during our lunch time. Then he gets "walked" again from 12.45-1.15. He sits in the classroom until 2.30 when someone "walks" him for another fifteen minutes. At four o'clock we go home.

He loves the boys in my class. It is amazing to see him going up and down the stairs between so many boys' feet on his way to and from our room. No matter what the children do to him he is never vicious - though he is as strong as a German Shepherd. Unfortunately for me, he pulls them all over the playground!

At home, life is different again. My first Border Terrier, Danny Boy, had the reputation of being the cleverest dog in Vancouver. He learned to add, subtract, multiply and divide any number below ten by barking the answer. This I taught him very laboriously. In two very short lessons of fifteen minutes duration, Daniel learned to count from one to six by imitating me. During the second lesson, I was able to say, "Daniel, what's four?" The answer would come back immediately "Woof, doof, doof, woof". Each night I mixed numbers. Then I began to say, "Daniel, what is four and two?" His answers were sometimes wrong if some noise or scent distracted him, but nearly always he was right. Then I began to subtract - six take away one; five take away one, etc., until he became perfectly sure of the answers. Then I gave him problems. "If you had three bones and I gave you two more, how many would you have?" and "If you had five shortbreads and John took two away, how many would you have left? "How many twos in eight?" "What is half of six?" His answers are uncanny. Other people try to do it. Real dog lovers can make him give the right answers, while he barks wildly for people without sympathy.

Like all normal people, he likes to talk about himself. This morning he became 8 months old, so he told me eight barks when I asked him his age. He knows that he has 2 eyes, 2 ears, I nose and I tail and of course 4 legs. He likes to say how many gentlemen and how many ladies are in a room. Last night I asked him how many people were wearing glasses. Five woofs was the right answer, much to the astonishment of everyone present.

Now comes a problem of a different kind. Daniel has turned the tables. Danny Boy hadn't the brains to realize that if he barked for something, he would get it. Daniel has! He barks to go out; to come in; to have more water; to have food that I happen to be eating. He goes to the front door and barks, but it never opens. Always he is put out of the back door. He plays with a ball and deliberately rolls it under a chair or out of reach then he barks until I get it for him. Now it has turned into a battle of wits between us. Just who has the stronger will power remains to be seen. He is only eight months old!

Mrs. Phyllis Westmacott

My Life with Borders

My first introduction to Border Terriers was in 1942 when we read an article about them in "The Field", and decided that Borders were the answer to a sporting terrier, good temperament, fun to take for walks and not spoilt.

My first Border was a dog, Kinsbourne Robin, sired by Callum out of Sunshine and going back to Ch. Blister. Unfortunately he was run over by an A.T.S. girl driving an army lorry. Shortly after, we acquired another from John Pawson, Kinsbourne Rusty, sired by Dipley Dusty, grandson of Ch. Foxlair and Ch. Aldham Joker. He was no show Border, but a great character and as tough as they come. In those days before myxomatosis we also had a young Dalmatian dog, Drummond, and they used to hunt the Hertfordshire hedgerows together. An old farm worker once told me he would rather watch our dogs working a hedge than go to the pictures. Rusty drew the hedge whilst Drummond stood a little way off and listened. One bark meant "I've found" two barks "It's coming out", and the toll was considerable. Rusty was a rare one for rats, of which we had a large number living amongst some experimental hops, belonging to a brewery, stored in an old barn. Once the lid was left off a large bin of goat food, and we saw a rat on top of the feed, so we carried the bin into the middle of the yard and dropped Rusty in. What we didn't know was that there were six rats in the bin, and he killed them one by one, the survivors running over his back whilst he did it. In middle life he was savaged by a couple of greyhounds whose owner had allowed them to run loose on the common land just by our gate, and he was nearly torn to pieces. However, with a good vet and careful nursing he recovered though he was a mass of scars, and lived until he was 12 when I had him put down as his heart was weak.

In 1954 I bought another Border dog, this time from Mrs. Twist, Hallbourne Boot Button, sired by Keymer Raven, and was persuaded by my vet, Miss Woodger, to take him to my first show in Luton, under Percy Whittaker. He had some success, I enjoyed myself and that did it, I became a dog show convert. One January with snow on the ground he was lost underground. I searched all the earths I knew and was afraid he had been killed, but a week later he arrived home with his paws raw and nails worn down, caked in clay. It was obvious that the earth had caved in behind him, but such is the resilience of the Border that he soon recovered.

In 1956 we moved further west on to the Chiltern Hills and I bought my first bitch from Mrs. Wainwright. Sprignell became my kennel prefix and Scylla was my foundation bitch. She was a daughter of Portholme Mustard, son of Ch. Boxer Boy. A game bitch and a delightful character who died too young. On one occasion she went to ground and emerged with the black part of her nose hanging loose after an underground encounter. It was sewn on again and a few months later you would have never known what had happened. Scylla had several litters and I kept a bitch, Clytie, sired by Ch. Deerstone Destiny. For the next 14 years we lived on the Chilterns and our land ran up to the vast National Trust area around Ashbridge and Ivinghoe Beacon, chalk downland and open woodlands. I had a lot of fun with the dogs as I used to take out a pack of three couples of Borders, a Beagle bitch (mine), and a couple of young foxhound bitches which I walked every year for our local hunt. They hunted anything which got up in front of them, hares on the open stubble, and in the woodlands, where we had shooting rights, the muntjac or barking deer lived. They used to come right down to the garden and their scent was irresistible. I often had a job to get the hounds and terriers back, and when baulked of their prey the little devils often felt like a good scrap.

Sprignell Lucy was a daughter of Clytie and Roger Clement's Hanleycastle Russ, a dog I always admired as a good type and with a super coat. I believe he lived to a very great age. She was another tough nut and was the dam of Rob Roy who is by Ch. Hawkesburn Beaver.

When we moved down to Dorset in 1969 and found ourselves with a "sure find" overgrown old quarry on our property we had terrible searches for terriers, as foxearths, badger setts and a returning rabbit population in what had been a nature reserve for 8 years proved too much for the Borders. They returned at all hours of the day and night, caked in mud with coats and faces worn bare. Rob Roy and Candy were down one earth for 36 hours and we only discovered it across the fields with the aid of Lucy. They emerged extremely pleased with themselves and quite unashamed. Finally we had to fence in the garden as dog searching took up too much time and always seemed to happen when we had visitors and the dogs knew I was distracted.

Coming to the present day once more the kennel has several youngsters who form a rather lively "nursery party" needing quite a bit of firm handling to turn them into well behaved and responsible Borders. From experience I know that it is not easy to train several at once, as no one owns up, when I sternly say "Who did this (penny)?"

or "Who ate that?" However I am aided in my training by my "Top Dog" Rob Roy who will stand no nonsense from any of them and has made that quite clear in a firm but non-aggressive fashion. But even elder statesmen have their female favourites, and our young bitch, Selina, fills that role very admirably although she has not been elevated to the House of Lords!

My husband takes reliable terriers in the summer to follow the Culmstock Otterhounds, hunting mink on the East Devon rivers, and in the winter they go with local Basset hounds, Beagles, as well as several packs of Foxhounds, all of which they greatly enjoy.

In the latter part of the summer we have a vast number of hunt terrier shows down in the West Country and most Sunday mornings we load up with a picnic lunch, flasks and terriers and are off to one hunt show or another. A call at a pub for "real ale" and then on to the show where the talk is about terriers, hounds and hunting in that order. Great people, great terriers and very good fun.

Sylvia Clarkson

Fifty Years a Border Owner

My only claim to write of Border Terriers is that we had our first 51 years ago and have had one ever since, the war years only excepted. We have never gone in for breeding, nor aspired to winning show prizes - but been more than content to keep one of these sporting little dogs as a pet.

Our first was Sim (after the Border raider Simeon Armstrong, though I've never seen the name elsewhere in the breed) who came of a famous line. His sire was Ch. Dandy of Tynedale, twice a Crystal Palace winner and a great grandson of Robson's Flint. I still have a letter from James Dodd from Oakwood, Hexham, dated October 1926, enquiring after the pup's welfare.

Sim arrived by train at Wolverhampton and well I remember my boyhood disappointment at the harshness of his coat compared with the silky covering of the Labrador and Cocker we already had. But Sim was to prove a stalwart character, able to hold his own with three growing children not to mention other assorted dogs. Alternatively spoilt and bullied at childish whim, he was expected to behave almost as a human, and often did.

The high point of Sim's year came at harvest, chasing - and very occasionally catching if cleverly slipped - rabbits out of the corn, cut in those days by binder whose ever decreasing circuits concentrated the then plentiful rabbits into the last piece of standing corn. Then all the dogs of the village had their chance!

The trouble with Sim was that he wasted so much breath screaming at his quarry - telling the rabbits what he'd do to them when caught, my father used to say. Ferreting he loved, too, especially when a bolter missed the net; and he was known to go out with the Abrighton Woodland Hunt. He was still going strong when I left the family home for the Yeomanry in 1939, fatally damaging his spine when going typically flat out after something on a frosty morning of an early wartime winter.

When we set up our own home in Kent after the war I was soon extolling the virtues of Borders to my Swiss wife, Erika. For a few years we were town-bound but then found space and Tinker arrived in 1950. He came from Mrs. Enid Burnley of Hutton-le-Hole, York, a son of Tweedside Red Playboy by Aldham Joker who also sired the maternal granddam. Tinker quickly became my wife's dog, so I'll let her tell of him, and his successor.

Tinker looked incredibly small to me, used to an Alsatian at home, when we released him from his special box at Kings Cross and Gillian, then aged 3, was of course thrilled with him. Though he really became my dog, he gave her wonderful company - and solace too when she called for him in the middle of the night when ill with asthma. Gillian would wander round the garden playing her mouth organ with Tinker close at heel howling for all he was worth. Singing we called it, and were convinced he enjoyed it!

He was the gamest little dog - in more ways than one, as witness the way he pounced on a rat dispatching it in one fell swoop, or was seen emerging from the bar of a nearby pub where he had tried to bestow his favours on a Great Dane to the entertainment of the customers. He was, alas, an awful roamer and that was his downfall. A boy took a pot shot at him with an airgun and by the time the trouble was discovered peritonitis had set in and poor Tinker never recovered from the operation.

So we went for a bitch next time, picking the boldest of a litter owned by Mrs. Marjorie Spicer, who then bred Borders near Fulmer in Bucks. Dusky, alias Bracken of Atholbrook and combining Grenlund and Chalkcroft blood, was born in 1957 and belying her youthful boldness, turned out the gentlest little bitch ever, indeed the only growls heard to emanate from her came when she found our second daughter Bridget in her Moses basket. The two became wonderful friends, Dusky suffering endless dressings up in made-to-measure outfits.

At birthday parties she would sit sedately on a stool at a coffee table, delicately fed off biscuit and sausage on a plate while excited children unwrapped her presents for her.

It was a sad day for us when at the age of 15 Dusky had to be put to sleep. But she had had a good life, perhaps the most disturbing interlude being the brief appearance of Josie, a guinea pig of which she became so jealous it had to be given away.

J Harris

Borders in the House

My first Border, Bess, was lost for 11 days in snowy weather just before I had her. She survived by the good offices of a farmer, who saw her and put out food and eventually caught her. She was only 8 weeks old and the exposure stopped her growth, she was undersized and only came into season once during the 13 years of her life. She was however a great character and a wonderful 'rabbiting' dog: never touched a ferret but when put in a hedge as a stop nothing else could pass her.

If sitting by me when I fired she'd give a little tail wag and stay put when I had obviously killed the rabbit : the areas I missed she would watch, and if a scrap of flesh flew up, she'd be off and either catch or mark to ground the wounded rabbit. If I missed completely I'd get a reproachful look and she'd sit still.

She was very attached to me and during the war would give me a great welcome when I came on leave. Whilst stationed at Woolwich I used to get home by bus - bombers permitting — and my wife and Bess would collect me by car at the bus station. One night I arrived having carried a nice smooth fox terrier bitch for some miles on my lap - to save her from the feet of passengers. On arrival as usual Bess jumped over the seat onto my lap the moment I got in the car: one sniff and back she went to sit on the back seat with her back to me. Fox terriers indeed!!

From that day she would completely ignore me whilst in uniform, her welcome was reserved until I had changed my clothes.

Judy was the one that persuaded me to start showing: she was a smartish red bitch and got quite a number of 2nd and 3rd prizes. My ineptitude as a handler was probably the cause of her doing no better. She had several litters and one I remember was born seven days early.

Whilst I was away at work she got out and went with her mother, Polly, to a foxearth up the field. They returned about 8.30 p.m., very bloody, very muddy and stinking of fox; they had evidently killed.

I did not think it a very good idea in her condition and told her so, however she assured me it was alright and proved it by producing 6 nice pups during the night. When I went to let her out next morning I was greeted with "I told you so".

About a year later I had a "breakdown" which kept me in bed on and off nearly nine months. Judy used to visit me and was much concerned at my condition. One day she sat on the bed gazing anxiously at me and then suddenly brought up her dinner just in front of my face. Luckily I did not scold her as I quickly realised what a compliment she paid me by treating me as her own puppy - all that nice dinner for *me!* After that I called her Nursey.

When my wife is out in the car I always know when she is returning: there are two points on the twisty road down to our house where there is no obstacle between car and house: one nearly a mile away, the other half a mile.

Any dogs in the house sit on the stairs listening and the moment they hear the car - quite inaudible to human ears - they form an enthusiastic reception committee. I've never known them make a mistake in identifying the car.

The vantage point on the stairs also gives a nice view of the road outside so that passing children and dogs can be suitably greeted. It also enables them to hear the telephone and they sing louder whenever it rings until someone answers it. This has gone on for many years now.

Biddy and Breezie live with a friend in Northamptonshire. I quote from a recent letter from her: "Biddy is now better, she was injured to the extent of 3 broken ribs and a damaged shoulder, the injuries inflicted by the heavy boot of a lout of 18 who broke into the next door house in the early hours of the morning. As I knew the old lady was in hospital I went to investigate: the dogs making such a row I knew something was amiss; I took a stick with me.

The lout came for me and Biddy stood her ground to protect me, whereupon he kicked her viciously; but she got up and still tried to protect me. I hit him with my stick and little Breezie held onto his leg and each time he tried to move just tightened her grip.

Fortunately I had rung the police before I went in, so that in about 20 minutes they came and carted him off.

Quite a do, but I was upset about Biddy, she's still tender over the ribs and limps a bit .... What spunky little dogs Borders are".

My friend later told me that the lout was fined £10 and ordered to perform some "Community Service" - only that, after a previous sentence to a detention centre!! I have heard since that Biddy is much better but will probably always limp. Brave little dogs and brave owner!

"BROOKEND"

Quick! What Shall I Do?

Border Terriers are lively active dogs, thriving on an open air country existence, and despite careful precautions by sensible owners, they may meet with major accidents or minor incidents, where immediate professional veterinary assistance cannot be obtained. In many cases, even seemingly trivial ones, prompt specific treatment by a veterinary surgeon will alleviate the condition more rapidly and efficiently than home remedies, but a good working knowledge of canine first aid ensures that the dog reaches the surgery in the best possible condition physically and mentally.

Unfortunately, one of the most common causes of injury is the road accident. Firstly it is necessary to restrain the dog, which is terrified and shocked, as calmly and firmly as possible, to enable a systematic inspection of the head, body and limbs for signs of injury. It may be necessary to move the patient, either carrying in the arms, or on an improvised stretcher or blanket, to the roadside or into a car, taking especial care to support injured parts to avoid further damage, and make the patient as comfortable as possible in a position in which breathing is as easy as possible, and keeps injured limbs uppermost. The patient must be kept warm by blankets or similar insulation, but not heated artificially, for example with hot water bottles. Attention to severe haemorrhage is a priority. Apart from obvious presence of blood, immediate signs are of shock: weakness, pallor of the mucous membranes, coldness of the extremities and rapid shallow breathing. Keeping the patient still will help to minimise internal bleeding. It is necessary to apply pressure in some form or other to sites of external bleeding. The simplest way to apply pressure is using a finger or thumb. If possible, the hand should be washed first, or a piece of clean material placed over the wound, to prevent introduction of germs. Care should be taken that any foreign bodies are not pushed deeper into the wound. Pressure may also be applied by a pad of gauze or cotton wool firmly bandaged into place. Applications of tourniquets, tight bands around a limb cutting off all arterial flow, should only be considered if less drastic methods are ineffective, should be applied just above the site of bleeding, and should never be left on for more than fifteen minutes at a time. Wounds when severe haemorrhage is not occuring should be covered by a clean dressing, pending proper thorough cleansing at the surgery. The dog may be offered a drink of water, if conscious, but not stimulants such as brandy. Fractures and dislocations should be immobilised as far as possible, by bandaging the limb against the body or applying a splint.

Several different types of wounds may result from injury. First aid measures aim to: control haemorrhage, cleanse wound thoroughly (with water plus a little salt or antiseptic) to minimise risk of infection, and then have the skin stitched up promptly, and antibiotics administered if necessary. Incised wounds caused by sharp cutting objects like broken glass have well-defined, clear-cut edges, and tend to bleed freely. Often these wounds require suturing, if large; incised wounds on dogs' pads, however cannot be sutured, and must be kept bandaged until healing is quite well advanced. A lacerated or torn wound arising from a car accident, barbed wire, or gunshot, carries a high risk of infection. Puncture wounds, from dog bites, nails, or thorns, for example, can be very deceptive, as the actual skin wound may be quite small but lead to a long narrow track deep in the underlying tissues. Again, infection is a common sequel. Two special types of wound are insect stings and snake bites. The former are, of course, painful, but can also be rapidly fatal if the dog is stung in the throat, as tissue swelling may cause asphyxia. Professional aid must be sought rapidly, as also in the case of adder bites. If the snake bites the dog in a limb, a tourniquet can be applied above the wound as a temporary measure.

Burns and scalds are extremely painful and dogs may resent interference of any kind. Treatment is better left to a veterinary surgeon. It is most important not to contaminate the affected area, and any dressings applied should be sterile, if possible, and dry. Shock is a complication of burns, and the patient should therefore be kept warm and as quiet as possible.

Poisoning in dogs usually results from ingestion of rodenticides, either in the form of the bait itself, or of dead poisoned rats. Symptoms vary widely depending on which toxic substance is involved, and so does treatment, so that if poisoning is suspected it is most helpful to collect a sample of the substance or contact the user to find out its name. An emetic may be administered to the dog, except in the case of corrosive poisons. A most efficient emetic is washing soda, given in the form of a lump about 1 cm diameter. Specific treatment will be given by your veterinary surgeon.

Heatstroke is a danger during the summer months. Dogs have only a limited capacity for losing heat from their bodies, and if this is not sufficient for the conditions, their body temperatures rise higher and higher, eventually causing irreversible damage to the tissues, and death. Dogs should never, never be left in cars in direct sunlight, even with windows open, nor exercised during the hottest part of the day in summer. If a dog appears to be becoming distressed, it should be cooled as quickly as possible, by giving it a cold bath, hosing down, or at the very least by wetting the coat thoroughly.

In cases of loss of consciousness from any cause, fits, and heart attacks, it is important to ensure that the dog is not asphyxiated by, for example, "swallowing" its tongue. Obviously professional attention will be required as soon as possible.

It is important to realise that "First Aid" is exactly that, all the conditions mentioned above are beyond the scope of home nursing, and the suggested procedures are merely intended as a stop-gap until the veterinary surgeon can be contacted. It is as well to remember to try to keep calm yourself in an emergency situation, since your own anxiety is quickly communicated to a sensitive canine.

E. M. Davey, M.A., Vet. M.B., M.R.C.V.S.

Thoughts on Working Dogs

How many of us go about our daily business knowing that every minute is full of danger? How many of us work in a foreign environment, under the sea, underground, somewhere man was never intended to go? This is the lot of the working terrier. He pushes his way into the darkness, through the damp and cold, over or round whatever obstacles he meets, with the sole purpose of getting within striking distance of a savage adversary. More often than not the terrier is giving away vital considerations. He is usually smaller than his opponent, he faces him in a position chosen by his quarry, and yet in spite of every odd, and in the face of often fearsome injuries, this noble animal will evict his opponent, or keep him at bay until the cavalry arrives in the form of the diggers. The sound of a terrier baying deep in his place of work is music to his admirers as thrilling as the cry of hounds. Who knows what danger the little hero is facing? We can only speculate.

Let us assume it is a fox. He hasn't the raw power of a badger but he makes up for this with his superior speed of strike and intelligence. He will whenever possible put himself in a position which the terrier finds extremely difficult. Very often he is in some little nook where he is able to strike at the terrier without reply. Perhaps the dog may have to turn a sharp corner or push his way forward on his back. The fox will take advantage of his position and is capable of inflicting some nasty wounds, and of course it is not unknown for a terrier to lose his life. In fact, it is on record that the famed Border Hunt lost a renowned terrier in this way many years ago after one of their longest ever hunts. Even though the terriers had followed the hounds all day, they were still to ground before any followers arrived, and on being dug out the following day one terrier was removed alive with the other terrier and the fox both dead. This is the type of action the terrier was intended for and over the years they have certainly set a high standard for today's enthusiast to try to follow, and it can only be maintained underground and out of sight. Not in terrier trials and the like for any dog will go to ground after a rat in a cage, which is a farce. The dog must face his opponent in his natural environment and towards this end I believe many working certificates are issued after some trivial "test" such as watching a dog go through a drain. This is simply not good enough, for it devalues the certificate for those who have really earned it, and the sooner some other method of awarding these is devised the better.

What about the badger? Now protected by conservation stupidity, he is worse off than ever. When kept to a reasonable level by responsible hunters he was far better off than he is now. Along come the men from the ministry with their evil gas, poor old brock gets no reprieve, no sporting chance. Far better were the old days when they were moved out of an area when they became too numerous. The terriers that face brock need to know their job for he is a terrible opponent. Thankfully he lacks the intelligence of the fox or no terrier would handle him. He will usually attempt to dig, but the dog who knows his job will prevent this, and when brock turns to face his opponent the darkness below is no place for a terrier lacking in courage or intelligence. The dog should not be crowded by other terriers backing him up as this can cost him dearly. He must have room to move and he must stick to his job as long as necessary. To leave brock for a minute or two is often enough to lose him for he can dig on and cover himself like some machine. The dog must be steady and if brock does charge past he must follow him, for brock will move through the sett like some thundering express train, and the earth will shake if he closes with the terrier. Injuries are almost unavoidable, and I look with great suspicion on the unmarked terrier for it usually means he is not venturing anywhere within reach of his opponent.

While the really hard dog will miss much of the season in the sick bay, the dog who bays too far back is a more serious crime to my way of thinking. They are what I call pretenders and I don't care for them at all. Old brock will soon dig on when faced with these for a bit of barking doesn't upset him too much. However hard the terriers work to brock he is virtually immune to injuries and I honestly believe the old days before the "protection" act were more beneficial to him. Unfortunately the actions of a few undoubtedly cruel "sportsmen" precipitated hasty harmful legislation when more thought could have been to the badgers' benefit. The true sportsman doesn't hate his quarry, or wish its extinction. Rather does he admire his opponent, and the fox and badger are in my opinion certainly top of the heap in the world of British wildlife. Let us hope that the "Gasmen" are not going to be responsible for the eventual destruction of the island's oldest inhabitant.

Author unknown

Type for Working

Lying at my feet, as I write this article, is a Border Terrier bitch called Morag. Morag is two years old and has bolted or killed over thirty foxes, has killed wild cats in Sutherland and is what any terrier man would call "dead game".

Morag resembles Borders as could be found in this part of the country at the turn of the century and it is from such stock that the pedigree Border Terriers have been bred. Morag and her parents are not registered terriers but the breeding of these game little dogs may be of interest to readers of this magazine.

Plainly, terriers like Morag are not kept for profit. In general, people prefer pedigree dogs and are prepared to pay more for them, although increasingly a really well bred working terrier pup will sell for more than an otherwise similar pedigree pup. Curiously enough, the same is not true generally of stud fees where an outstanding worker commonly earns a higher fee than his pedigreed cousin. This is not quite so strange as it appears because the working terrier owner is never keen to see any Tom, Dick or Harry with a terrier as good as his own, whereas the pedigree stud tends to bask in the glory of his progeny.

Secondly, the working terrier man, for obvious reasons, does not attach quite the same importance to appearance as does the pedigree Border enthusiast. However, I happen to believe that the Border Terrier standard reasonably describes a useful type of working terrier although I also feel that the standard has been mis-interpreted to some extent.The working Border has a relatively longer muzzle. I am quite sure that anyone who has seen, as I have, a short muzzled Border come away from a fox with an eye hanging out of its socket and the jaw bone broken, would agree that a rather longer muzzle than is currently fashionable, is to be preferred for terriers which may be worked.

It is, quite certainly, impossible to make a terrier go to ground and tackle a fox, so if the dog is required for work it must have an inherent desire to do so. Nobody should be "conned" into believing that with training any Border Terrier will make a worker. It is just not true. I do not doubt that occasionally a good worker is produced from stock which have not been used for work for generations, but generally speaking, working terriers are bred from working terriers.

Morag's sire, Tinker, belongs to my good friend Harry Bragg and runs with Johny Richardson's Blencathra fell pack. He travels to meets with hounds and is kennelled with them. It is therefore essential that he is good natured: a quarrelsome terrier would not last five minutes. Incidentally, in the opinion of that vastly experienced and knowledgeable huntsman, it is the quiet little terriers that are the gamest. In Harry's words "Tinker has yet to be beaten by a fox and has been in every hole in Blencathra country". By that Harry means that Tinker, who has worked with the Blencathra for six seasons, has managed to bolt or kill his fox every time.

Cindy, Morag's mother, now lives in Sutherland with another good friend Nicol MacNicol. This terrier is practically identical to one depicted on an 18th century print. She is a wonderful little bitch. Anyone seeing her rolling about in the house might be forgiven for thinking her a soft touch, but this terrier has worked foxes, otters, badgers and wild cats with distinction. One reason why I gave her to my Highland friend was that Cindy was so keen on explorations sub-terrestrial that there were occasions when she was merrily barking her head off in inaccessible parts of the enormous earths we have around here when everybody else had gone home! Morag is exactly the same.

This enthusiasm for work is the hallmark of a good terrier; it is a quality which passes from parent to progeny as surely does appearance. No matter how experienced a judge of terriers may be, there is no way of assessing working ability on looks alone. If readers wish to maintain the wonderful reputation Border Terriers have for work, there is only one option open to you - you must work your terriers and breed only from those game enough to have a go. May I add, in conclusion, that my friends and I will be only too pleased to help those of you who wish to work your terriers. Borders are part of our hunting heritage, let's keep it that way.

William Gray

The Earth Stopper

In 1967 I made the following notes on the well known print showing Arthur Wentworth of Bulmer near Castle Howard, Yorks.

The original oil painting together with two others by the same artist, Nathaniel Drake, are in the possession of Mr. John Joliffe Tufnell of Langleys, Gt Waltham near Chelmsford, Essex.

They were probably commissioned by Mr. William Tufnell Joliffe since they show respectively that gentleman with his hounds at Nun Monkton Priory, his Earth Stopper and his Bailiff.

Regarding the print, there are at least 3 versions : First, a mezzotint published by Robert Sayer in 1767 - engraved by Valentine Green. I have a copy of this one. Second, a print published by Laurie and Whittle (successors to Robert Sayer) in 1794 engraved by R. Laurie. Mr. Tufnell has a copy of this one. In 1801 J. Scott engraved a variation with the two terriers in front of the pony : this was published in Daniels Rural Sports.

The Mezzotint by Green (No. 1 Version) is entitled "Arthur Wentworth of Bulmer near Castle Howard, Yorkshire, aged 75, Earthstopper to Charles, late Earl of Carlisle, to Henry Brewster Darley, Esq., and now to Wm Tufnell Joliffe and Mann Horsefield Esq"

The fourth Earl of Carlisle kennelled his hounds at Londesborough, south east of York and hunted what is now the wold side of the Holderness Hunt in which Castle Howard was situated. Mr. Henry Brewster Darley kennelled his hounds at Aldby Park in the same country from 1733 till he retired in 1765 in which year the wold side was incorporated into the Holderness County (Reference Bailey).

It appears that Mr. Darley may well have succeeded the Earl of Carlisle as Master.

There is no record as to when Wentworth entered the service of Mr. Tufnell Joliffe. Mr. Tufnell had assumed to name Joliffe — presumably to do with property of some sort. He kennelled his hounds at Nun Monkton Priory some 10 miles north west of York. Possibly Wentworth entered his service when he started that pack as the picture was painted some time prior to 1767 when the print was published. It was presumably in 1765 when Mr. Darley gave up - or possibly earlier .

Mr. Mann Horsefield must have been a joint master, the county hunted was on the borders of the present Middleton and the York and Anstey Hunts.

Wm Tufnell Joliffe was a bachelor and on his death his estate passed to his brother Mr. Tufnell of Langleys the direct ancestor of the present Mr. J. J. Tufnell.

I have gathered these facts (and suppositions) from Mr. Tufnell and various correspondence in "The Field".

The two terriers shown in the print might well be Borders - badly drawn as is the pony - in the original oil painting they are very much more recognisable as Borders. The strain may well have been the Lowther terrier strain, brought across by the Earl of Carlisle but equally easily it could be true Border strain brought down from Northumberland - in which case this must be the oldest known picture of Border Terriers. It is of interest that both blue and pink coats are depicted.

H. D'O. Vigne

Borderitis

"Do they all live indoors?" visitors are apt to ask. Yes, they all live indoors. The house would be very dull without them, a lot tidier perhaps, and it would be nice to sit in a chair and not come up covered in little red hairs, but dull. A drift of Borders about the house is constant entertainment and amusement, and I can get as much satisfaction watching their antics as watching most TV programmes, more in fact. My husband insists, to strangers that is, that he is not a dog lover, funny that when he sits by the fire in the evening at least two sleep happily on his lap, and that all little puppies are carried about and kissed and talked to by this so called non-dog lover!

As I write, the family is disposed in front of the fire. They lie in a long row on their sides, noses pointing to the blaze. Grandfather, (Mr. Boggs to his many friends and admirers) clad in his voluminous winter attire looks relaxed, but one eye is slightly open so that he can keep tabs on what is happening in the household. Mr. Boggs is super intelligent, he understands many words, we tried spelling some but he learned how to spell, we even translated some into school-room French but he is better at languages than either of us. He runs the whole house and the tribe of relatives most efficiently. He has taught them all to get exactly what they want, when they want it. He has taught them the correct procedure for dealing with all visitors and how to attract our attention when the phone rings and we do not hear it. As a telephone answering service he is beyond price. He is also chief ratman, though he is often thwarted in his efforts here as the two cats are super efficient at this job and often leave their home work on the back step, I never know whether it's a gift or a feline "Harvey Smith" gesture.

Mr. Boggs has a crows' nest on the top landing where he shouts down the news of what is happening on our patch, and on the fields and farms opposite, his communication efforts stir his relations to excited conversation, perhaps it is as well we have no neighbours. His daughter Barbie, lies dreaming, she always dreams as soon as she falls asleep, her little paws are digging, her whiskers twitch, she squeaks and her eyes roll horridly under half open lids, she is mousing, her days sleeping and waking are spent in pursuit of MOUSE. To Barbie, Mouse lives everywhere, even when he doesn't, she once got an idea that Mouse lived in the gas oven and drove us mad for weeks scratching at the door. I even put her in to show her Mouse did not live there, but she was not convinced. Mouse to Barbie lives in the larder, down the back of the sofa, in our slippers, behind the wardrobe, and everywhere outside. If she ever catches Mouse she swallows him whole like an oyster. At night she sleeps rolled up in an old dressing-gown like a parcel on the end of my bed, suddenly in the middle of the night she will hurtle off to find Mouse. under the bed, it is very disconcerting.

Boggs' eldest granddaughter Huggy Bear, who has always found life very bewildering and would not know Mouse from a frying pan if it got up and hit her, sleeps the deep, untroubled sleep of those with no conscience. Her sole concern is the gathering of tasty morsels to assuage her incredible appetite. She gathers strength as she sleeps so that she can stand more firmly on the step of the pedal bin to make the lid fly up when she extracts all the delicacies from within. It is the only intelligent thing she has ever done. Huggy Bear is very feminine and very loving. She is also very beautiful. Once when I was showing her in an AV class under an elderly and much respected all rounder, he cupped her face in his hands and said, all soppy, "What a lovely face, like a little flower !" Huggy, I regret to say, has been very conceited from that hour. Huggy has always wanted to be a mummy, I think she had it worked out that you got three meals a day when you were in this state. So we let her be a mummy, but disaster struck and poor Huggy had to be unzipped one Sunday morning in a hurry, it is her first and last go at motherhood, she will have to try other methods of getting little extras. Her two surviving daughters, the Munchkins, now nine weeks are curled up together. One is brash and mischief seeking, one is rather shy and when it is time for bed gets under the side board and peeks out knowing I cannot abstract it, maybe it is not shy, just cunning. We have not made any moves to sell either, they are rather charming, I feel they have decided to stay. Next to them sleeps the five month old Jet who sleeps a deep exhausted sleep after a long day spent committing great wickedness. It included disembowelling a full waste paper bin, pinching her mother's bone, ripping the cover off the magazine rack, and doing a sinful thing behind the chair in the sitting room. She is no doubt gathering strength for a similar day tomorrow. She is beautiful, engaging, fast on her feet, cheeky, and altogether charming. She gets away with murder everytime. So there they all are, except when my daughter comes home with Barbie's sister, Cissie Stick Ears, a mighty hunter and traveller, who has also won prizes and produced Huggy Bear who actually went to Crufts and won a 2nd prize. Cissie is very full of her own importance which Barbie will not stand for, we keep a close eye on them, it is the only time that Barbie lets up on her relentless quest for Mouse.

Peggy Grayson

Then and Now

Recently I was asked by a would-be Border owner and exhibitor about presentation of the show dog and during the conversation I remarked that far more trimming is done now than was general practice when I first became interested in exhibiting. That conversation led me to think of what changes had taken place during the past 17 or 18 years, and to wonder what the regular exhibitors in the 1920's and 1930's would think if they saw the breed at a Championship show now - would they welcome the changes or shake their heads and hold up their hands in horror?

Probably presentation and handling show the major superficial differences since 1961. I say superficial, as I am not considering anything actually involving the breed standard except for a passing query on coats.

I can recall in those days there were three types of presentation. Some dogs were shown literally "in the rough" (and this did not appear to prejudice their chances of winning - judges seemed more critical of shortage of coat rather than too much), a large majority were tidied up only round head, neck, feet and tail, and just a few were turned out really very neat and tidy. My memory may be playing tricks, but I seem to think dogs had thicker coats in those days, and, if this is so, are we breeding out the really thick and dense coat, are there more single-coated dogs being shown, or is it perhaps just the modern method of presentation, always wanting to show elegant lines that makes owners strip out more frequently, and sometimes even before the coat is fully grown?

Regarding handling, it now appears to be the norm to top and tail in the ring, whereas it used to be the exception. No doubt it makes things easier for the judge to have a line-up of static dogs all neatly placed and motionless, but, in my humble opinion, it does nothing for the dog as it seems to me to lose a lot of its Border character when positioned and held by its handler. Perhaps the time factor plays a part with large classes and another breed waiting to follow in the ring, but if the Cairn people (who usually have a larger entry than we do) can show their dogs naturally, why not Border owners? We do still have a few handlers who do not resort to stacking and seem to get the best out of any dog, perhaps due to a natural ability plus much time spent training the dog to respond. These folk have all my admiration (and envy).

Concerning presentation and handling, I suppose it is really a matter of opinion as to whether we have gained or lost something over the years, but there is one department in which I feel today's exhibitors are the losers. This is difficult to explain as it is something rather intangible and hard to put a finger on, but I do think we have lost a little of the camaraderie there always used to be around the Border Ring. People tend to get into cliques more now (possibly due to there being more exhibitors), and there does seem to be more back-biting and less genuine appreciation of other people's dogs. Where we used to have a free and easy atmosphere, the whole business of showing now seems to be taken far more seriously, which again is understandable when it costs so much to compete at Championship show level. But let us stop and think. Why do we go in the first place? There is no compulsion, so presumably it is because we enjoy showing, and surely that is what it is all about - a very pleasurable (even though expensive) hobby.

So may I make a plea for 1979 - that we all try to grow a little like our dogs, not in looks I hasten to add, but in character and also that we let them show some of that character in the ring, the happy-go-lucky, no-nonsense, carefree "joie de vivre" which is the essence of the Border Terrier.

Molly Nicholl

Summer Reflections

Since the days of King Henry II the advent of Spring with the warmer air and lengthening days has caused eager anticipation to rise in the breasts of those who have enjoyed the pleasures of otterhunting. However, from last year the do-gooders, or kill-joys of our age, tolled the final bell for otterhunting in England, although this still continues in Scotland.

From my toddling days I have been a follower of otterhounds. The emptiness of last summer was brought home to me for the first, but by no means the only time, when I saw some people leaning over a bridge, looking at the. river. Automatically, I put my brakes on, but no, they couldn't be watching otterhounds, not any more, so with sunken spirits I went about my business. How dull our countryside will be when there are no packs of hounds to hunt it, only specimens kept so that the rare breeds do not follow the Unicorn and Dodo into extinction.

It is not my intention to discuss the ethics of otterhunting, but I will tell you what I miss. Firstly, the companionship of a host of friends drawn from all walks of life who shared one great interest, otterhunting, and also of course, an interest in the countryside and what went on in it. I have grown up alongside these people and known three generations of families all pursuing the same interest.

There is now no reason for these folk to meet together, so that bond is broken. As we hunted, we talked. There was plenty of time for discussion. We learnt about all countryside lore, wildlife, farming, horses, gamecocks, the local population and anecdotes about characters long since gone. We talked about past events, forthcoming events, politics, religion, money, how to run a business, how to make our gardens grow.

Otterhunting was a leisurely pastime, conducted at human walking pace, not too fast, as hounds must draw every place and stone where an otter may have landed during the night. And there were long intervals sitting on the bank while the terriers worked or the endless holes were dug in the fields so as to insert the terrier at the right place in the land-drain. We leant over bridges for hours, studying the water currents, spotting salmon and observing.

What privileges we enjoyed following hounds through land that is not normally accessible to trippers and tourists. Each river has its own character and how well we learnt every inch of the terrain - where to wade across for easier walking on the other bank, which corners to cut if one felt lazy, how to negotiate the fences, which impossibly steep-banked woods to walk round rather than through. We even learnt the drainage system of the fields where otters used the land-drains.

We enjoyed passing the time of day with the fisherman and hay-makers who we encountered. We observed wonderful birdlife - dippers, oystercatchers, wagtails, the blue flash of a kingfisher, a sandpiper, the clever 'broken-wing trick' of Mrs. Duck which never failed to entice some foolish young hound into pursuing her hopefully, whilst her ducklings quietly camouflaged themselves until she returned safely to gather them together. We saw the wretched gull hanging in a tree suspended by a broken fishing cast, in which it had become entwined and we freed it.

The flowers of stream, river bank, woodland and moorland tarn we knew. We nibbled raspberries and blackberries, filled our hankies with horse mushrooms. We knew the smells of the river bank, crushed wild garlic in the shady woodlands after it had been trodden on, the smell of muddy, wet otterhound and sweet meadowsweet and honeysuckle.

We saw salmon, lampreys, trout, crayfish, minnows and eels. We walked into wasps nests, we were eaten alive by midges, bitten by clegs, and stung by bees, but we also saw dragonflies, mayflies, gorgeous butterflies and other insects.

Most of you have seen the pure bred otterhound with their water-proof jackets, folded ears to keep the water out, large noses and deep, sonorous voices. Otterhunting was the best way I knew of watching hound work at close quarters and experiencing the ancient skill of man pursuing a quarry with the aid of dogs alone and no mechanical implements.

These hounds could, with their well developed noses, hunt where an otter travelled the previous night or even the night before that. This scent is known as the drag and as the hounds came closer to their quarry, so their music would get stronger as they spoke with more certainty. Hounds cannot hunt drag on the water, so the hound music is spasmodic, hounds speaking wherever the otter had touched land during his nocturnal wanderings. The drag may have been hunted all day without ever reaching the otter, or of course the whole day may have been blank - no sniff of an otter, so no music.

Once an otter was marked to ground and bolted which was when our terriers came into use, the hounds could hunt the scent both on land and water. The current of the water of course affected the scent, carrying it on it, "wash" is the term for scent floating on the water. An otter can travel very fast on land and a bold dog otter would sometimes take to the land for a while and give the hounds a good run around a wood. How richly those booming voices echoed in woodland.

Lakes were also hunted and provided a different sort of sport, long swimming hunts. Otters hunting on lakes would show themselves more often, surfacing and often lying on the surface casually watching hounds. I remember one which had given us a good hunt, sitting in the middle of a small tarn watching us all eat our lunches as much as to say "can't catch me". We didn't.

We had our exciting moments apart from the thrill of the chase. The mad farmer's wife brandishing a very sharp carving knife; the human remains found in the river; the grave-digger who would insist on squaring the edges at a dig; the wallet which was accidently dropped into the top of the field drain, which was opened in several places, and the owner rushing down the field shouting "there it is" as it passed each opening on the flow of water to catch it at the mouth of the drain as it sped into the flow of the river; the otter which went to ground up our lady secretary's skirt; the otterhunter who was struck by lightning; the one who was swept away by a strong current to be fished out by a kind man downstream; the famous judge of Borders who slid down a bank on her BTM not realising there were broken bottles in the soil; the hound rescued from a whirlpool by a brave young man; the silly hound puppy who swam on to an island in a lake and refused to leave, and the naked doctor who swam out to collect it, and the screams of terror from the puppy when it saw the pale naked form arising from the water.

Yes, we had fun. Those days may be gone for ever, for me mink-hunting is for a man and his terriers, not for noble hounds, but "they" can never take away the experience or the memories of those happy summer days - not always hot and sunny but even when blank and wet, never dull or boring. And how the terriers enjoyed it.

Anne Roslin Williams

Mistaken Judgement of Working Character

I have been badgered into writing an article for this year's publication. I went through the old books and every aspect appeared to have been covered some time or other. At last inspiration came via Anne Roslin-Williams' breed notes Jan. 12, the relevant passage being "an item caught my eye regarding an American Working Trial where a Border was penalised for hitting the cage containing the quarry and backing off every seven or eight seconds".

I remember years ago reading an account of a working trial written by Leo Wilson. It took place in Sweden if I remember right. Presumably the American Trial was run on the same lines. The dog was put in an artificial drain at the end of which was a chamber, a den with a removable lid in which was caged a tame fox from a local fox farm. The winner was a big smooth Fox Terrier which attacked the cage so fiercely that they only just got the fox out in time.

If you are asked to judge do you give a shriek of joy and jump on the band wagon or have you the courage to say no, I don't know enough about it, or even give me a bit of time, and then start to do your home-work. To get back to the point, in Anne R.W.'s report these judges had not done their homework, they elected to give judgement upon a subject they knew nothing about. After all, you may say, what was there to judge. Just if a dog was brave enough to approach a fox in a cage or not, and so this verdict on the "dodgy" Border damned one of the best working breeds, because it used its brains.

We are not told who these judges were, the chap from down the road, or some eminent judge in the world of dogs whose opinion carries weight, praise is soon forgotten, but disparagement in any form lingers on. "I would like to have a working Border but it does....or if it didn't"; if and but, two little words but two of the most meaningful words in the language.

When a fox goes to ground, unless the terrier is running with hounds there is a considerable lapse of time before he is put down. First, the digging party has to get there, hounds have to be taken away, and usually the hole cleared out where hounds have been scratching before he can get in. Moreover the ground has to be examined for some distance round to find any other exits there may be, and in bracken or thick undergrowth one may easily be overlooked and the fox get away unless a careful search is made.

Meanwhile the fox has had a rest and gets the added advantage of choosing his ground, be ready to bolt if the dog intimidates him, or wedge himself in a small hole with his back to the wall, get his head down and prepare to sit it out.

The aforementioned fox terrier that Mr. Wilson saw will rush in regardless and do battle, will probably get very severely damaged so much so that it may have enough and come out.

Now for the "dodgy" Border. He gives tongue, darts and feints to and fro until he irratates the fox into making a mistake and dropping his guard. The fox lifts its head and snaps back, the right moment has come, the opportunity is there. The dog dives in low and seizes the fox by the lower jaw or throat and the fox is helpless, unable to bite back. The dog will attempt to draw but if the fox is too tightly wedged in he will stay latched on till dug down to.

This is when the "bleeper" comes into its own. The dog wears a tight collar with a small attachment firmly taped on. The other half is above ground, switches on like a torch and is moved around until it ticks. The area is reduced until the tick is pinpointed, and progress can be followed and digging started immediately. In any case you know where he is.

The reader may think I have rambled on, and castigated judges pretty strongly when I don't judge myself, but against that I do know something about working terriers. Since the last war I have used several generations of my own, and seen a lot of other people, some of them very knowledgeable who have been kind enough to impart information and allow me to suck their brains. So when I saw the Border damned for its merits I felt I must put pen to paper, which I much dislike doing, and uphold the breed.

I believe this book goes to America, I only hope some of those who were at the trial will read this and inwardly digest.

B M L Eccles

Good News, Bad News

A well known Border Terrier judge consulted his vicar as to whether he could get similar employment in the next world, since he has so much enjoyed his judging in this one.

"The vicar he was no fool. He'd been to a great public school". After a week he met the parishioner and said : "I have found out some information for you, some good and some bad. First the good news. They are very short of good Border judges, so there is plenty of work which will keep you busy for years and years".

"What about the bad news?"

"Well, I'm sorry to say, your first judging engagement is a week on Saturday".

Mr. Wattie Irving with Ch. Rising Light.

The Irving Connection

The names Irving and Musselburgh are synonymous with Border Terriers and the long association of the Irving family with the breed is remarkable in that it is unbroken since 1924 to the present day.

With the granting of approval by the Kennel Club for Mr. Andrew Irving to award Challenge Certificates to Borders, the Irving family have achieved an extremely rare distinction of three generations of a family becoming Championship show judges - the late Mr. Wattie Irving, his son Andrew and his son Ronnie.

Only two other examples of this triple honour come to mind, the owners of the 'Ware' Cockers and the 'Watteau' Smooth Fox Terriers. There may be others, but not many.

This therefore seems an appropriate time to record the history of the Irving family's association with the breed which started in 1924, just four years after the Border Terrier was granted official recognition by the Kennel Club.

In 1924 Mr. Tommie Lawrence, Station Master at Hawick in Roxburghshire, made a present of a Border bitch to Andrew, the young son of Mr. Wattie Irving. At that time Mr. Wattie Irving was Station Master at Riccarton Junction, a village between Hawick and Carlisle in the very heart of the Border country and in the area covered by the Liddesdale Hunt. Riccarton was a railway village and nothing more, having thirty-five houses inhabited only by railwaymen and one schoolmaster's house. It was surrounded by Border fells with no approach road, only the railway. What more natural breed for the Irving family than the Border Terrier, the native terrier of this remote district.

This bitch was Station Masher, bred by a Mr. A. Fox, but records do not show how she came into Mr. Lawrence's hands. She notched up quite a few wins at the local shows before becoming Ch. Station Masher, in Mr. Wattie Irving's hands. She became the foundation of the kennel which has been carried on since that day. She was what we would call a blue and tan, but was registered as "grizzle with a dark back". Her breeding was Oxenham Pincher (Ch. Grip of Tynedale ex Flora Ford) out of an unregistered bitch, Jed (Scamp ex Teviot Nettle).

She proved her worth as a brood bitch. Mated to the famous Tinker (who was owned by Miss Bell-Irving, and was the first of the breed ever to win a C.C.) Ch. Station Masher produced Arnton Billy, a rather large dog by the standard of the day. However he did a bit of winning locally and sired several litters in one of which was a bitch, Fancy, who produced Ch. Heronslea in 1930 who in turn sired Ch. Wedale Jock.

Mated to Ch. Barney Bindle, Ch. Station Masher produced Ch. Kineton Koffey which Mr. Irving owned in partnership with Captain C. R. Pawson and sent to Captain Pawson to augment the ranks of the breed in the south.

From another mating back to her own great-grandson, Whitrope Don, Ch. Station Masher bred that well-known Champion of the 1930s, Ch. Joyden who won ten C.Cs including at least one each year for a period of seven years, and her final one at the age of nine.

Ch. Kineton Koffee

Whitrope Don sired Rab o'Lammermoor, another influential stud dog owned by Mr. Irving, perhaps best known as the sire of Ch. Fox Lair and Devonside Diversion, from these two stem two important lines of descent to the modern Border.

Other Borders owned by Mr. Wattie Irving before the war included Din Vic, Din Shiela (2 C.Cs), Winnie o'Dryffe (2 C.Cs), Greatmore Leo, Honest Jock, Hunting Sally, Hunty Gowk, Knowe Roy, Lady Pat (2 C.Cs) Liddesdale Wendy, Miss Shena, Red Billy, Wind'im, Wood Nymph and Darkie Bet, all names well-known to students of pedigree but, owing to the lack of a prefix, not readily associated with Mr. Irving.

Winnie O'Dryffe

After retiring from the railways in 1948 Mr. Wattie Irving had fewer brood bitches but owned a number of successful stud dogs. His first big winner after the war was Ch. Rising Light who won 10 C.Cs and sired two Champions. Mr. Irving recounted how this dog won his title, and to spare, before he, the owner, ever handled him to a C.C. win, as he used to be despatched by rail to the nearest station to the show and handled by anyone available before being returned, with his C.C., by rail ! Of course. the Railway system was more obliging in those days, but what a superb temperament the dog must have had to show, and win, for a stranger.

Next came Ch. Alexander, Ch. Rab Roy, Ch. Brieryhill Gertrude and Ch. Bright Light, the last three all bred the same way by Miss Galbraith. Ch. Bright Light still holds the post-war bitch record for C.Cs won with eleven (*True at the time but now held by Ch Dandyhow Cleopatra owned by Mrs Kate Irving - Ed.*)

Since the 1960s and following the death of Mr. Wattie Irving, the kennel has contained Ch. Bounty Tanner, his son Ch. Arnton Fell, Ch. Llanishen Penelope and her daughter Ch. May Isle Misty and Penelope's two grandchildren, the litter mates Ch. South Box and Ch. Din Merry, all owned by Mr. Ronnie Irving with the exception of Ch. May Isle Misty which he owned in partnership with a cousin, Mr. Bottomley.

Ch. Hawkesburn Beaver

Mr. Wattie Irving's son-in-law, Mr. T. Mervyn Gaddes who died late in 1979, was also a Championship show judge of many years standing who had officiated at both Crufts and Carlisle, as will have both Mr. Wattie and Mr. Ronnie Irving by the time this appears. Mr. Gaddes owned Ch. Hornpiece Salvia, which he acquired from Miss Hemmingway and bred Ch. Hawkesburn Beaver. Miss Grace Gaddes (now Mrs. Grace MacDougald) owned Ch. Gay Gordon.

Another member of the family is Miss Hislop, who co-owned Dryden Keryna, mother of Chs. South Box and Din Merry, with Mr. Ronnie Irving.

Ch. Hornpiece Salvia

For historians, it is a pity that the kennel has never had a prefix, although the name Musselburgh has long been associated with the kennel. The kennel moved there in 1931. When Mr. Ronnie Irving married Miss Kate Sullivan of Dandyhow fame in 1978, the Border folk impressed upon him that he must look for a house only within the boundaries of Musselburgh, or lose his right to the unofficial prefix. However the problem was circumnavigated by leaving a branch of the famous kennel in Musselburgh with Mr. Andrew Irving.

The reason for not having a prefix, as did not many others in the early days of the breed, was that there was a certain amount of controversy over whether recognition was in fact a good or bad thing for the breed and those taking a prefix might be considered to be seen to be too pro-recognition. The late Mr. Wattie Irving, however, claimed that as he, like most people, bred as many mediocre as good Borders, he preferred not to be closely associated with the former!

As a final note, a clue to the rather strange seeming names might be enlightening. Din is not, as one would be forgiven for assuming, a loud noise, but a fell near Riccarton, as is Arnton. And the South Box was one of the two signal boxes at Riccarton Junction.

T. Gaddes

Conformation of Body and Mind

My first Border Terrier came to me as a small puppy thirty years ago - a good representative of the breed sired by Ch. Swallowfield Garry. Many of the intervening years have been spent in the less trod parts of the world which precluded a personal canine companion but included working G.S.Ds and Labradors. It was close observations of the adult working dog that allowed study of the end product of man-ordained matings.

Planned animal breeding should be directed at producing an end product as good as, if not better than each of it parents. Genetics allows prediction of certain traits in the offspring of a mating. Genes, the bearers of characteristics, have been likened to a pack of playing cards. A mating is the shuffling together of the genes of each parent. The offspring carries a full pack up made of a proportion of cards from each of the parental packs.

The Standard laid down for each breed of dog includes coat colours and the size and shape required to enable the breed to fulfil its original purpose. Those that judge the animals we produce obviously must ensure that the dog or bitch conforms to these standards as much as possible.

The intriguing part of animal breeding is 'the Joker in the pack' of genes. To make a fair assessment of the value of breeding material (parents) we should assess the whole litter for defects. Perhaps these may be of little moment in the household pet but disaster in working or show animals. It would be of interest to know what percentage of each mating carried faults either physical or mental to render them unfit for showing.

Surely there is more to it than that? There are animals who may closely conform to the breed Standard but which find difficulty in whelping, lactating or mothering their litter. Such characteristics may be inherited. In certain breeds of dogs there are well known inherited defects in structure of some part of the body - e.g. eyes, hips. The relative importance of these in the mind of the breeder varies because there are a number of characteristics which are linked together. So often one hears of the recipe for producing the 'super dog'. Attempts have involved effort, time and money but I know of none that have proved entirely and consistently successful. The 'fixing' of one characteristic may well lead to the loss of another equally valuable asset. The end product of genetic juggling may be a physically sound dog but this serves little purpose if the same animal is unable to reproduce itself or has 'little between the ears'.

My title includes both body and mind. The combination of the mind is commonly called temperament. In this field perhaps, in addition to heredity, environment plays some part in forming the end product. One has read (H. G. Martin in Dog Training Weekly vol. 16 no. 8 24 Feb. 1978) that by the changing over of litters at birth one can predict the temperament of the pups in each litter in that the pups' temperaments are moulded to that of the bitch which rears them, each pup having a temperament similar to the bitch which reared them and not necessarily to the bitch from which it was bred. This observation was reported recently when two G.S.D. bitches, one aggressive the other timid, were mated to the same sire at each of two successive heats. The first time each reared her own puppies but on the second occasion the two litters were swapped. The results were reported as follows:

Rearing Bitch	Temperament of Dam	Puppies Reared by Dam	Puppies Changed at Birth
A	Aggressive	Aggressive own pups	Aggressive (Bitch B's Pups)
B	Timid	Timid own pups	Timid (Bitch A's Pups)

This observation gives food for thought but it would need to be tested many times before it could be accepted as 'the rule'. As in all breeding matters there is the chance element, 'the Joker in the pack'.

I do believe that two factors control temperament, firstly genetic and secondly environment. From the genetic side each parent contributes a potential for a good or bad temperament in their offspring. Subsequent to birth the potential develops according to the environment in which the puppy is brought up.

Today we hear about giving young puppies the chance to socialise with humans, other dogs and a host of environmental possibilities which the dog may meet during its adult life. There is little new in this. Do you remember Black Beauty spent part of her early life in a field beside a railway line ? At first the passing of a train caused terror of the unknown snorting monster but it was not long before she treated it with the same contempt as the sheep with whom she shared the field. They were already acclimatized to that particular environmental factor.

I hope the above may stimulate thought and discussion. Let us take heed that in our dog breeding our end products, as well as slipping neatly into the physical mould described in the breed standard also retain the physical stamina to perpetuate themselves as well as that conformation of mind which is essential to the make up of a working Border Terrier.

Gordon Willde

Changing Times

Regarding the article by Molly Nicholl 'Then and Now' in last year's Year Book. I must now agree with her when she says the showing of Border Terriers has changed over the past eighteen years. I have shown Borders for twenty five years and have possibly seen more changes, many of which I personally consider are not for the better..

As Molly Nicholl says, "topping and tailing" now seems the normal thing. In my opinion this may be an advantage when the Border is seen from a distance on the ground, but it does not in any way alter the dog whilst being "gone over" by the judge. All experienced judges should be able to assess the dog's good and bad points (of conformation) by close examination and touch; faults in movement and the conformation of the limbs will be identified when the animal is walked. "Topping and tailing" should not influence judges in any way - it cannot change the true conformation of the dog.

On the subject of Border coats - I believe that Borders should be clean and tidy when shown - not shorn as many are today. Some, so smartly trimmed for the show ring, would really feel the cold winds or hail of our east coast. If they were expected to stand around waiting to work here, they would need a good run round to stimulate the circulation before they were capable. This should be taken into account when inspecting coats as, after all, the order is a working terrier and so should be able to work in any weather conditions.

I realise that all show animals should be exhibited looking their best, but there can be no comparison between showing farm animals, which will be either molly coddled from show to show or destined for slaughter in a few hours, and showing Borders which can be put at a show today in sunshine, and working in pouring rain and mud tomorrow.

I would hate to think that we are getting two types of Borders - one for work and one for show. Too many working breeds are becoming divided - please exhibitors and judges, keep the Borders as one breed.

Regarding the attitude of people around the showring - again I agree with Molly Nicholl - the change is for the worse. Gone are the days when the old hands were glad to help and advise the newcomer. Today, only a few with a knowledge of the breed seem willing to pass on sound advice, and many of these appear to be the people who have already sold a puppy, or taken a stud fee, from the inquiring beginner. Surely the beginner can obtain opinions and advice without buying or begging.

In what I would like to call "the good old days", the majority of judges would walk around the benches after they had judged, and were ready to discuss any dog, be it winner or loser. Few of the present day judges do this. One is left to speculate as to the reason for this change. Dare the judges not face the losers, or is it simply that the beginners know it all, and so succeed in stopping some judges from offering (sometimes) valuable advice. I hope that it is neither; but so many things remain unexplained in a fast changing world.

Syd Grantham

Fox Hunt in Australia

In August of 1979 a group of Border Terrier enthusiasts gathered at Brisbane, Queensland, Australia for the purpose of exhibiting their dogs at the Brisbane Royal Show. It was the first time that such a gathering had taken place due to the vast distances between us with some of the people travelling over 1500 kilometres. It was gratifying for all concerned to be able to muster eight Borders for exhibition this year. The total number of Borders that my wife and I played host to was twelve, ranging in age from three and a half years down to four weeks.

During this time a friend of mine who owns a small parcel of land close to Brisbane was telling me he was having trouble with a fox harassing his chickens and of his intention of trying to shoot it. Half joking he made mention of my funny terriers and suggested that I bring a couple out to see what they were made of. Taking up the gauntlet I replied, "name a day and we will be there". Over supper the subject was discussed with my visitors and it was decided to make it a field day for our Borders and it would give us a good opportunity to test our dogs on entering. Four adult dogs were chosen plus two seven month old pups to gauge their reactions. Only two of the dogs had been to earth previously, one of them being Mr. Tom Morrow's dog Ha Ha who is quite accomplished with fox, having dispatched two one week before arriving at my place.

A preliminary look at the area was undertaken and it was decided it would be very unlikely that we would encounter a fox at earth as the climate is rather warm and there is plenty of cover for fox to live on the surface. The only chance would be to catch one napping in the heat of the day or a vixen with cubs. The terrain is vastly different from the Borders' native land. It is semi-tropical, very scrubby. Plenty of fallen timber, criss-crossed by small creeks and loads of cutting vines which wrap around the ankles. The earth is very sandy and easy to dig in and plenty of openings were sighted so the dogs were sent for. Mr. Tom Morrow was placed in charge as he is from the Border Country of Scotland and has had experience working Borders while living with his parents. It was not long before the first opening was reached and Tom's dog was let off. Like a shot he was gone. He emerged ten minutes later to inform us that the earth was empty. It was decided to try my three year old bitch who was very excited. Without hesitation she entered to return shortly to report finding nothing. All four adults were entered in turn each not willing to accept the previous dog's word that the earth was empty. By this time the pups were very excited straining on their leashes so were allowed to go to the mouth of the earth. They could not work out what all the fuss was about and looked at each quizzically. The day progressed and many happy hours were spent watching the dogs working their way through the scrub, crossing creeks on fallen logs and entering every opening they came across until they were thoroughly exhausted. I have to report that no fox was sighted but the day was well spent. My friend did not solve his fox problem but he no longer refers to my dogs as funny little terriers and is proud to relate the day's proceedings to all he meets. Whatever we lack in our Borders we do not lack in temperament, willingness and ability to work. I look forward to the day when the number of Border Terrier enthusiasts has grown from six to sixty in this country and the eventual formation of a breed club and what a day it will be to attend the first speciality show.

K. W. Iggleden

Coundon - or How it All Began

My first Border Terrier was born in 1933 and was by Ch. Dinger and breeding went back to Tinker, Ch. Station Masher and Gem of Gold. He was bred in Hunt Kennels. He was six months old when I had him and was told he had been to ground with his dam! I was not surprised that he was interested in nothing bigger than a rat hole. He would sit and watch one until forcibly removed. He died of hard pad at 5 years old.

I then had a puppy from Mrs. E. W. Lowrie by Ch. Wedale Jock x Morning Dew. He caught his first little rabbit at 4 months - the first of many and always little ones.

I always wanted to breed dogs, but met with parental opposition - so when I bought a bitch Portholme Beatrice, called Sally, they were horrified.

"Did I realise there would be puppies - more mouths to feed". I registered my prefix, and Buster and Sally had several litters level in size and colour. Buster had a few visiting bitches, but would not mate with more - perhaps brought on the wrong day. I took Sally to another dog, but she refused him, although left for several days. I brought her back and she mated with Buster straight away, so faithful were they to each other!

My first show girl was Minnie of Coundon, but she was not a success as a brood. I bought from Mrs. Twist Ravensdowne Roxana, bred by Miss Fair. I called her Zoe. She was fascinated by the telephone and used to sit on my lap and listen in to the other voice. In those days the exchange was manual. If I was in the garden out of earshot and Zoe heard the bell ring she used to whine to me in great agitation. I would rush to the telephone always sure I was wanted.

Zoe's first litter was by Ch. Hallbourne Brick of which I kept Coundon Jet, who was sold later to Mrs. Harold Sinclair to make room for Trudy. Tim was from the next litter by Ch. Billy Boy. Jet was bred to Scarweather Atom owned by the late Major Glynne Powell from where came the famous Hanleycastle Russ whose line still goes on. Tim was bought by Miss Long and became Ch. Winstonhall Coundon Tim. He got his 4th C.C. at Leeds in 1962 under Mr. Robert Hall. Trudy became a champion and was B.O.B. at the same show - this was my greatest day! Trudy had a daughter Coundon Troena by Ch. Portholme Macsleap.

In 1964 she made a profit of £16.46 over entries ! It has never happened before or since! She eventually won her title.

I only keep bitches. Her first litter was all bitches which I let go being in no hurry to expand the kennel. Sadly her following two litters were all dogs. Things went wrong and she had to be spayed. I managed to obtain a grand daughter of Troena's by Dandyhow Brussel Sprout. She wasn't a successful brood and her show career was spoilt by being bitten in the ring, which she never forgot. She still enjoys life at 12 years old.

I had Llanishen Rosemary from Mr Dennis Wiseman, who became Ch. Llanishen Rosemary of Coundon. Rosemary has a comic and very small daughter. In 46 years I have never been without Borders - and by the time this Year Book is printed maybe I shall have some more !

Nancy Turrell

A Border Family

Having prepared for two litters of puppies expected within ten days of each other in the house (as all my four legged friends are), the nurseries ready, one awaits events.

First Bobward Little Dorrit (Bunty) produced milk and gradually decreased in size. On a check up with the Veterinary Surgeon he pronounced "No pups - false pregnancy." Poor Bunty became very frustrated and the more my other bitch Eignwye Fern of Lairdarch (Scylla) showed signs of motherhood, in every way, the worse it worried Bunty. The great day arrived, Scylla produced six lovely puppies, but Bunty's milk increased.

Scylla's first outing to the garden was joined by Bunty also and to my surprise, and I may say, under very careful supervision and a constant watchful eye, I watched Scylla and Bunty return together and both, without hesitation or sign of aggression, got into the whelping box and settled together as if they had both produced the same litter. They continued to go out together and race back to see which could get to the pups first and have the pick of the bunch to nurse, but with no unpleasantness.

The relationship was wonderful to see and so rare - Scylla feeding the pups and Bunty washing them, alternately, sometimes pups with each of them. This happy relationship lasted until the pups were on their feet and Bunty had dried up, then becoming their governess/playmate instead.

Scylla would not allow her great pal Pearl nearer than the outside of the whelping box where she would sit for hours on end, listening to the squeaks and jostling inside, her head moving from side to side. Pearl knew she could go no nearer.

Their old grandmother Bobward Faerie (Wendy) is accepted by all nursing mothers and is trusted by all, and at a later date the pups will pull her about, she washes them and they curl up and sleep with her.

This relationship is unique, even with my own Border family. Bunty's daughter Lairdarch Bobward Pearl, when she has pups, will not allow Scylla or her mother (Bunty) anywhere near the whelping box so, even in one canine family, some can be very unpredictable and possessive, as the majority of nursing bitches are. Great care must be taken at all times not to let other dogs near a nursing bitch. One should in no way take a nursing mother for granted but treat her with great care and respect or one may find her deserting, or destroying the whole litter. I have been lucky with my lot!

Felicity Carr

Working Enthusiasts

Whilst most would agree it would be detrimental to split the breed into two distinct types, the working and the show type, we would acknowledge the existence of various types of Border Terrier owners. The owner principally interested in showing his dog is well catered for in the S.B.T.C. This club also holds functions for owners who are not show mad, but enjoy the company of their Borders and who aim to breed good quality puppies.

A third type of owner is the working enthusiast whose primary interest in Borders is as a working dog, fulfilling the task for which it was used originally, for foxing. I'm sure we have many such people amongst our members, but they seem to be reluctant to make themselves known. I am making a plea for working enthusiasts to speak up - advertise yourselves. Tell us about your dogs, send us pictures of your dogs with their thick Border coats not tidied up. I am often asked where "proper" working Borders can be purchased, so advertise your dogs in the Year Book, there is a demand for your product. But, two pleas to you:

1. Please register your stock, and use only registered stock in your breeding programmes. It is no longer possible to register a dog from unregistered stock however good. By breeding with unregistered stock you are doing the breed no service.

2. Breed according to the standard laid down for the breed many years ago. If you require a terrier with short legs and a short thick body, don't breed Borders, but pick another terrier breed for your working activities.

I would like to see more working enthusiasts coming to Kennel Club Shows. After all, you go to Working Terrier Shows where the standard of judging sometimes leaves much to be desired. I say, come to some shows, express disgust at some of the dogs being shown (we all do!) but look carefully and you might see one or two that aren't too bad.

Finally, I would like to urge breeders not to refuse to sell pups for working, but to consider all potential buyers on their own merit, there are good and bad owners in all fields of interest. Keep your very best stock to breed from by all means, but please don't fob working enthusiasts off with poor stock, a working animal must be sound in mind and body.

Marie Sharp

A Badge of Distinction

Having been the owner of two Portholme Borders and having recently acquired Bobby, of Rhozzum breeding, I have been press-ganged into writing a few of my true experiences of the interest and curiosity aroused by my Southern Border Terrier Club badge, both here and in Australia.

Its prominence was first brought to my notice about three years ago on Eastbourne sea front when I was asked about it by a party of people and when I told them, one old lady asked "Do you judge at Crufts then ?" Later I was asked what mob I was in by someone who thought the badge was like that of his regiment, the Royal West Kent Regiment.

On another occasion, it even attracted the Bishop's attention for, when the service was over, he came and asked me all about our Club and its badge.

I recently spent three months in Australia where I spent a pleasant time with Robert Bartram. I didn't wear my badge often but once had quite a hard time persuading an Aboriginal woman that I was not evil, but that my badge was a proud possession.

When I did wear my jacket, the badge aroused great curiosity, none greater than at Bahrein where we had a fuel stop. Whilst in the airport lounge at dawn, a party of Arabs came up. One was a Sheikh and he kept pointing out my badge to his entourage. They all began pointing to it and talking loudly in Arabic, which I did not understand, I got up to go to the plane and the Sheikh and his party followed behind, still pointing. I didn't know if I was going to be offered a few thousand barrels of oil, or cash, for it or whether they thought I was a person of high esteem. I never shall know as they stopped when I went to the embarkation point. I did glance back and they were still pointing and talking excitedly. Both on the trip out and back I was questioned and searched three times at the Security check because of the badge's metal content.

Many more such incidents have occurred - only the other day I had to visit my doctor and even he asked me about it and seemed glad to tell me that he had once owned a Border.

I am very proud of my badge and its significance, that it creates such interest. I have a safety clasp on it now, having nearly lost it twice.

Leslie Dumbrell

The Rules of George V

When I bought my G.S.D. puppy over 20 years ago, the breeder gave me the following set of rules upon which the late King George V tried to base his life. She told me that if I remembered them I would enjoy working my dog in competition, and on looking back I know she was right. I think they apply equally well to showing a dog, so you might think they are worth reading.

- Teach me to be obedient to the rules of the game.
- Teach me to distinguish between sentiment and sentimentality admiring one and despising the other.
- Teach me neither to proffer nor to receive cheap praise.
- If I am called upon to suffer, let me behave like a well bred beast that goes away to suffer in silence.
- Teach me to win if I may and if I may not win, then above all teach me to be a good loser.
- Teach me neither to cry for the moon nor over spilt milk.

Elizabeth Rhind

Brave Border

Sir,

I want to boast through your columns about an astonishing Border Terrier. This remarkable creature plunged into the River Coln at Bibury in pursuit of a wounded cock pheasant. The river was swollen, but undeterred both of them swam up stream, the cock bird by flapping his wings. The little dog eventually caught him and dragged him ashore and then dragged and carried the bird in stages to hand.

C. R. Hall

(Printed by kind permission of "The Field")

Would You Like to Show Your Border?

Let us assume that you have a nice young Border dog or bitch and you would like to take him or her to a dog show. Of course we know that all Borders are nice and yours is a very special dog, but it would be fun to see how he gets on in competition with other Border Terriers, so how do you start ?

Well, first of all you, must find a show not too far away, preferably with Border classes, but if not, Any Variety Terrier classes will do quite well for a start. Look in the two dog weekly papers, "Dog World" and "Our Dogs" or ask other terrier breeders if they know of a show coming on. Entries often close 4 - 8 weeks before the date of the show so that catalogues may be printed etc. It is easier to begin with a Limited or Open show as exhibitors bring young and inexperienced dogs to those shows, they are not all stars of the dog world. The atmosphere is more relaxed and a novice dog will not find too many strange noises.

These shows are unlikely to be benched so you must keep your dog with you all day - unless you can leave him in your car, and that depends on the weather as even when it is cloudy and dull a car soon gets very hot. It is much easier if you have a dog travelling box or crate where the dog can sit in comfort, survey the show, get used to all the other dogs. You can put him in it and watch the judging, have your lunch or a drink in peace.

The classes you enter before the closing date for entries printed on the schedule depend on the age of your dog to a large extent. Puppy classes, under 12 months usually have a good entry of youngsters and for a dog over 1 year, the Novice class in a small show is a good place to start. Special Beginners class may also apply to you.

If you have not prepared your dog and its coat two or three weeks before, the last minute or evening before the show is too late. You should see that his coat does not look too long, wild and untidy. Borders need dead hair removing two or three times a year. A new coat will grow through the undercoat in about 6 weeks unless you are lucky enough to own a Border who always has a new coat waiting under the old one. You ought not to give him a bath just before a show, it will make his coat soft, in fact with regular grooming unless he has a good roll in a cowpat or something similar he will rarely need one. Keep the scissors for trimming round the feet to make them look neat. See that the toenails are not too long they throw the foot backwards. Level off the coat as far as possible. A "Magnet" comb helps with this, it just grips the hair and resembles a hacksaw blade, the ordinary stripping comb is not suitable for a Border Terrier. Do see that the tummy is also trimmed of loose hair, scissors may help with the most tender parts. I often see Borders looking fine on top but wispy underneath, and their owners tell me it is because the dog objects to grooming. Here the answer is to start this trimming at the puppy stage, later on is often too late, the dog struggles, you give up and he is the top dog, not you! Of course I need not mention the awful fact that he might be rather plump, so watch the diet and cut it down when the waistline vanishes. It is unwise to give your dog a large meal on the day of the show, he will travel and show better on an empty stomach.

You will need a show lead, a simple nylon one with a sliding clip will do nicely. Avoid the pink and purples, they are not for Borders where plain dark brown is more suitable. You will also need a clip to wear and show your ring number card.

Have with you in your pocket a few small titbits to attract his attention if he looks bored as some judges are very slow, but don't throw them down on the ground, you may upset the dogs near you and you won't be very popular. Squeaky toys are not a good idea for the same reason.

I hope that you have been able to find some show training classes near you before your first show, so that your dog will not mind the judge handling him and looking to see that his teeth are correctly placed in his mouth. If he nips the judge you certainly won't get a prize so practice beforehand. Make him walk on a lead up and down in a straight line at the pace which makes him look his best whilst moving. A candid friend is a help here, you can't see it yourself. Standing still in line with the other dogs he should have his forelegs level with each other, and the hind ones slightly extended and also level. Head up to show off his nice neck and shoulder line, and if his tail droops and comes out under his chin, a few encouraging whispers and a titbit may help to give him confidence.

The moment when you have a chat with the exhibitor next to you and your dog is sniffing the ground and standing all askew is the moment when the judge looks round at you, so keep an eye on the judge and the Best of Luck.

Sylvia Clarkson

The Mystole Diggers

We are not Australians, but we earned our title on Saturday night.

After their walk on Thursday, only Bramble the dog returned with Liz as the two bitches, Mouse and Rebecca, had gone hunting. This is not unusual, as the countryside is crawling with foxes, and Border Terriers could wish for nothing better. Around 7.30, just as we were going to dinner, Rebecca returned, but no Mouse. Friday came and we discussed the ability of Borders to survive. Saturday, and still no Mouse. We had of course gone out on Thursday night with torches and Rebecca had shown interest in a hole in a steep bank covered with scrub and saplings. On Saturday, coming home from the walk, Rebecca turned off in the same direction and, encouraged by the question "Where's Mousie ?", went again to the same area where there is a complex set of burrows, earths and setts, all interconnected and honeycombing the root systems. Liz swore she could hear a response from her shouts down a particular hole, and so I set off with digging tools shortly after 4 o'clock on a rainy Saturday afternoon. Pat and Hugh joined us on the way out, and after more listening Pat, too, was certain that she had got a response; and so we started digging.

By 5.30 we were obviously not going to get very far without help and so Liz went to Cliff, the farm foreman, who came back, half-an-hour later with a tractor, his wife, his boss Tempest, and his son Andrew. We used the tractor to remove a young tree and got down to digging again. After a while the cries from Mouse were becoming clearer, and we had all, including the doubters, heard them. It was also clear that we had some way to go and we would have to dig along a trench rather than a burrow if we were to reach her. Anyhow, by this time we had exhausted our jokes about Oflags and Stalags and so we cut down from the bank to our burrow 6 ft below.

"It's high time we had some sandwiches, and bring my bottle of whisky, too".

Off went Liz and Jennifer while we continued in the dark with what was becoming a fairly big excavation.

"I can see down the tunnel and it forks in another 4 ft. She is down the right fork".

Removing a bank of earth 2 ft. wide, 6 ft. deep and 4 ft. long takes time, and when we got to the fork there were two alternatives to the left and two to the right. By this time, Liz had returned with sandwiches and bottles; also Len and Jim, together with more torches and shovels. We all had a drink and a sandwich and the women went to the working face to listen. They pronounced firmly that she was round to the right - and we hoped they weren't wrong. We could now hear Mouse's cries without sticking our heads right down the hole, but it still seemed a long way, and so Cliff sent for his other son Stuart who returned with his friend Jeremy. This was very welcome as by 10 o'clock some of us were feeling weary; the pick and shovel are not tools that come naturally to the office worker. Someone suggested that we should leave it and start again in the morning but this was firmly slapped down, and we wondered instead if we would be eligible to join the Miners' Union on the strength of this excavation. Strangely enough, nobody wanted to, and we dug on.

"It's a long straight hole now and I can see 8 ft. down it".

Clearly it was time to pass the whisky bottle round again and the excavation continued. We had reached the top of the bank by now, and were well into Farmer Lay's beanfield. His combine had done this corner and so we had no anxiety for the safety of his machines. We had by now turned the corner to the right and were filling in the trench behind us as we moved forwards. Even so, there is a limit to the number of people who can work in a 2 ft. width.

"Never again", said I, "will I criticise the British workman when I see two of them at work with eleven looking on." and this was the size the team had become. Nothing daunted, we followed the burrow with Mouse's cries becoming clearer all the time. For the umpteenth time someone said "She's just round the corner", and so it seemed.

"Let's get finished by Sunday".

We never made that target, but around 1 o'clock I was working in the trench myself and at last I could see Mouse in a chamber behind a dead fox. Her eyes were glinting in the torchlight, and she was crying continually. Most of us had got our second wind by now, and I chiselled away at the hole until I could get my arm far enough down the burrow to pull out the fox. I had warned Liz that I thought Mouse might well be injured, as although I could see her, there didn't seem enough reason for her not to push the fox out of the way and get by. However, all the torches were on the hole as I dragged the fox out and following, on her own four feet, came Mouse walking out of the hole.

What must have happened was that the two bitches had killed; and in their manoeuvres in the dark, Rebecca, who is admittedly more slender than Mouse, had been able to get out, but Mouse had not been able to follow. It may be that Rebecca had tried to move the fox and in the dark of the earth only blocked the exit. However it was, she had undoubtedly shared the kill, which was a young dog fox. Rebecca had appeared quite miserable in Mouse's absence, but delighted to see her again and we made a big fuss of her as it was little short of a miracle that Mouse had been found. To understand Rebecca's indications, to hear a very very faint response (which to me might well have been the beating of my own heart) and to reach this gallant little bitch after she had spent 50 hours below ground was both satisfying and stimulating. We had not had much food, but we had got rid of a bottle of whisky, half a bottle of sherry and not a few cans of beer, in our 15 yard dig.

Next morning we buried the fox in the chamber, together with the cans and bottles, and chuckled to imagine the reactions of the archaeologists finding them in 250 years' time.

John Power

Borders in Colorado

Let me introduce myself and tell you how I first got to know Border Terriers. I'm a 35 year old, female geologist (a rare breed) working presently for the U.S. Geological Survey in Denver. Just prior to moving here 4 years ago, while still teaching at a college in Washington state, I decided to get a dog - my first. I wanted one well suited to my personal and professional life styles. This put unusually severe limitations on the possible choices. I ski tour and backpack for pleasure; my Survey job was going to entail 3 to 4 months a year of field work. Field work means geologic mapping of an area. The area may have other people, cars and dogs, or it may be very remote. The mapping may mean long days in the truck, usually on bad roads with much popping in and out to sample rocks, or a full day (12 hours) on foot over rough terrain miles from the truck and even farther from civilisation. Lodging could be a motel, cabin, trailer or tent.

Obviously I needed a dog with endurance and surefootedness, one that was adaptable, trainable and good around other dogs, and particularly a dog with a good spirit. Not too impossible a set of requirements until I add that the animal must be small for two reasons. (1) space in truck or tent; and (2) weight. I wanted to be able to carry it should it get hurt miles from the truck.

My search started at the library where I saw my first picture of a Border Terrier. The description sounded good. I observed several obedience classes - no Borders - but the instructor knew of a breeder just over the line into Canada, a Mrs. June Monaghan. When I called she just happened to have a litter. I went to see them and of course returned with my first Border.

Now I have three Borders and they are exactly what I wanted. They absolutely love field work and I love them. Each has been to beginners obedience classes and received 2nd and 3rd out of about 40 dogs. They quickly learned the rules of the truck, how to swim streams, climb cliffs and keep track of me as we hike so they don't get lost.

Cliff climbing even includes stepping off ledges onto my shoulders to be ferried down a stretch too steep for critters with short legs and no hands. Although a real test at times, 'No' has succeeded in meaning don't chase the cows (or deer), and leave alone snakes, porcupines and dead things. The Borders have been wonderful companions and great "field assistants". I hope to always have one with me.

One of the most hair-raising adventures I've had with my Borders was in southern Utah. The dogs and I were camped with another geologist, Jim, beside a dirt road on Bureau of Land Management land. We were packing to leave when I heard an incredible shriek. It had to be one of the dogs but I hope I never hear it again. I ran in the direction with rattlesnake on the brain and saw my female Rima, trying to come towards me. She was snapping and pawing. My heart nearly burst - she was in a coyote trap. I grabbed her and pinned her down to keep her from ripping her foot off. Jim grabbed the trap but in horror we realised that neither of us had any idea how it released. We struggled; Rima struggled, Jim, with strength born of anger, finally collapsed the springs to release the trap.

I carried Rima to the truck and got her settled while Jim unchained the trap from the juniper tree only 25 ft from the road. It had been baited with odiferous tar and hidden by tree litter. As our adrenalin slowed, our minds still raced. What if I had rested there in the shade and caught my hand in it? I couldn't have opened it and even if I got it off the tree, how far could I drive on bad roads with a trap painfully clamped to one hand? What if I'd had a child with me? What if it were the dog's nose instead of a foot?

We took stock. Rima's hind foot looked good; I couldn't feel a break and the skin was intact. Luckily the trap had closed on the leg bone and not the toes. My index finger was bleeding. It had been gnawed on by a pain-crazy dog at one point, when she worked her head loose from my grip. We doctored the finger and headed towards the nearest Vet - a day and a half's drive. By noon Rima, wanted up and successfully limped to a bush on her own.By evening she was fully recovered and rough-housing with the other dogs. Tough lady, I however, spent a miserable night with a badly infected finger.

We've had other adventures together but I'll save those for another time. It's a life style I suspect few Borders have and I hope that other owners will enjoy hearing about it.

Kim Manley

(Reprint by kind permission of the Author and the Editor of "The Borderline" - Border Terrier Club of America)

The Beloved Companions

Our magazine is, rightly, concerned with the great Border breed, its champions and high standards.

Until 1967, my wife and I had never owned a dog. We were then living in the Royal Naval College, Greenwich, and some friends of ours, long-time breeders and showers of Staffordshire Bull Terriers, thought we ought to have a puppy. By train, Hanleycastle Wee Juggler arrived. We did not know then, but he was a "big" Border, with great and lovely paws, a noble face and body - a survival, I now suppose, of the otter-hunting strain. He was never allowed to soil the R.N. College grounds and went for walks in Greenwich Park. Even thereafter, he would never soil our garden but always had to be taken for long walks outside it.

He used to go the Ministry of Defence Police post at the R.N. College, where he had a saucer of "Policeman's Tea", though oddly enough he never retained the taste for it. When we considered a pet name, one of our policemen said "He's a real "Bosun"; and so "Bosun" he became; (Dandyhow Brussel Sprout ("Veg") was his ancestor).

Early in his life he was jumped by a one-eared Greenwich moggy who tore his nose. Thereafter he retained a hatred for the feline race and once, to our mortal embarrassment, he killed a kitten.

In 1970, our younger daughter thought she would like a Border. So, inevitably, as she was a working girl, we looked after her - "Farmway Red Sparrow", house-named "Tiffany". She had to be spayed, for we are not breeders and for a brief period we went through the trouble of a dog and a bitch, in season, in our house.

Both of them have given us the utmost faith and love. Bosun, the independent, single-minded plodder; Tiffany, after a slightly vicious start, a most affectionate bitch with all the Border character and standards.

Faithful, great "bed" dogs (as "Dandyhow Brussel Sprout" was), lovable, alert, real terriers; they have lightened and enriched our lives.

Breeders may look down on us, but how very much we owe to Mr. Clements and Mrs. Aspinwall, the former for letting us have a dog who would never have succeeded in a show for, as in Fats Waller's words in the song "Your feet's too big"; the latter for a gem who could have been a Champion (indeed her mother was and her pedigree is full of them, as was Bosun's).

Bosun died last November. We know now that his great heart had been failing for some time. In the last days, because he would not foul his nest, he used to go out into our acre garden and lie on the frosty grass, alone with his nose in the air. Time and time again we carried him in. He was not in pain, for had he been, we should have taken the necessary action at once. In the "Middle Watch" just as I was about to take over, he died with my wife holding his paw, a faithful Border to the end.

Tiffany remains a joy and a delight, at 11 years. With all the characteristics of the breed, she is an independent old lady - still loving "beds", though not allowed to spend the night on them.

So, many thanks to Mr. Clements and Mrs. Aspinwall - and I hope they know that there are other things than the show ring, or "working" .... we certainly do, and are infinitely grateful for it.

Captain W.R.H. Lapper, R.N.

The Bawdy Terror

I was heartbroken when I lost my beloved dachshund, my dear companion inexplicably struck down with incurable paralysis at the tender age of four. I felt bereft and it was probably a blessing that Abigail, my two year old daughter, was ill at the time. Feverish and irritable, she demanded my attention and I nursed and placated her in a daze, all the while feeling numb with grief.

Having at last rocked the fretful infant to sleep, I was less than delighted when the doorbell rang. A workman stood in the porch with a bedraggled puppy under his arm. "It's been wandering on the building site for a couple of days", he explained "I took it to the village shop and they said bring it to you". I groaned inwardly, surely I had enough to cope with at the time. "O.K. leave it with me", I replied, wishing I were made of sterner stuff. Looking relieved, the fellow made a quick exit leaving me convinced I must be mad. Shutting the door I placed the scruffy pup on the floor for a closer inspection - a bitch, around five months, some sort of terrier - a quick look through my Observer Book of Dogs and I found it - a BORDER TERRIER. Feeling knowledgeable, I rang the Police. I couldn't bring the dog in, I explained, I was nursing a sick child. I was quite willing to keep it until it was claimed, I was amazed to hear myself saying. The voice at the other end sounded relieved. The relevant details were given and I put the phone down feeling sure I would regret what I had rashly said.

As hastily as possible I fed the obviously hungry pup. The minute she had finished her meal and been popped into the garden to relieve herself she tore indoors and climbed up onto the settee with Abigail where a day bed had been made during her illness. Greeting each other like long lost friends they were both asleep in minutes.

For five days the puppy and my daughter were inseparable. Abigail, as two years olds are apt to do, made a speedy recovery. The two of them played, slept and made mischief together.

Having contacted all the local animal societies and drawn blank I began to believe in miracles. The puppy had obviously been abandoned and had been heaven sent to me. My faith was short-lived. The doorbell rang and a family stood there. They had heard through the grapevine that I was looking after their lost Border Terrier. The puppy greeted them with great enthusiasm and within a few minutes one very happy family had driven away leaving behind a completely miserable one.

The search was on. We MUST have a Border Terrier. The family for once were unanimous. Luck seemed on our side, a litter was advertised in Horse and Hound some fifty miles away. I picked up the phone and dialled the number. The man at the other end informed me that there was one bitch left. I bought it over the phone and promised I would put a cheque in the post. The honest and level headed man at the other end of the phone was unhappy at my buying an unseen puppy and suggested we meet at a town halfway and do a deal at a pub called The Black Fox. This was marvellous. I could have my puppy that evening instead of waiting the endless few days until the weekend.

My husband was unable to come that evening and, filled with trepidation (for I am extraordinarily shy of walking into pubs alone), I set off. Having reached the town without difficulty it remained for me to locate The Black Fox. I thought I had followed directions but when I should have been in the right area the only pub around was The White Swan. There was nothing else for it but to walk in and enquire where I could find The Black Fox. Nobody had heard of it, and feeling I ought to explain myself, I blurted out that I was meeting a man about a dog. When the gales of laughter had subsided people tried to be helpful. I was given directions to The White Horse, The Golden Pheasant, The Black Cat and The Red Lion and several other animal/colour combinations that the town boasted. I tried them all, feeling more and more desperate and just as I was ready to give up I once again tried the White Swan. Unbelievably, in the corner of the bar stood a man with a puppy under his arm. Very apologetically he told me that he was sure The White Swan used to be called The Black Fox. Realising his mistake he too had toured the town searching for me. More by luck than judgement we had at last found one another.

Midge is an unqualified success. She is everything I could wish for in a dog. Abigail calls her a "Bawdy Terror" being unable to get her mouth round the correct pronunciation. I think, on reflection, it describes her well.

Carina Lewis

A Life is a Life

I have been asked by your editors to write an article. They supported me loyally when I was in their position - but what have I to say that has not been better said before?

Only having worked my Borders in a small way, I cannot speak with the authority of those brought up to hunt. Likewise from the ringside I have watched beautifully trained Borders moving and showing to perfection. Those of mine that won did so in spite of, rather than because of my showing skills.

This leaves me among the many who kept Borders initially as housedogs, but some urge has compelled us to try to breed them, although still wishing to keep our friends and companions at our hearthside.

I have made many mistakes at cost to my dogs. Possibly my experiences may help some novice, starting on the same path, to weigh the pros and cons, or possibly realise that breeding is not for them. Nothing can surpass the rapport between a Border and his master built up from long years of companionship.

This perfect unity and peace of mind cannot be reached as owner of several dogs. The reward for that activity is mixed with some inevitable heartbreak. Better perhaps to raise prize cabbages, unless one is a born stockman, and the fruits of a breeding programme are paramount.

To build a kennel is very exciting. If one selects initially a type that epitomises one's true picture of a Border Terrier - and let no-one advise you on this, as you must follow the dictates of your own eye - then by breeding back, not too closely but truly, to the same ancestry one stamps, as we all know, this type on to one's own stock.

What is more warming then to overhear perfect strangers recognising some dog they are viewing as typical of one's own - or the buyer of one of one's puppies phoning to tell of a similar experience ? One imagines one has arrived. There, alas, is the pitfall. Ambition so easily creeps in, and the housedog owner is pitchforked out of her depth into the larger kennel area. Miss World, alas, is always so young. We oldies do not stand a chance. To keep in the picture one's dogs must be "kept on the move". Homes are found for those not fulfilling show expectations, or for the brood bitch whose litter was disappointing. If the homes are carefully chosen, most of these dogs are delighted to be "onlys". This is the only way a large kennel can keep going over the years, with perhaps an old favourite or champion kept as a housedog. The youngsters are mainly kennelled till sorted out.

If, however, the above is not for us, how do we proceed with our housekept Borders? Full of enthusiasm, it is decided to breed a litter, and inevitably one keeps a puppy. A mate may even be bought for the original dog or bitch. In no time there is a cluster of housedogs. If the initial stock was wise and kind, and put the youngsters in their place as they arrived, an hierarchy builds up, especially if you leave a good age gap between acquisitions, so that sibling rivalry cannot occur.

As numbers build up, meticulous fairness must be practised as jealousy is easily sparked off. I once started trouble by tossing a bitch a pill each morning. On the fifth occasion her neighbour expressed extreme disapproval, imagining I was giving titbits ! Now, on the rare occasion anyone has a pill, they all get a bit of cheese.

Once you have built up a close-knit family it is criminal to interfere through ambition or an overcritical eye. Improvement is for future breeding programmes. As with our children, one must love them as they are and be thankful.

Perhaps a relative desperately wants one of your older bitches and you know it will get individual attention if passed on, and so with some pangs you let it go, with perhaps a sneaking feeling that you will now have space to buy from another kennel an animal with the one virtue you feel your own kennel needs, to bring it to perfection.

Do not be misled. You have broken up a well knit interdependent family unit. There is no certainty that the stranger will be accepted. If she is submissive she may get by, but if she takes up a challenging position there will be disagreements. One's dogs learn to accept a "passing stranger" in their midst but permanent integration of an adult is a more delicate matter. In the wilds one would not expect a stranger to be automatically welcome on the territory of an established pack. When we build up artificial numbers of housedogs we must remember they are DOGS and respect their instinct. It is not often realised that dogs can have a lifelong devotion to each other, and no more than humans will welcome having their friends chosen for them.

Our first Border was absolutely devoted to the little bitch we subsequently bought. She copied everthing he did - not the least of which was to make for the grass verge by the roadside and to sit tight on hearing impending traffic, an exercise which I taught the dog in one twenty minute pram walk. He remembered the next day and ever afterwards. I am certain he knew it gave me time to collect up my toddlers, knowing he had taken himself to safety. He was incredibly intelligent, due I am sure to undivided attention from us. He astonished our neighbours by firmly shepherding my baby toddler back home every time she strayed through the flimsy rails surrounding our temporary naval married quarter. He had been taught our boundaries and she must keep within them too.

The bitch, alas, was killed when left at a Hunt Kennels during one of my husband's moves. We were miles away, but I suddenly knew that she needed me desperately. I could not get to her until too late. It was unforgiveable on my part. Desperately sad, we bought a replacement bitch but the old dog would not look at her, she was NOT his wife.

Beaver and Chipmunk were another pair. They might be physically at different ends of the house or garden - but should a gate be left unlatched, in no time both had vanished. Telepathy between them I am sure, as not one of the other dogs had moved a muscle. They got into awful scrapes amongst the Duke of Beaufort's fox nurseries and the badger earths. Generally one had given up hope before they eventually emerged several hours or days later, tottering on the edge of a large earth working. Beaver would be badly marked up and Chip so clay encrusted that one had to open her mouth and seek her one uneven tooth to be certain of identity.

Where we live now there is an old earth by a field path at our back garden gate. Old Mulberry and Buffalo found this immediately we arrived here and always sloped off at the end of each day's walk. In their own good time they followed us home for their supper, hoarse and exhausted. Mulberry died last year, Buffalo has not looked at the earth since. He sleeps most of the time and eats his heart out.

The above illustrations may appear disconnected from the start of my story. This was somewhat triggered off by hearing that a member of a Border forum had been shot down recently by querying whether a Border should be sold to a non-working home. I gather consensus was "Yes, of course Borders make ideal pets".

This set me thinking "'What is a pet and what is a good home, and what is a fair life for the puppies we produce ?" "'What is work ?"

Work to fox is not easy for most pet owners. I will stick my neck out and say it is for the knowledgeable and skilled only. But having said that, I believe that a Border is happiest continually in the company of his master. No opportunity should be missed to use his intelligence in any useful way and let him take part in all that goes on. He will not miss a trick and reward you beyond belief.

Selecting suitable homes from enquiries received by phone and letter is heart searching. They are so pernickety about your kennel, and you are so suspicious that the pup will end up too fat, toothless and unexercised wheezing on a cushion, or it is only being bought to keep the children quiet during holidays, will be neglected during term time, and receive less and less attention as the children grow up and follow their own pursuits. Best of all is to have an enquiry from someone whose sadly beloved has died at a ripe old age, walks are unbearable without a dog, and nothing but another from you will do. Long may such folk exist to enjoy all our very special Borders.

Felicity Marchant

An Introduction to Border Terriers

For many years I have lived with, bred and shown terriers, but dare I say it, not Border Terriers but Jack Russells and "Jack Russells". I wanted to have a pedigree terrier, for a long time, but my husband, who really wasn't a "doggy man" said that he would do a lot for me but if I expected him to prance around a show ring with a box of chalk and a hair brush I could think again.

I often used to see little brown dogs when I attended hunt terrier shows in the West country and to me they all looked alike.

A little over a year ago we visited a well known Border Terrier breeder to buy her last Jack Russell. While we were there she showed us her Border Terrier puppies. It was love at first sight and we returned home clasping a fluffy little brown bundle. Ten days later I went back for another one, only this time it was a nearly black bundle.

At first the "Jacks" were very suspicious but quickly accepted "the girls" as part of the family. One Jack Russell dog I had used to howl if he was separated from his girls, he was reared with them and I'm convinced he thought he was a Border.

A few weeks later a friend of mine decided she wanted to part with a nine month old Border dog. I was rather short of cash but I knew the friend wanted to buy a table with the money she hoped to obtain from the sale of the puppy. I offered her an antique table and as she handed over the dog I was told, rather acidly, that the table would last a great deal longer than the dog. So it may, materially, but the pleasure of the dog will last for many a year. He was called "Casius" when he came to live with us but later was to become "Castle Lad of Clystlands".

Early last year I arranged to attend a Jack Russell show in Manchester and, because the Championship show at Belle Vue was the day before, I decided to enter "Cas". I'd never attended a Championship show and didn't know what to expect at all. As the day approached I became increasingly apprehensive.

Was the dog good enough? Am I going to make a complete idiot of myself and the dog? Shall I chicken out and leave Cas at home? In the end I decided Manchester was a long way from home in Devon and if I did make a fool of myself so what, nobody would know me anyway. To my very great delight and astonishment Mr. Frank Jackson awarded Cas a reserve. I was over the moon. The next day one of my Jacks was awarded the reserve championship at our Club show but somehow that faded into obscurity in the knowledge that one of our terriers had actually achieved a "reserve" at a Championship Show, I drove back to Devon on Cloud 9.

The following May, Cas was awarded two firsts at the Birmingham show. This time my husband showed him (he'd discovered he didn't need chalk and a hair brush in a Border ring) while I took my turn at staying at home with the family. After the classes my husband rushed around the show ground until he was able to find a telephone which worked, so that he could tell me the great news. He forgot that Cas would have to be shown in "Best of Breed" and arrived back to the ring in time to find Cas being shown, very kindly, by Mrs. Aspinwall.

Because we were so new to the ways of the "pedigree world" it took us some time to discover that Cas had actually qualified to be shown at Crufts in 1982. When we made this discovery we just couldn't believe it.

At the end of August my husband showed Cas at the Exmoor hunt show and Cas won the cup for the best Border which Master very proudly brought home. Two days later my husband died.

Since then much has happened, very sadly I have had to find homes for many of our terriers. However, I still have a "car full" and that includes my five Borders - the boss dog of whom is Cas. I've entered him for Crufts and although I don't expect him to achieve much, I can't get over the fact that he will be mixing with "The Cream of the Dog World".

Even if I were never to attend another show, I won't ever be without my Borders. I've kept Jacks for well over twenty years and couldn't part with them now either, but this I do know, if I'd started to keep Borders in 1959, instead of Jacks, I would never have become involved with the Jacks.

In my so far limited experience, I find the Borders combine all the qualities of a good terrier with great loyalty and intelligence. They have working ability as well as pet ability. It's marvellous to own terriers the aim of whom is "to please". On this count alone they score many points against the Jacks whose main aim is "to please themselves".

As for Border Terriers all looking alike - I wonder how I could have been so stupid for every one of my little brown dogs has a "certain something".

Ruth Hussey Wilford

Don't Use the Dog Next Door!

How often breeders receive a telephone call - "Have you a stud dog? My Border Terrier came in season about a week ago and I would like her to have a litter." The caller then goes on to try and find the nearest and cheapest dog with no thought for the suitability of that dog in trying to breed a decent puppy. Matings should be planned well in advance of the bitch coming in season, so that, at the first signs of such an event, her owner can notify the owner of the prospective suitor and make a firm booking of his services.

The owner of the stud dog should be asked if the bitch would be acceptable for mating (no one is obliged to allow their dog to be used) and an enquiry made as to how much the stud fee would be. It is bad manners to haggle over the stud fee and this should be paid immediately after the mating.

The owner of the stud dog will want to know the breeding of the bitch at the time of enquiry about arranging the mating. The pedigree should be to hand anyway, as all matings should be planned with regard to the bloodlines shown on the pedigree. How does the novice breeder select the dog? The one-dog pet owner will not know any of the current stud dogs. If possible, it would be a good idea to visit a championship show or a breed club show to see as many Borders as possible. Notice those you prefer, and mark them in your catalogue. Maybe they will be sired by the same dog, or some of them will come from one kennel.

Fix firmly in your mind what your priorities are in breeding the litter. What is there about your precious bitch that could be improved ? Of course she is perfect, but could her ears be rather large, her nose a shade narrow, or is she a bit aggressive? Having established this, look at the Borders at the show to see which excel in these points, and what is the calmest dog present.

Talk to people. Take along your pedigree and explain what you want. Don't make any firm bookings or promises, just listen and try and sift through the possibilities later. Good breeders do not push their own stud dogs at you, they will try and suggest the most suitable. Of course there are some whose little eyes ring up the cash sign at the thought of a stud fee but most try to be sincere in their attempts to help.

It is advisable to use an established stud dog, especially with a family pet bitch who will be very humanised and sometimes very difficult to mate because of this. Also, use a dog who gets good sized litters. Some do seem to be more prolific than others. There may be a very nice and suitable pet Border dog owned by your best friend which would be so handy to use, but a maiden dog and a maiden bitch with novice owners is creating awful problems over the actual mating.

If it is not possible to visit a show, or hunt terrier show (you will see some good Borders at those too), study the pedigree of your bitch. To spot the bloodlines, read the lines horizontally, not the columns up and down.

If the bitch is the product of an established breeder it would be sensible to consult the breeder who will know exactly what dog to recommend for that line. Failing that possibility, try and trace the owners of, say, both the grandparents. Show them the pedigree, and describe your bitch, and what your objective is. Very often the two people will come up with exactly the same solution. Study the pedigrees in the Year Books. Try and find some similar breeding to your bitch and see what has tied up well with that. Very often you will find the same pattern of blood lines merging well together. Then do some detective work to locate the dog and ask advice about it. If the bitch comes from a well-known bitch line (look at the bottom line of the pedigree, does the same prefix appear along the line ?) then it would be a good idea to try to select a dog of similar blood. This would be line-breeding which is the pattern followed by most dog-breeders. Line-breeding is the mating together of relatives or descendants of one dog or family, thus concentrating on the good (and bad) points of that line with a little unrelated blood as well.

In-breeding is the mating together of close relatives, i.e. brother, sister, half-brother, half-sister, grandfather, granddaughter, father, daughter, mother, son. This is not recommended for the novice breeder as one needs expert knowledge to use this method of breeding successfully. Besides which, it is difficult to sell the resultant progeny to the general public who have been brain-washed against such methods by press reporters.

Outcrossing or the mating of unrelated stock, is, for this reason, theoretically preferred by the novice breeder. It is a very chancy way of breeding stock and anyway impossible in Borders. Most Borders trace back to several well-known dogs - it would be difficult to find a pedigree which did not contain Ch. Future Fame if written out showing enough generations, and there are other dogs who appear again and again.

As many Borders from well-known kennels do not carry prefixes or affix, it is important to know which dogs are related. Sometimes a Border pedigree can appear to be more or less outcross breeding, but in fact contain many full brothers and sisters, which will be revealed if the pedigree is traced further back. It is a good idea, for this reason, to write out a five generation pedigree of the prospective litter and study the pedigree to see just what the resultant breeding looks like. If you have several dogs in mind as possibilities, write this out for all of them. It often finalises the choice to see the full pedigree laid out.

However much advice has been sought, the final choice must always rest with the owner of the bitch, who must accept responsibility should the resultant litter not be up to expectation. Do look for positive points such as good type and, most important, good temperament, and above all, use a dog you like.

Be prepared to travel to the best available stud dog, and to take a day off work so that the bitch can be taken, at a time convenient to the owner of the stud dog, on the right day for mating - not the nearest weekend to it. Be prepared to pay a realistic stud fee. If you can't afford it you should consider seriously whether you should breed a litter at all. Puppies are expensive to rear properly and it is not unknown for things to go wrong leaving the breeder with no puppies and a very large vet's bill.

At times of recession there are not so many enquiries for puppies as before and it would be advisable to consider whether it is necessary to breed the litter at all. A few four month old remnants growing in appetite and wickedness are a very different kettle of fish to those dear little eight week old puppies which can easily be contained in a fenced off corner of the sitting, room. Don't expect other breeders to sell your puppies for you. The responsibility lies with those responsible for bringing them into the world. Maybe the stud dog owner will pass on any surplus enquiries, but if there are none, he can't. Obviously he has to sell his own litters first.

Under no circumstances should the bitch be taken for mating should she in any way be off colour, suffering from skin disease or having had an infectious disease within the past six weeks. She should also be free from fleas, lice and other vermin.

Back to the telephone calls - be tactful. Don't tell the proud owner of the stud dog that you think his dog the best of a mediocre lot, or that you actually prefer another, but that it is not available. I was incensed recently by one caller who asked if there was a dog nearer than my "pride and joy" - thirty miles was such a long way to travel for his services. It took me the best part of twenty-five years to produce him, yet she could not spare an hour to travel to use him!

Anne Roslin-Williams

A Profile from the Past

I have been asked to write some of my memories of Hester Garnett-Orme for our Year Book. When we first met, she lived with her father at Pangbourne near Reading. She told me that Clara Butt, the singer, had lived there at one time and used the very large hall to practice in. Hester was very house-proud so all the dogs lived in very nice kennels. She had a well kept garden with the help of her married couple who were with her for years.

After her father died, she bought two cottages at Great Horwood near Bletchley, Bucks. One was for her couple. We never discovered whether she could drive her car, but Sergeant used to bring her to the Shows.

Under the prefix of Raisgill, Hester's Borders may be found in many early pedigrees. She bred the dam of that well-known dog Ch. Deerstone Destiny, and owned Ch. What Fettle at one time. When the war came, neither of us could do any dog breeding, so we started researching Border Terrier pedigrees. I used to write to all and sundry to help trace the various dogs they had owned or would know about, then check what they sent me and send it on to Hester for her to go into, which she loved doing.

Thinking back, I had very few refusals as most of the old breeders were very helpful as far as they could be, so many of the old dogs had the same names one after the other and could only be checked by dates and owners. Like all pedigrees, dog and human, there's usually a dead end which leaves one guessing.

I had a lot of letters from Willie Barton, we have a picture of his dogs in the Year Book of 1964. His dogs were all kept indoors, much to his housekeeper's annoyance he told me. I also had a reply from J.M. Strother in 1942. He had a bitch called Juppy born in 1911, by Adam (unr.) and Vic (unr.) and was showing dogs in 1920. He told me he thought I knew more about Borders than he did.

From all this information Hester compiled invaluable records of the breed which were left to the Southern Border Terrier Club as they are unique and quite irreplaceable. They can be consulted by arrangement.

After the war we started showing and breeding dogs once more, also editing the Year Book, starting with Hester, Miss Eccles and myself - as we know, quite a job.

Hester also published "Border Champions and Challenge Certificate Winners", an important collection of pedigrees, in 1953, and "Border Tales" compiled from past Year Books in 1967, also bequeathed to the S.B.T.C. She gradually got tired of shows and got keener on the working side and took up otter hunting, but she did carry on judging at Championship Shows including Crufts in 1967. She was President of the Club 1949-1952 and thereafter continued as a Vice-President until her death in 1971. She has been called "Annalist of the Breed", having collected and preserved so much valuable information about Borders and their breeding.

Kathleen F. Twist

The Judge's Angle on the Breed

First of all I don't think Borders are an easy breed to judge as they differ from other terriers in many ways and one must always bear in mind as the Standard points out that they are workers.

I first awarded CCs in 1949 when I gave Future Fame his third CC and Dronfield Berry the bitch CC. I have judged all-terrier shows and when in Holland judged the Long-legged Terrier Group along with 2 co-judges. I found this Group easier to judge than Borders (except that a Boston Terrier was in the Group and it is not classed as a terrier over here). To me it was easier because all the terriers were good ones and our winner eventually finished Best in Show.

I try to judge according to the Breed Standard and whilst a good Border head is very important, I want a well-balanced dog free from exaggeration. My pet abomination is one with a very short muzzle accompanied by protruding eyes and ears set high; this gives a Griffon-like appearance; fortunately nowadays this type is rare.

Because the Border is a working terrier it doesn't mean it should not be presented in a fit, clean and tidy condition. Mr. Wattie Irving told me the story of a man who had been showing a big, rough looking dog which didn't win so the exhibitor questioned the judge's decision and said "Remember it's a working dog". The judge's reply was "I'm a working man, but I've had a wash and shave before the show". So to me, presentation and showmanship does play a part but that doesn't mean a poor specimen, well-presented and showing well, should beat a good one that is a bit shy and not very well presented. I remember many years ago awarding a bitch her first CC, she wasn't a show lady but in my view her good qualities outweighed this. The following year she won the CC at Cruft's and beat one of my dogs for Best of Breed.

I take judging seriously and from some photographs I have seen I tend to look a bit grim sometimes! When last in the States my wife was to judge the Sweepstake Classes and as I knew some would be shown under me later, I got well away from the Border ring and sat on the grass. I was wearing my judging badge and as a lady came past me she made a remark something like "It's not all that bad you know" - reckon I must have been looking pretty serious but this made me smile.

One of the most pleasing aspects of judging Border Terriers is the attitude of exhibitors and this seems to apply also when judging abroad. I remember at one show in the States I said to a group of Border people that I thought Borders were good at choosing their owners.

At one show however, some years ago an exhibitor who was quite a character was very cross with me and after the judging came to see me to enquire why the bitch CC winner had beaten his exhibit and of course he didn't agree with my explanation. He must have overcome his disappointment as later at two Annual Club Meetings he proposed me as judge for their Championship Show but I was already booked for other championship shows. A few years later he had 2 unbeaten bitches at a show and asked me to take one in for him. I tried very hard to get him the CC but didn't manage it. Later he came to me and without a word pressed a Border Terrier key ring into my hand - one of my happy memories.

What I find disappointing is when what seems a good specimen on the table turns out to be a very poor mover. I didn't pay much attention to exhibits at shows prior to having a judging engagement so that I didn't ever subconsciously assess a dog beforehand. In any case one can't judge from the ringside as even dogs I have regularly shown against or seen from the ringside may have virtues or failings that I only became aware of when I actually judged them. It is very satisfying when the exhibits are of good quality and a special pleasure when one comes across an outstanding specimen. I have never given a puppy a CC as the unbeaten puppy always to me lacked that finish that the older good exhibit possessed. I have awarded puppies the reserve CC and if I had continued judging there might have been an occasion when I thought a puppy could beat the opposition.

In my judging career I remember some very good dogs and some very nice exhibitors and this is the satisfaction and pleasure that judging has given me.

Robert Hall

The Midwife

Tess, our first Border, had produced three litters of four pups, thankfully without complications. Liz, a daughter from Tess's second 'family' was now two years old and expecting her first offspring. At six weeks she became very big indeed and by seven weeks was just managing to waddle along after the other dogs. (She, like her mother before her, made it plain that it was more distressing to be left behind than to follow at a snail's pace). The most anxious moment we ever had through taking out an in-whelp bitch was when Tess decided to go to ground for the first time a few days before her pups were due - it resulted in us having to dig her out with anything that was available - and all this because of a rabbit skin and a dried up dead hedgehog! Well, Liz managed to keep going until the last moment though by this time she looked as if she might explode. Apart from her sheer size she was fine in herself - all we hoped now, for her sake, was that there were a large number of small puppies and not just a few big ones. Her due date was August 22nd and now follows a summary of events:

August 20th: Quiet and refusing all food. 3.30 p.m. - going back and fore to her box looking generally uneasy. 4.00 p.m. - ate a good meal - behaviour normal - slept soundly all night (in our bedroom).

August 2lst: 8 a.m. - went straight into her box downstairs. Not interested in food at all.

Noon - began to tear up papers in her box - looked very sorry for herself.

Midnight - first noticeable contraction followed at 12.30 by a large contraction. The first four pups were born without complications at 1 a.m., 3 a.m., 3.30 a.m. and 3.45 a.m, respectively. We did however have to break bags and sever cords, as Liz showed no inclination to do so.

Meanwhile, Tess, who had been in the kitchenette throughout the first few hours, was behaving very anxiously so we decided to let her see what was going on. She calmly observed proceedings at close quarters then gradually inched her way into the whelping box (suitcase) and, commenced to help Liz clean up the puppies. At 4.05 a.m. another pup appeared and to our amazement Tess proceeded to break the bag, cut the cord and eat the afterbirth. 4.30 a.m. another pup and a repeat performance. The last two pups born at 5.15 and 6 a.m. were delivered by Liz unaided - having learnt by mother's example. We will never forget the touching scene of our two bitches and the complete faith they had in one another. I must admit that when we were very tired and Liz was exhausted - Tess calmly took over as midwife and helped us all out. She helped Liz with the little ones for the first two days and then faded into the background leaving a proud mother with her contented pups.

P.S. Had Liz shown any displeasure at Tess's presence we would have removed her immediately but she was obviously relieved to have her there. However, we would certainly not want to encourage anyone to 'try this out' as we realise the results could be disastrous.

P. Phillips

Danny's Adventure

As it was nearing the end of the school holidays we decided to take our son, daughter and a friend for an evening trip to the coast and the amusements on the pier. We arranged to call for them at the entrance to the pier in a couple of hours and took our two Borders onto the Downs for a run. It was a beautiful evening and the sea was calm, and Ben and Danny scampered around happily for an hour or more. Thinking we would have time for a coffee we fastened Ben on his lead and called Danny who had been a few yards from us only moments ago. Although only 18 months old Danny is normally very obedient, but there was no sign or sound of him. We searched and called for half an hour by which time it was getting quite dark. We then decided to call for reinforcements from the pier, so I stayed with Ben calling and whistling while my husband went to get the youngsters sending two of them along the beach, and returning along the top of the Downs. We contacted the Police and with the help of a flashlight searched until 1 a.m. with no success.

Next morning the others set off for the coast again with spades in case he was stuck in a rabbit hole, while I telephoned every organisation I could think of who could possibly help. We spent a miserable day with Danny still missing at the end of it.

At 5am on the Sunday morning we were up again and cutting up an old Border Terrier Year Book (sorry) to select any pictures resembling Danny. We pasted these on cards offering a £50 reward for his safe return. Once again the family set off and searched the streets, Downs and beaches, then put the cards in newsagents windows and around the town, returning home to await the right telephone call.

All our friends phoned making us jump up hopefully, then finally at 7.15 p.m a fisherman called to say he had found a little dog stuck on a ledge up the cliffs the height of a two storey house. He had climbed up to rescue him and got growled at for his trouble, but got Danny down and had taken him home with him. Later that day his daughter saw one of our posters and took down our telephone number.

After a visit to the Vet for an injection, and with a few cuts and grazes, Danny seems none the worse for his experience, and we are a very lucky family to have him back with us.

Brenda Gravener

Working Terriers

The Border Terrier is probably one of the oldest working breeds in existence today. There is a picture painted in 1693 of the Cottesmore Hunt having on it also two terriers resembling a present day Border, running with hounds.

The Border Terrier has also been known and worked in the Border district of England and Scotland for hundreds of years, and has only been given his title in recent years. One of the reasons why he was given the title of Border Terrier was because he was widely used for terrier work by the Border foxhounds, who were mastered by the Robson family for generations. It is said that the Border Terrier's ancestors are Bedlington or Dandie Dimont Terriers, though the truth probably is that the Border was the original breed from which the others have sprung.

One of the physical features of a good working Border Terrier is his jaw. It should be very short and strong. He should also be game to the last ounce, and be able to run with hounds and horses all day. Border Terriers are earth dogs and were originally used for working fox, badgers and others. Nowadays the majority are used for ratting and keeping vermin down. Although unless he is also good underground, he cannot be classed as a working terrier.

Oxcroft Tally and her son and daughter (Ryswick Ranger and Ryswick Raspberry) all have slept with hounds at the Hunt Kennels, and run with hounds and horses. It not only disciplines them, but settles them to other animals, traffic and noise.

The only disadvantage is that you must expect accidents; for example having your Border trodden on by horses with shoes on and the ever increasing problem of traffic. Apart from these accidents above ground, you must expect marks and scars on your Border below ground. Even the most experienced terrier will receive a medal or two.

Besides the thrill of working my Border and seeing him go to ground, marking his victim, it gives me personally the greatest pleasure, seeing my own terriers running with hounds and horses across country on a hunting day.

A. P. Willis

Three for Dinner

Whilst shopping my son decided to buy a marrow bone for our two Borders and had it cut in half so they would not squabble. He gave them their portions well apart on the lawn and came indoors but within a few minutes Ben was beside us. This seemed strange as bones are usually top of the hit parade, so we all went to look out of the window. As we got there the bone keeled over, apparently on its own, but on closer inspection we found our tortoise on the other side having a good tuck in! Ben would not take it away from her so another bone had to be bought.

Brenda Gravener

Bustle

An animated flue brush has just belted in and out of the room as I write, it is hotly pursued by Mr Boggs enjoying an evening game with the youngest of the family.

I did not really intend to buy another puppy in January. After all, I always go to Gil and Mary to see the new litters, and I take care always to leave any spare cash at home so that I do not get tempted. But I had fallen for the mother of this particular litter when I saw her as a pup, so I was halfway to parting with some cash before I arrived at Ridge Hill.

The three bitch puppies came into the warm kitchen wide eyed and curious. "Gil thinks the best bitch is the big one", Mary volunteered. The big bitch was trotting about, tail wagging. No. 2 was investigating the cupboard doors. No. 3 sat and leaned on a table leg and looked around with an enquiring expression. Our eyes met. "You", she said to herself, "look like a soft touch", and sneaked over to sit on my shoe. "That's the little one", said Mary, "we think she might be a bit shy". A bit shy! That Mrs W. is the laugh of the year!

The small person was soon safely curled up inside my husband's coat, and being borne home in silence. No, we had not meant to buy one, but you know what Borders are.

Our three came shrieking a welcome as we came in, then stopped. Something was up. What was THAT inside father's coat? We took it into the sitting room and put it on the floor. Barbie took one horrified look and, rolling her eyes, fled into the study exclaiming, "A puppy! My God, how could they?" Mr. Boggs got up in the rocking chair, turned his back, and rocked himself gently to sleep. "If I don't look at it", said the expression on his back, "it will go away". Dear simple Huggy sat on the sofa and fixed the newcomer with her blank and unwavering stare. "Once upon a time", she was thinking, "I had something like that". I picked the puppy up and put it beside her. She sniffed it, rolled it over and began to wash it thoroughly. In ten minutes they were curled up together fast asleep. Huggy from then on decided that she had again given birth, but this time it was much easier, it came fully made. And from that moment she has loved it as a daughter, washing it, playing with it and punishing it as required. Punishing it! Yes indeed, for if ever a puppy was the personification of naughtiness, that was Bustle! She was also and still is, the most delightful, enchanting person to live with. I have never heard her growl or utter a hostile word, she lives in peace with the whole world, but she is so lively and full of spirit and true Border character.

Coming at a time of deep snow her first two or three weeks meant she had to stay in or she would have disappeared in a snow drift. She took to sitting in front of the Rayburn, leaning back so that she was in contact with the warm stove. This did extraordinary things to the coat on her back, causing it to crisp and curl, and as she never progressed anywhere except at a flat gallop, she quickly earned the nickname of "the animated flue brush". I think one of her ancestors was a mountain goat, nothing is safe, and she can spring from a standing start on to any table, especially if there is food thereon.

It took a week or so before Barbie would deign to acknowledge her, or speak to me. She was deeply offended that we considered it necessary to import another when we had her, but about then Stove Mouse invaded the house, and she had to vacate the 'huff seat' in the study to dislodge him; and when she found a small attendant willing to learn how to take the gas stove apart without really trying, she decided to accept Bustle from then on. She now treats her like a grandchild, rolling her on her back and holding her firmly down with a paw while she says such horrible things in such a loud voice that poor Huggy retreats to a corner, and Boggs covers his ears to avoid hearing the language.

As for Boggs himself, well, he dearly loves a game with anything, animal or human, and the little mite had only been with us a few days when in a shame-faced way he came up to her and laid his bell-ball at her feet, poking it with his nose and inviting her to play. The riot now caused by this early lesson sends books, papers, and tea cups flying about as they career around over and under the furniture, while Huggy sits and barks at them, for it is her turn next. Huggy, who has never played with anything, not even her own puppies, is won over by this charming devil.

Bustle's greatest ally is the cat, a twelve year old neutered female who has brought up all the Border puppies, and cuddled all the litters, and is slightly confused as to whether she is a cat or a terrier. Although Huggy gave up washing the puppy after a week or so, the cat still offers this service every evening, with Bustle pushing her face into the cat's fur so that she can get free ablutions.

Destruction is Bustle's middle name, not only does she take and destroy things that do not matter, like logs of firewood, paper sacks and Bob's old slippers, but she takes things that do matter and has her way with them. We now have a wide selection of coats, macs and jackets, minus pockets and collars, several decimated hats and caps, gloves with no fingers, shoes with no uppers, and two antique umbrellas now no more than skeletons. The wall in the kitchen is bare of paper and several worthy mats have disintegrated after her ministrations. Biros, letters, papers are all fair game, as for waste paper baskets, they are her spiritual home. She is however, delightful to take out, and so well behaved that tales of her devilment fall on deaf ears as friends look at the flower-like innocence of her face. At her only two shows she behaved impeccably, but her VHC at WELKS rather went to her head and her surrogate relatives lost no time in punishing her for her big headedness.

"I suppose", said Mary, when we last met, "you will breed from Bustle next year?" Breed from Bustle - the spawn of the Devil? You must be joking! Come to think of it, a few little Bustles around would be rather nice!

Peggy Grayson

Tarzan's Terriers

One morning in February 1983 I received a phone call from an animal agency, asking if I would be interested in doing some film work with my two Border Terriers, Jasper Button and Eaglemount St. George. They could tell me nothing about the film, only that the location was at Hatfield House and filming was due to start the following day. That same evening I had another phone call, this time from the director confirming the arrangements for the following day. A car would be calling for us at 6.30 a.m. to take us to location and filming would begin. The film was to be called "Greystoke - Tarzan of the Apes."

Next day we arrived at Hatfield House and met the other dogs who were to appear in the film: two Staffordshire Bull Terriers and two Scottish Deerhounds, they all got along famously. We were at Hatfield House for two weeks, where the dogs just sat around in arm-chairs, beside log fires and occasionally greeted their Master (the late Sir Ralph Richardson), at the door.

Believe me it wasn't easy asking two nosey Borders to sit in a chair, when there were new surroundings to be explored. I spent a lot of time lying flat on the floor, out of the sight of the camera and under the bed. The scene with the bed called for me to position the dogs on the bed and wait outside, an actor then knocked on the door and entered the room. Being two good housedogs, they barked and flew off the bed each time the door was knocked. The director, Hugh Hudson, decided that I should lie under the bed to reassure the dogs each time the door opened. I'm pleased to say this worked after a couple of takes, but then in the next scene the director wanted them to jump off the bed when somebody entered the room. This was all very confusing for them. In another scene the dogs were sat on a chair in the main hall. Enter Tarzan in a distressed state looking for Jane. Exit Jasper Button, who thought he was in trouble and being shouted at. After this, every time the director shouted for action, Jasper would disappear to the nearest corner and stay there. After Hatfield, we travelled to Kelso for two weeks filming at Floors Castle.

Now this is where the fun begins for the dogs. They have to chase after a carriage and pair, but we have another problem. They have been taught not to chase horses and cattle, so all the dog owners - all ladies I must add - get into the carriage and crouch on the floor with a blanket thrown over us. The dogs see us get in and we keep calling out to them, this we did about four times with success. I didn't want a repeat performance of horse chasing whilst out walking. Our next experience was with a talking parrot. The director wanted the dogs sat in a chair and just behind that was the parrot in a cage. They had never seen a caged bird before, especially one that talks, so there was just no way they would face the camera when the parrot said "Hello, come on then." The entire film crew were on verge of hysterics, in the end the director shouted "Cut".

The dogs enjoyed it all very much, especially all the fuss and attention they received from the film crew and actors; James Fox tells me his aunt has two Border Terriers.

Jasper and St. George took everything in their stride, behaved perfectly and did not disgrace me in any way - not even in the chauffeur driven limousine that collected us each day. Jasper did object to being photographed by Vogue magazine; St. George co-operated as usual and lay like a lord on the four poster bed.

I sometimes think we asked too much from them and I expected to end up with two neurotic dogs. However, with a good run in the woods between filming, we all managed to preserve our sanity. At the end of filming the dogs were very tired, as sometimes we spent 12 hours a day on the film set. An actor's life is definitely not for me. The conditions they work in are not at all glamorous, in fact sometimes they are very difficult and unpleasant.

I do hope the film is a success, as everyone worked terribly hard and they were such charming people, they all deserve an Oscar. It was certainly a month I'll never forget.

Maureen Bundy

Border Beaters

I suppose the most interesting thing about using dogs for a job, if you are a breeder too, is seeing how your breeding ideas have worked (or sometimes not). Whilst doing this so many things are learned, many of them almost unnoticed at the time but which one realises later.

It is not by any means the boldest young puppy that makes the best worker. I have found rather the reverse. It is the pup that does not rush forward, but that watches you from the side, that will be the first to learn your ways, sense your thoughts and eventually go through fire and water for you, doing its job of work 100% as a natural thing.

My Borders have a real terrier's life. From their puppyhood they are among all sorts of livestock including poultry and therefore become safe with all those at an early age. Equally early, they learn from their elders about catching mice, moles and rats. They then move on to bigger things.

Letting them "hunt on" in woodland I can tell from their voices what they have found, as well as their individual voices. I think they consider rabbiting great fun, mink something to be dealt with as quickly as possible, foxes even more so, while for sheer enjoyment I am sure they would vote for shooting squirrels - I suppose because at last they get hold of the maddening creatures that normally rush up trees and make rude noises at them.

The first mink mine caught was a great surprise as I did not know there were any here. On a normal exercise walk the terriers started hunting a steep slope running parallel to a stream. I saw something brown slip downhill and go to ground quite near the stream in a small rabbit bury. The dogs were *very* excited and started digging, making good progress in the peaty soil. Then a noise like a cat came from the hole and I almost called them off as they are not allowed to chase cats, but at that moment something bit one of the terriers so hard that she hurled herself at the hole and a moment later started feinting from left to right. Suddenly she went straight and was shaking something madly. It was a male mink and a large one but she killed him in seconds. Since then they have had ten others, but we have seen none for over a year now.

One reads in books that foxes are not the natural enemies of dogs. This is not true of my lot. They hate foxes and their hackles go up and their expressions change the moment they smell one. If on the line of one in the open their voices are noticeably sharp and urgent. I have two lurchers as well who are of course silent hunters, but the moment they hear the "fox voice" they are gone in a flash.

This is pheasant country - steep hills and a lot of woodland. There are several big shoots locally and the gamekeeper of a neighbour comes from the North, is a great Border fan, and very northern blunt. Having seen me and my pack several times when he first arrived and eyed them, he asked if I'd like to try them beating for him on shooting days. He later confessed he was afraid I'd go poaching!! Anyway the dogs love it and are super at it, yet they never look twice at a pheasant here. They behave far better than they do at home, spread out in line and never move until the whistle blows. Of course they mop up any vermin as we go and on one hysterical occasion a Border retrieved a live pheasant from a lake because it wasn't going to admit a Springer Spaniel can do anything better than a Border Terrier. The bird was alive and swimming. The terrier took it by the wing and they made the shore, cheered on by guns and beaters alike!

I am very lucky that I have the opportunity to work my dogs in ideal surroundings. Borders are terriers, bred for work and I fear sometimes for their future. So many are sold as pets or purely for showing nowadays and I'd hate to see them lose their ability or will to work as that has kept them free of so many hereditary defects SO FAR. Only work can prove soundness in my opinion. I suppose ideally I'd like to see none made a Show Champion unless it also had a working certificate. Also I'd like to see pet owners encouraged to do something with their dogs. Mine are all complete lap-dogs indoors and in spite of what I have written now, I have no lust for blood - just a great interest in my dogs' working ability.

I have just been given a Dandie Dinmont puppy as a Christmas present. Are any worked nowadays? This one has already shown she has a nose and she is very bright. I will see what she can do.

Alison Mountain

Stripping a Border

This is the text of a talk given at the Teach-In at Lane End, December 1983.

Stripping a Border is far easier to do than talk about, but I'll have a go at explaining the general principles of keeping a Border coat neat and tidy for everyday purposes. To keep it looking good throughout a showing season is another thing, and I am not sure I have fully mastered that art yet.

You might well ask why strip a Border?

Why not leave it as nature intended, it is after all supposed to be a natural unspoilt breed. I think that nature intended the Border to push through undergrowth and squeeze down holes, during which activities, any dead hairs in the coat get pulled out, leaving a short weatherproof covering. A shaggy coat holds rain like a sponge besides collecting mud and balls of ice in the snow.

When should the coat be stripped?

The answer is when the hair has died it will be pale in colour and easily plucked out. This may be once, twice a year or more frequently because every Border's coat is different. The factors Which affect the coat are 1) the environment, 2) feeding, 3) heredity. By the environment, I mean whether the dog is kept in or out. I have found that it makes little, if any, difference to density or texture of coats whether the dogs live in the house with central heating or out in unheated but cosy kennels. Where I live is a couple of miles from St. Harmons which is frequently the coldest place in the country according to the newspapers, so if climate is of prime importance to coat quality, then I should have the thickest, harshest coats of all. Feeding affects the coat not only in that a properly balanced diet is reflected in a healthy coat, but some diets seem to make the coat too greasy, some too dry. I have recently completed a month's experiment feeding a couple of dogs on a complete food instead of their usual tripe. Their coats became smelly and greasy.

Heredity plays the most important part in coats in my opinion. If the parents have good coats, then the offspring tend to. What is meant by a good coat? The standard says it must be harsh and dense. I like it to be harsh and dense always, not just for a couple of weeks and thereafter increasingly soft and shaggy.

I have brought along Token to demonstrate stripping. Her coat does not perhaps look too untidy, but there is an outer fuzz of paler hairs that are dead and are contributing nothing to keeping her warm and dry. When this fuzz is removed, she has a new coat underneath. Let us set about stripping her.

What do we need?

1) A firm table, not wobbly, of a suitable height and with a non-slip surface.

2) An overall or similar to which hairs won't stick.

3) A Hoover plugged in ready to clean up the debris if weather does not permit working outdoors.

4) Your own finger and thumb and a pair of small scissors.

Start at the head, using one hand to hold the dog and its skin and the other to pluck, pulling small tufts of hair in the direction it is lying. The head and neck seem to take ages, then you seem to whizz down the back, and you think you're home and dry when you come to the area round the tail. This is always more sensitive and the hairs more reluctant to leave their follicles, and the dog increasingly fed up about the whole thing. But persevere, tuck the dog under your arm to restrain him, and take smaller tufts of hair at each pluck. Then strip down the legs and do as much of the feet as possible. Some strip down the tail, others start at the tip and work towards the base - whichever way, don't denude it, otherwise it will resemble a rat's tail. Finally finish off the feet and underbelly with the scissors.

So much for Token and her easy-care coat - what about the all-or-nothing type of coat which grows long and parts down the middle? These are sometimes soft and silky or so harsh and wiry the hairs cut into your fingers. I have found it best to comb them through every day which drags out much of the hair, leaving fewer to strip.

To help with difficult coats, you can rub a chalk block over the coat and on your fingers to get a better grip. Some people find that rubber gloves enable them to pluck without producing so many blisters. Some swear by a Magnet stripper which has a hack-saw like blade that needs blunting before use as it can cut the coat which does spoil it. Beware of any stripping knife that contains a blade as it ruins a Border's coat.

To finish, I'll try and answer your questions, but to anticipate a few common problems:-

1) Soft top knots - yes, I know they are hard to pull, but use chalk for a good grip, take small tufts at a time, and don't be afraid to do just the head and not the rest of the body.

2) Ears. Keep the "velvet" look by stripping as the hairs grow, doing inside the flap as well as the outside, so that they hang properly.

3) Will I end up with a bald dog? Very unlikely - the undercoat will still be present unless it is a bitch rearing a litter. These sometimes lose all their undercoat and if you strip her then, she will be bald.

4) Whiskers and eyebrows. Strip according to what appeals to you. Look at pictures of otters and carve out the shape of an otter head from the hair on the head.

Marie Sharp

Coat Colour Inheritance in Border Terriers

Colour is not a matter of great importance in a dog intended for the type of work expected of Borders but it is of interest and most breed enthusiasts have their colour preferences. Speculation on how colours are transmitted from one generation to the next led me to read all the books I could find with references to genetics and Border colours, only to discover very little has been written on the subject of coat colour inheritance in the breed. In an effort to find some answers I carried out a small survey and explored the findings of geneticists in terriers of similar colour which enabled me to formulate some theories. No doubt these will give rise to disagreements but I would welcome discussion and debate on the subject particularly from those who have knowledge based on many years of practical experience.

Colours: The Kennel Club Breed Standard states "Colour: red, wheaten, grizzle and tan or blue and tan". Grizzle and tan, usually referred to simply as grizzle, is by far the most common colour, reds appear to be fairly numerous, and blue and tan, although relatively small in numbers, does seem to be enjoying something of an upsurge in popularity at the present time.

Red varies from light tan to a really rich red shade. It must be a pure colour with no dark hairs in the coat although the dog may have dark points.

Wheaten is a distinct pale colour rarely seen today. In fact two well known authorities in the breed have told me that they do not believe they have seen a true wheaten for over twenty years.

Grizzle and Tan describes the colour in which the dog is basically tan, or red, in any of the shades seen in Border Terriers with varying amounts of black tipped hairs distributed in the coat. There may be so few dark hairs that the dog appears red until examined closely but on the other hand there are those that have so many that they resemble blue and tans. Between the two are varied effects, some I would describe as resembling tweed, others have a less even pattern but some most attractive variations can be seen. Although there is only one named colour in the Standard there is a tendency to describe dogs having the deeper red coats as red grizzle and those with an abundance of dark tipped hairs as dark grizzle.

Blue and Tan is a dark or blue back extending up the neck and down the sides. The blue must not be a dense unbroken black and the skin and undercoat should be blue. The remainder of the dog should be a light tan but some are a rich red colour.

This is just a brief outline of coat colours, there are many other details and factors such as white patches, greying and dark points to be taken into account in considering the genetics of colour inheritance. Novice Border owners should not be surprised if the colour of their adult dog does not match that given on the registration certificate as many whelps are born dark and the eventual colour may not have been established by the time the puppy is registered or even when it leaves the litter.

The Survey

Of the breeders approached, 27 responded with information. The period covered was the three years 1980 - 1982. The total number of litters recorded was 120 producing 470 puppies. There were 1152 Border Terriers registered with the Kennel Club in 1981 and allowing for the fact that there are probably a number of unregistered Borders, it will be seen that the sample was very small so the findings must be treated with caution.

The results of the survey and a study of genetics, leads me to believe as Miss Garnett-Orme wrote, that the agouti alleles are responsible for the main coat colours in Border Terriers.

There appear to be two groupings, one producing grizzle and tan, red and wheaten and the other blue and tan, the first group being dominant. The presence of another gene would account for the quantity of black tipped hairs in the grizzle and the recessive of this for the red. There is probably another factor responsible for wheaten. My theories are in fact born out by the survey but I would hesitate to call them conclusions and in considering the possible outcome of matings one must always allow for the laws of chance. My expectation is that grizzle and tan to grizzle and tan matings will result in all grizzle puppies or approximately 75% grizzle and the remainder blue and tan. This occurs if both parents are carrying the recessive gene for blue and tan and pass it on to their progeny. Grizzle and tan to blue and tan may produce up to 50% of each colour or all grizzle puppies depending on whether or not the grizzle parent is carrying the gene for blue and tan.

In theory blue and tan to blue and tan matings should result in all blue and tan puppies. Unfortunately there were no such matings in the survey but I have recently heard of two which resulted in entire litters of blue and tans.

Red is a difficult colour to comment on since people's definition of it varies. I believe that the gene responsible for the absence of dark tipped hairs is recessive to the one responsible for them, so that red to red matings should produce all red puppies. The confusion arises when dogs with very few dark hairs are described as red. Grizzle and tan to red matings could result in about 75% red puppies.

The above is a condensed version of a full paper written on the subject and I may have over simplified it in an effort to be brief and avoid technical jargon. Studied in depth, what at first appear to be "little brown dogs" in fact have a fascinating range of colours in them and I hope to publish the paper which covers all aspects for those who are interested in pursuing it further.

References:

The Colour Question. Paper by Miss H. Garnett-Orme in S.B.T.C. Year Book 1966.

Border Tales. Compiled and edited by Miss H. Garnett-Orme.

The Border Terrier. - Miss Anne Roslin-Williams.

Genetics for Dog Breeders. - Roy Robinson.

The Inheritance of Coat Colour in Dogs. - Clarence C. Little.

Diane Swales

To Mate - or when to Mate That is a Question

I have been asked to write some words from my own experiences on deciding when an in-season bitch is ready for mating.

This is a perpetual problem for a kennel without a dog of its own (where bitch and dog will leave one in no doubt when the time is ripe). It is frustrating and often expensive for the bitch owner to travel long distances to the chosen stud dog, only to find the bitch unresponsive or the experienced stud dog completely disinterested. He knows, wise fellow, that the bitch is not ready, even if no-one else does!

This state of affairs presents a headache for the stud dog owner also. Is the bitch 'going off', or in fact brought too soon by an over-eager or inexperienced owner, and not yet 'come on'? If the latter is correct perhaps the bitch can be left a few days - or returned at a later date. All additional trouble and expense.

The bitch owner is questioned carefully, but is rather vague as to when the season started. Visits by a neighbour's dog, or stains on the bedding perhaps, brought the matter to notice. Friends are consulted, all of whose advice differs, but no-one feels there should be delay in getting to a stud dog. Are not stray dogs calling already? (Avoid this menace by carrying your bitch out of doors and clear of your precincts before putting her on her feet well up the road, or carry her to the car and drive a short distance before exercising.) No-one disputes the fact that while a bitch is attractive to a dog all through her season, she is only ready to stand for him and be mated over a comparatively short period, and it is over this day or two that her maximum ovulation occurs and the breeder must ensure her mating.

Veterinary Surgeons, for whom my respect is profound, and whose advice on gynaecological disorders and progress of pregnancy are spot on, can be non-specific on the exact readiness of one's own bitch for mating on a particular day, unless they have made a speciality of breeding. They will confirm that a bitch is in season which usually lasts 21 days, and that on the 10th - 12th day is usually around the time that a bitch may be mated to advantage.

We can argue with none of this, but there are exceptions, commonly slight, occasionally major (of which more later). The bitch owner must be aware of what to watch for, before embarking on fruitless expeditions.

To be fair to the veterinary profession I must confess to finding recently and so late in my day, a man understanding exactly this breeder's problem. He will take a swab from a bitch early in her season for microscopic examination. The nature of the discharge alters as the season progresses and from these findings he will probably advise a second visit and swab at a stated interval, when advice will be given on progress of oestrus and date to visit the dog.

This is a splendid service and invaluable for the novice owner or for the experienced breeder with a bitch difficult to get in whelp, or season of unusual span. However, such advice does not yet appear universal, judging from feedback from others I have advised to seek similar help from their veterinary surgeons.

For those folk I give my own following guide lines which have served me well over the years. Matings between my own kennel mates have never missed, so there must be some proof in the pudding!

USUAL PROCEDURE OF SEASON

Around six to eight months a bitch will commence coming into season. An observant owner may be warned of the event by the bitch possibly being slightly attractive to a dog or slightly flirtatious a week or two ahead, and nearer the time inclined to spend extra pennies when out for a walk.

Stage 1.

Pinkish discharge (NOTE THIS DATE). The vulva will look fairly normal at first, but as the ensuing week progresses it will enlarge and swell to quite hard. The discharge becomes bright red and copious, if all goes by the text book (usual), about ten days after initial start the vulva, although still large, will soften. The discharge loses its colour, becomes straw coloured and almost clear. If a hand is passed down the bitch's back towards the tail she is likely to turn her tail and brace her hindquarters. She also may 'ride' companion bitches in play, indicating her arousal. All these point to readiness for mating.

I do not like amateur internal examinations, but if doubt still persists a scrupulously clean little finger may be gently inserted into the vaginal passage, which, now it has softened will be 'open' and allow easy access of the little finger up to its first small joint. Now is the moment to confirm with the stud dog owner (having alerted him immediately your bitch started her season, so that he may book her in) that your bitch is ready for service.

Advice, which I followed with success, was that the day after a bitch has achieved 'readiness' is the ideal for mating her. Borders appear willing to stand over a few days, although I believe there are breeds with very limited periods of acceptance.

Variations on the Theme.

1. Duration of the Season

Classically 21 days. Some bitches appear to prolong the waxing or initial start of their seasons, and take far longer than the average 10 - 12 days before 'readiness'. Watch the progress of vulva enlargement, and softening and behaviour, and mate accordingly. Whatever you do, DON'T let the bitch loose in a pack of dogs after the statutory 21 days of season. Wait until you are sure she has returned to chastity (28 days overall or more if necessary) or you may be in for a nasty surprise!

2. Although the vulva enlarges no discharge is noted

Perhaps your bitch keeps herself very clean, or has naturally less copious discharge. Watch progress of vulva and mate accordingly. I have had this experience. It can vary from season to season. If ever discharge is unusual or offensive consult your Veterinary Surgeon AT ONCE.

3. Bitch is flirtatious very early in season

Perhaps you didn't notice her coming on? If willing and physically ready, take to dog at once. I mated a visiting bitch happily (for her!) on her 5th day. For interest I tried the dog two days later and she wouldn't look at him. She had seven puppies. Conversely, I had to wait 21 days before mating successfully another bitch. Less intense variations are common. I always mate when the bitch is both ready and willing.

4. Will repeat matings ensure a large litter?

If the bitch is brought at the correct time to a regularly used fit and fertile dog, it is wisest to be content with one mating if satisfactory in every way. If the bitch is a maiden, and perhaps shies at penetration, or only a sketchy mating is achieved, a second mating within 24 hours, or 48 hours at most, can be given. A dog's sperm count is legion, and can lie in the reproductive tract for that period to fertilize any ova shed. Repeat matings over several days can result in puppies conceived of differing ages. This can be a whelping hazard. No less is the headache for your veterinary surgeon if your bitch delays whelping. Is she overdue to the first mating - or holding to the last? There is strong evidence against such practice on all counts.

I hope the above may be helpful to new or novice breeders. Perhaps the good friends who advised me so generously long ago may recognise a few of their wise words. My grateful thanks as always.

Felicity Marchant

A Couple of Border Cases

Time and time again we had thought of dog ownership, always dismissing it on the grounds of a) lack of garden space, and b) having to leave the animal alone in the mornings while we were both out at work. At one point we almost took a Jack Russell advertised in the local rag, but fortunately the dog had already found a new home. "Fortunately" because it allowed us to take stock of the situation, but not for long. Seven days later we visited the Three Counties showground at Malvern at the event of the WELKS show. It just happened to be the day that the terriers put on their smiles and it wasn't long before we fell in love with some loveable, small but sturdy looking terriers which, in all honesty, we'd only seen previously in the Lake district.... Borders, of course.

The expressive, friendly look on all their faces pushed us closer still to the inevitable. We then got chatting to a couple of Border owners, (not a difficult thing to do since every owner we've met since loves talking about their animals). During the course of conversation we mentioned our reservations at leaving the dog alone during the mornings, to which came the reply "most dogs get 'left alone' for about 8 hours every night". We didn't need any more reassurances and promptly set about finding out more. Five minutes later we were in the company of Mr. John Creed who suggested a few words with his wife, Pamela, very well worth while since a litter had just arrived.

About seven weeks later we were winding our way through the country lanes of Batheaston, eventually arriving at the beautifully secluded Star Fall Farm. Two minutes more and Pamela presented us with a very difficult choice - two little black

bundles - a little wiser now, we regret not having had the pair. Anyway, the choice was made and with the expertise and knowledge synonymous with such a reputable breeder, all the paperwork, diet sheets etc. were exchanged and we were on our way - now three of us.

Being complete novices, we knew not what to expect, but during the months that followed our eyes were well and truly opened. I've no doubt some Borders are quite faultless and innocent during their puppyhood. But not this one - Pepper, the interior designer (or re-designer), who insisted on rounding off the plasterwork on the corners of our 'L' shaped kitchen, removing wallpaper that didn't really need stripping, turning full length curtains at the French windows into half length curtains (both curtains sheared off at exactly the same length). She then decided to dig rabbits out from underneath the carpet. In an attempt to relieve her obvious boredom at being left in the mornings, we took the only course open to us - we decided to give her a little sister to play with - or half sister to be precise - since Pamela Creed's "Be Friendly of Bannerdown" had provided another litter, amongst which was another smashing bitch. So it was we trundled off to Batheaston again (the three of us) and duly returned later with another one in tow. The family was now complete.

Despite her early gnawings, Pepper has tempered a little (only a little) but Minty, who we hoped would be the calming influence, is the epitome of the devil, and although number two in line, has placed herself firmly number one in pecking order. As for the devilment, anything Pepper did before, Minty can improve on.

Since the dining area adjoining the kitchen is carpeted, we used to put a plastic type garden trellis across the dividing line between carpet and floor covering, a deterrent which worked very well since whenever it was touched it rattled, much to Pepper's dislike. Enter Minty, all brawn and no brain - in a kamakazi attack the trellis was flattened. The trellis was then replaced with a door, on its side, (the things we do), supported on one side by a chest of drawers and on the other by the tumble drier. This proved for a while to be an effective barrier. Until, that is, the brain exceeded the brawn. Minty, by pulling down the loading door of the drier manufactured a perfect set of steps by which to climb up onto the kitchen units, whereupon the tit-bit bowl full of a variety of biscuits and doggy nibbles was completely demolished, but not before cups, saucers and a multitude of bits and pieces was kicked onto the floor. On arriving home at lunchtime, and after administering verbal abuse at the offender, I was horrified to see fragments of banknotes amongst the rubble at my feet. A yard of sellotape and half an hour later the notes were restored to their original shape though they tended to look more like pieces of plastic. It took careful scrutiny by several bank staff before they finally accepted them as legal tender (though I doubt that they were ever circulated again).

As soon as we thought Minty was 'adult' enough, we brought the barriers down finally, thus giving them the additional space of both kitchen and dining area to play in - the carpet still being in a holey state from Pepper's previous diggings.

What a delight it was when finally we got a new carpet laid and the room once again had a certain respectability to it. The delight lasted but four days. On the fifth day I made my usual lunchtime entrance to find the pale brown carpet was now white. During an obvious mischievous fit, one of the little horrors had managed to enter a cupboard and remove a box of Polyfilla, whereupon the only obvious thing to do was tear a hole in it and run around the room shaking it between their teeth. Everything in the room was covered in a layer of white dust not to mention Minty's beard which by now was starting to set in little white spikes. A hasty phone call to the product manufacturer assured me of the non-harmful nature of the contents. After carefully cleaning and vacuuming the carpet, the following day Pepper decided to dig a hole in it!!! so it's back to the barrier again until we eventually replace the carpet with some form of Border-proof floor covering.

You may or may not have noticed, but there is no mention of children in this short history, that's because we have no family, thus we treat our two Borders as parents might treat their children. We worry about them when they're ill, we shout abuse and scold them when they're naughty and could sometimes throttle them when their innocent play causes so much damage. But despite all things we love 'em, and hope to write again about their escapades.

We shall continue to show them in the hope that they may pick up some better habits from their many cousins.

Eddie Wheel

The Terrier at Work

Having worked various breeds of terrier to foxes in almost every type of terrain in the U.K., I feel qualified to comment on the special skills possessed by the best working terriers.

Many armchair hunters will go to great lengths to convince you of their vast experience of working terriers. They usually "do not work them nowadays but only kept workers at some time long ago." These people justify their over-trimmed, unmarked terriers' pretty looks and immaculate coats by saying "The clever workers never get bitten". No comment exposes the "fake" more quickly and makes respectable working terrier enthusiasts shake their heads in disgust, than this one.

It is of course possible, and frequently happens, that a terrier bolts a fox without getting "marked". This usually occurs when the terrier is entered quietly into an earth or drain holding an unsuspecting vulpine, who, when surprised, decides that discretion is the better part of valour and promptly vacates his residence.

Quite a different prospect awaits the terrier when the fox has been hunted by a pack of hounds for many miles before taking refuge in some deep earth or rock pile. In these circumstances it takes a good hard terrier to bolt such a tenant, the fox preferring to take its chances with one terrier than venture forth to face the baying pack of hounds awaiting his emergence. The terrier must then be game enough to "mix it" with his adversary to persuade him to bolt or be killed where he lurks. In doing so the terrier will almost inevitably receive considerable punishment from his opponent.

It is not however only the fox's bites that can spoil a terrier's looks for showing. Its coat can be damaged whilst working its quarry in confined spaces many of which are wet and cold.

For these reasons almost all Borders seen in the show-ring today are never given the opportunity to experience the true vocation for which they were bred. Their owners, of course, will rarely admit to this, preferring to offer excuses such as "no time due to business commitments" or "no opportunity available". These same people will find time to exhibit at most championship shows up and down the country and almost anyone can find work for a good terrier with local hunts or working terrier clubs. The real reason is that these owners are just not interested in working their terriers for fear that they might be spoiled for the show-ring! Of course no sensible owner would want their terrier to be punished. However sooner or later the best workers will receive some damage for their efforts. I maintain that the best working Borders should be capable of bolting or killing a fox. I say the "best" because it is no easy task for a terrier to kill an adult fox. Indeed some experienced breeders maintain that this is impossible. I disagree as I have owned terriers who have destroyed foxes in a one to one encounter. Indeed my well known dog "Dodger" has killed some good foxes who have refused his invitation to bolt. These terriers are exceptional and must be bred for and not merely left to chance breeding.

The ideal working terrier should not however immediately take hold of its quarry as soon as he locates it. The terrier should lie close to the fox constantly baying to bolt him or hold him at bay until you dig to him. However should he be in a deep spot the terrier must become "harder" and kill him if he is to be accounted for. Such a terrier is highly prized amongst the Northern Fell packs who are required to control foxes and not merely "show sport". The next time an owner boasts of his terrier's working prowess, carefully examine its beautiful head for the tell tale signs of the true worker. They will not necessarily be great scars as terriers are remarkably quick and efficient healers provided that they receive prompt and competent attention to their wounds. However scars are not even proof of a terrier's working ability as they can be the hallmarks of a foolhardy or fighting terrier.Now that the reader is totally confused I can say that a terrier's working ability can only be determined in the hunting field where his natural instincts will come to the fore.

Good Hunting.

Ron Hillcoat

Chubber

I am the proud owner of a Border Terrier bitch named Chubber. She has reached the great age of nineteen and half years old, having been born on 7th June 1965. She is still hale and hearty, having all of her senses, hearing, eyesight and a keen sense of smell.

I have always worked terriers, mainly of the Jack Russell type. I was given Chubber's mother who was in whelp when I received her. She whelped her puppies on 7th June 1965, one of which was Chubber. Chubber has had a hard working life and was entered to fox, badger and otter and I can quite honestly say she was one of the best working terriers I have ever had the pleasure to own and work.

One day Chubber was with me, out with the Meynell Hunt, and hounds had a fox "to ground". Though the Meynell had their own Terrierman he was nowhere around and I put Chubber in the earth. This was the first time Chubber had gone to ground but she bolted the fox within three minutes and she was only 9 months old, though I don't like entering any terrier until they are 12 months old. Chubber did several seasons with the now defunct Hawkstone Otterhounds, even now I have to keep an eye on her when near water for she will jump straight in. I have dug many badgers with Chubber in the past, though badger digging is now illegal as is otter hunting.

Chubber was not fully retired as Hunt Terrier with both the Beaufort and Berkeley Hunts until she was 13 years of age but she really bolted her last fox this last spring, a huge dog fox, though that was nothing to do with me. I was walking with her through a local wood when I suddenly missed her so I retraced my steps to where I last saw her. There was no sign of Chubber but to my dismay I found a fox earth. I knew where she was when I saw the earth so I lay down and put my head inside the hole and I could hear Chubber faintly, baying to fox deep underground. I was extremely worried. I was so worried that I shed tears for I did not know what to do, but as luck would have it the fox bolted from another hole about nine feet from the main entrance to the earth and within five minutes Chubber came out of the hole from which the fox bolted. She fell over exhausted but you must remember she had passed her 19th birthday at the time! I can quite honestly admit I have never had a more fearless and gamer working terrier than my little Chubber.

I have one deep regret and that is that I only wish I had bred and worked the Border Terrier instead of the Jack Russell type. Chubber is a blue and tan but soon I shall have a rare coloured Border, a pure white one. Should any of you have a working Border Terrier, take great care of him. I have proved there is not a gamer terrier than the Border.

Lesley Drew

Working Border Terriers with a Pack of Mink Hounds

So much has been written in the past about working with Border Terriers that I thought I would tell readers of another aspect of hunting where the Border really comes into his own. I have two and a half couple kennelled with the Northamptonshire Mink Hounds Terrierman Mel Freeman. He is a great man working with terriers who will tell anybody he prefers Borders to any other type. He has worked the Border with the Woodland Pytchley Hounds for whom he was terrier man for quite a number of years.

Taking the Border to the hollow tree

The Border working with a pack of Mink Hounds has to run with the pack for anything up to six hours a day, sometimes three days a week during the summer months, in addition swimming alongside hounds, so he has to be fit. He is not just carried by car and popped into a drain or earth as most terriers are when out with a Fox Hound pack. His harsh double coat is a great asset to him when hunting through large patches of nettles, brambles and reed beds and when required to swim, climb willow trees and enter drains often three quarters full of water. Therefore it is important for the Border to meet the Breed Standard to be ideal for the job.

One day last season hounds had hunted a mink for just over half an hour but then could not own the line. However Ragsdale Huntsman (Copper to his many friends) marked at a nine inch drain, which had seven inches of water in it. On being told to "Push him out" he swam into the drain, which was fifty yards long, and after what seemed a long time, succeeded in bolting a large mink which was later accounted for by the hounds. On numerous occasions Copper, Crusty, Tally, Tarka, Boatman and Banker have marked a mink when hounds have gone past and they have killed just as many mink as the hounds this season. Many people who have been out for the first time have been amazed to see the Borders working so well and have said to me "I never thought Borders worked like that." Most people will have heard by now what a vicious killer the mink is and of the damage they are doing to the wild life along our streams and rivers. Fish, wildfowl, small birds and gamebirds all suffer from this predator.

Fording the River

Apart from hunting the mink there is a lot of pleasure gained from walking along the brooks and rivers of rural England and seeing the wildlife while watching the merry little Borders working. I will conclude by saying that the Border is truly a working terrier as during a day's hunting they need to be prepared for anything, floods, strong running rivers etc. go to ground when needed and not be quarrelsome with hounds. What more could anyone ask of a working terrier? If any member would like to have a day with us in the summer they have only to contact me or Steve Dean. I can assure them they will see some happy Borders doing what they like doing best.

Frank Wildman

Border Terriers on the South Downs

To dig a hole eight feet deep in solid chalk takes a long time and a lot of energy. I have dug several of late - the callouses on hands and my white stained trousers testify to this! "All this to unearth a fox, is it worth it?" you may say. It is when the fox in question is a habitual raider of poultry houses and a killer of new lambs. Many of the South Downs farmers are going back to sheep farming as the only commercially viable way to use their steeply banked, scrubby land. This environment with its gorse cover is very suitable for rabbits and consequently attracts their foremost natural predator - the fox.

The fox, however, doesn't confine his activities to the hills. He or she (both known as Charlie!) finds easier pickings in the farmer's hen house; they often scale six foot high chain link fencing to do so. Or they frequent the lambing fields and hope for a still-born lamb, or in some cases, as I witnessed this year, will kill the lamb as it is leaving the ewe's body. All in all a particularly unpleasant creature is Charlie. I have a small kennel of Borders whose main purpose in life is to stem Charlie's assaults on the domestic and farm animal population of Lewes and surrounding countryside. Unlike Hunt terriers my dogs do not see the regular work that spells a short life and disfigurement. I only work on demand - however that too can be a painful process as the scars on my dogs' muzzles, chests and legs bear mute testimony. I "enter" my dogs to work at around two years of age. Prior to this they are taken over the hill near my home and allowed to play in a disused earth. This gives them confidence underground. Some pups refuse this otherwise unfamiliar environment and are subsequently branded unfit for work, when all they have is a distrust of the unknown - a jolly good thing in my opinion and one which has saved a lot of dogs' lives in the past.

Borders are fortunately blessed with a large amount of common sense and, unlike some other breeds of terrier, don't usually rush in without thinking. My working dogs are keen without being foolhardy, and prefer to bay at Charlie rather than get involved in a fight. However they do say it's the exception that proves the rule and my tiny bitch Tess (Tried and True) would agree as she would sooner battle it out than enter into discussion. She will face anything and won't give an inch - I can only foresee a short but eventful life for her.

Noggin (Severn Showgirl) is a very cautious bitch, a careful worker and reliable. She "sings like a lark" if Charlie is at home and her warcry (known to all Border owners!) carries through many feet of tunnel. We can dig to her confident of finding our quarry at the end.

Tangle is the mainstay of my team. She's not perfect by any means but she has the ability to extricate me from all sorts of difficult situations. She has common sense and an incredible amount of bravery and fortitude. She keeps the younger dogs in line and resolves kennel disputes in seconds. Tangle is also disobedient, bad-tempered and frequently unclean in the house - hardly a paragon of virtue but I think the world of her.

My bitches are all small, spanning easily behind the shoulders. I should be happy to see more judges spanning the exhibits in the show ring, bearing in mind these dogs should be capable of performing the task for which they were bred, even if not, in many cases these days, intended for it. I avoid the large strains of Border as I consider them a liability to themselves (and myself ....) underground. Their natural enthusiasm causes them to try too hard in tight places and getting stuck is the result. This can lead to a slow death by suffocation at the very worst, or a badly perforated snout if Charlie is still at home.

I am fortunate that my work and my interests coincide, and that I have access to many thousands of acres of land. I have sympathy for the many Border owners who tell me that they would love to work their dogs but have no opportunity to do so. These incredibly game dogs are so much at home by the fireside that it is easy to forget their true vocation - until a burst of aggression reminds us that the placid easy-going hearth dweller is really a tiger in disguise!

The miles of rolling downland behind my home stretch down to the sea, and in the folds of the hills are a multitude of clumps of gorse that rather inadequately hide the white scars of fresh diggings in the chalk. Not all the diggings are Charlie, however, as he finds the hard work of making a home in the hillside not really to his liking. He often enlarges a rabbit burrow or cohabits with black and white Brock the badger. Often whilst waiting in the half light of evening for the pigeons to fly in to roost, I see his portly short-legged body pushing its way through the undergrowth, oblivious of my presence and in truth probably unperturbed even if aware! Brock is a relatively harmless old chap and only causes trouble with his habit of tunnelling in places that man considers to be his own. I rather feel that Brock might have the better right to tenancy. Nowadays Brock is rightly protected by law from interference with his diggings. However Charlie uses these deep tunnels as though they were his own, and his rank and bitter smell clings to the area around his home. Neither is Brock famous for his personal hygiene and although he airs his bedding every day he still carries an aroma all his own ....

We also have a lot of marshland nearby that is home to a savage little predator - the mink. Borders are ideally suited for mink hunting as they have a natural affinity with water. Has yours been digging in his water bowl lately? My bitches regard a mink hunt as the greatest fun imaginable! As we walk the banks of the innumerable streams and ditches that crisscross the marshland, they stop and "mark" the offending mink by scratching at their holes. This often leads to an exciting chase. I always carry a gun on these outings as I see nothing exciting or sporting in the kill and prefer to execute the coup de grace as humanely as possible. Borders can also be used in conjunction with ferrets to catch rabbits or rats. Rabbiting is probably the pet Border's favourite pastime! I only use Tangle for rabbiting and keep the other two purely for foxing as it is upsetting to dig for hours through solid chalk only to find a bunny in the hole .... Tangle has the reputation of being able to catch something on almost every walk on the hills. On one occasion she jumped on a crouched hare and was dragged across a field before she gave it best.

Borders who work fox are usually very hard mouthed and the results of a rabbiting expedition rarely appeal to the cook in the family .... As I sit and look out at my dogs in their runs and the windswept and rolling downland beyond them, I consider myself very fortunate to be able to work my Borders on the South Downs.

Ray Hatley

One Man's Borders

My love affair with the Border Terrier goes back nearly forty years. In 1945, at the end of a tour of operational flying, I was posted to an aerodrome at Finmere in Buckinghamshire, for a rest in an instructional job. Not far from the perimeter of the flying field was a pub whose landlord was a retired hunt servant, and in his back yard were four Border Terriers ... probably the first I'd seen, and certainly the first that I had really noticed. It's surprising how first impressions stick. I can still remember being charmed by their looks and behaviour, and saying to myself "I'll have one of those one day" ... but it was to be a long, long time. The war ended. I went civil flying at first and then into journalism. I acquired a wife, then a family, and over the years two dogs or rather bitches, but they were just the handiest pup when we needed one - the Border vow lay dormant. There then came a period of ten years when we were dog-less. The children had departed, I had a job which took me abroad a lot, circumstances were against dog-owning. This period came to an end with a more settled job. I began to think of Borders again and went as far as reading text books on the breed. Finally, fate took a hand.

Every year I attend a trade dinner in Hull on a Friday night, and as it's in April I stay in a pub on the East Yorkshire Moors for the Saturday and Sunday to walk, and return south on the Monday. I buy Saturday's "Yorkshire Post" to check what the latest generation of journalists have made of the speeches at the dinner, and look through the Classified Ad. columns which are full of country things on a Saturday. And there it was, a litter of Border puppies in a village which would mean a detour of only a few miles on my route home. I decided to push fate to the limits, and didn't ring the number till Sunday. There was one puppy left, a bitch. The owner had to go to work the next day, but it was only a few miles away, he would take the pup and its dam with him and I could call there. Before I left on the Monday, I begged a fibre-board case from the pub "just in case".

I found the place I was looking for and there, in the middle of a vast hangar-like building where buses were being repaired, I found my owner and not one but two Border pups confined in an industrial-size litter bin. Prospective clients had failed to collect the pup reserved for them the previous evening, so I had a choice - both bitches. One was dark, the other a lighter sable with the dark ears and eyes of the breed, and a tiny spot of white hair in her chest - straightaway I called her Sandy. Here really were the seeds for disaster. I was doing everything against the book - in spite of the time lapse I was making the actual purchase on impulse from a breeder about whose reputation I knew nothing. The pups' pedigree had been prepared and I recognised the names of several of the bloodlines from my reading. I couldn't "think about it and come back". I liked the look of the dam so I took a chance and bought the lighter-coloured pup. She went into the cardboard case with a piece of the Union Flag which had been her bedding in the litter bin! She was ten weeks old. There followed six hours of the wettest drive south that I could remember. The rain sloshed down and the M1 was murder. There was complete silence from the case on the passenger seat. We stopped at the service area at Leicester and I loosely looped some binder twine (which was luckily in the boot) round her neck and carried her over to a grassy patch, but she was much too bewildered. In the two further hours it took to get home, there was one whine from the case. I stuck my finger through the air-hole in the top, got it chewed a little and all was silence again. Arriving home I put the case on its side in our conservatory while my wife and I had tea. Very slowly and nervously Sandy emerged, ready to run back at any noise. Gradually she got bolder- and came over to us - she had joined the household.

One can argue for ever about whether a working breed should become a household dog. Heaven knows how many Borders, Lakelands and Jack Russell-types are born annually ... it must be thousands, and I don't suppose more than a half per cent get the opportunity of going to ground. But it depends on the household. I come from Herefordshire farming stock, spent a lot of my younger days on farms and now spend a lot of time at weekends walking the Chilterns, either on estates where I am welcomed by the keepers, or on the miles of public footpaths in the area. There is a large garden at home. I reckoned a Border could fit into this life style without sacrificing its character.

From early on it was obvious that Sandy was going to be very biddable and trainable. At the start I decided that I wanted only three basic things from her, but they had to be right. For the occasions when she had to be on a lead I needed her to walk reasonably at my side and not pull. Out in the country she had to be absolutely steady with all stock and pheasants, and because we would be walking lanes where cars come occasionally, she had to come to me immediately she was called and "sit" and "stay" when she got to me. The last was the easiest. A happy pup that likes you will always come to you. You can build on this by getting the action associated with a call and rewarding the result. Steadiness with stock was a bit harder. When she was seven months old, we went to Northumberland for a week of hill walking - something I have done for a number of years - (coincidentally basing myself at Rothbury where the Border breed is said to have originated). The hill sheep of the county proved to be the ideal teaching aid. They usually graze close to the foot tracks and if a pup does start a chase, they bound away, leaving it standing. Sandy only started two chases and has been steady with all stock ever since.

Pheasants were the hardest. The two estates where I walk release thousands of pheasants. She had to be steady walking a ride with newly released birds a few yards in front. By calling her in to walk at heel and "nagging" the instant she looked ready to break, we won the day. I have a few Maran hens at home. They usually spend their time in a fold unit which is moved around the lawn. Occasionally they are let out to roam and Sandy ignores them too. Now if we are walking a hedgerow and she scents a pheasant she will flush it, but we can walk through a release pen and she will stay at heel. The text books say that Borders have very good noses, they jump well and have good balance. They don't like water and are usually gun-shy. Mine fits the first two but is the opposite for the last couple.

She will find game anywhere. If we walk a hedgerow she usually lopes along with her tail horizontal. If she winds anything her tail starts to feather. She then points for an instant with her tail arched over her back and a paw raised. Then it's in and flush what-ever's there. You can read a dog's thoughts by watching its tail; I wouldn't want to own a docked breed! She has killed a few rabbits by working very thick blackberry clumps. Normally they just bolt but the odd one seems to freeze and then she chops it very efficiently. Up in Northumberland we were walking the perimeter of a tussocky grass field with wire netting on the field side of the hedge. She put up a rabbit from about ten yards into the field, it bolted towards an obviously familiar scrape under the wire, missed it in its rush and almost bounced back off the wire into her mouth. Sandy considered that one a gift!

She loves water. I think it all started when I had only had her for a few months in the summer of 1983. There were spells of hot weather in that year too and in the evenings we often walked a Thames towpath with some gently shelving shallows coming to the bank. At first she just paddled to get cool, got bolder and with only a little encouragement started to swim. Now she enters any water she can find and swims very strongly, her broad head and short muzzle looking very otterish in the water.

I am lucky enough to work in the country. Sandy often comes to the office with me, spends the day snoozing in the guests' chair and walks to the local woods with me at lunchtime. On one occasion she disappeared down a disused badger sett, but just when I was thinking of going back to the office to call for digging volunteers (I would have got one anyway - there's a part-time gamekeeper on the staff!) she reappeared. There are so many stories that surround a growing puppy - like the time she was lost and really showed a lot of intelligence getting back, but perhaps another time. Everyone has their ideal dog. Some want a dog that will share a freezing cold hide on the saltings, another needs an unobtrusive companion for a London flat. Many spend a lifetime looking for their ideal and not finding it. Sandy is rising two and I know I have found mine. When she is nine I shall be seventy. I hope our joints will stiffen in unison so that our walks in the Chilterns and the Cheviots shorten by mutual accord and that maybe she will produce a family or or two along the way which will give someone else equal pleasure.

Bill Potter

A BORDER TALE

I have a little dog,
Tiggie is her name.
I comb and brush her daily
But her coat remains the same.

She looks like a Koala
Or a shaggy mat on legs.
You see, she's rather plump as well
From the chocolates that she begs.

She should be slim and sleek
And just fourteen pounds in weight,
I really cannot understand
How she got into this state.

Could it be the many friends
Who can't resist the plea
Of those bright brown eyes
That seem to say "Please, just one more for me"

I really shouldn't pass the buck
Nor try to lay the blame
On others, for I'm just as soft
And have been - since she came.

T'was ten long years ago I fell
For this little Border Terrier.
Of course, I knew not then
That she'd become a Hedgehog worrier.

But with all these faults -
Of hair and weight and begging from my friends,
I'd hate to be without her,
So there the story ends.

For "Borders" are the nicest dogs
Their tails like flags unfurled.
I once was told they're known as
The "Wee People of the Dog World".

N. Thompson

Mental Unsoundness in the Border Terrier

Hoist by my own petard, caught in the elephant-trap I set myself, that's me. Last year, writing an article for the Year Book on unsoundness, I rashly said that I was confining myself to physical conditions but that I could write a complete article on mental unsoundness. The Editor pounced, so here I am, trapped.

Mental unsoundness manifests itself in numerous ways, different breeds showing different traits. For example, sharpness of temperament would be an unforgivable unsoundness in a Labrador but extremely necessary in a Pit Bull Terrier. Everyone who knows a Border Terrier soon realises that they are a law unto themselves where character is concerned. A noticeable trait which denotes their courage is their habit of staring into space, refusing to look you in the face or flinch in any way when the Vet is sticking a needle in or dressing a wound. It is a mental unsoundness in a Labrador if it will not look you directly in the face even if you are a stranger, but a normal habit in a Border. Loved ones, yes, but stare straight over the shoulder of a stranger, this is a point of honour in the Border breed. This is just an example of Border character, and most certainly is not a mental unsoundness, which to me in a Border ranges from ring-coyness, a form of self-conscious stage fright, to outright bad temper.

To start with the various types of ring-shyness, first there is the nervous dog who hates everything except complete peace and quiet in his own home and even there is in his bed or under the chair if strangers call. This is a very bad unsoundness, entirely mental, and one has a potentially dangerous dog, because if cornered he will panic and may eventually bite in his frantic desire to be left alone. Another facet is the coy wriggler who "wets her knickers" and rolls on to her back when asked to be handled. You note I say "she" because this is usually a bitch's trait and is normally very often seen in a puppy when it is not an unsoundness, unless it continues into later life and proves impossible to cure by careful setting-up or table training. If it persists in an adult, then there is mental unsoundness somewhere, even if only slight, but for show purposes the bitch might just as well be cow-hocked or chronically lame because she will shrink away or keep turning round to face the judge when the latter goes round behind to view the hind quarters. And worse still, if challenging for a top award and the handler gets a little tensed up with the C.C. in prospect, then this unsoundness comes to the fore and instead of putting more and more in, the bitch will pack in instead and under pressure lose the award.

A strange facet of this particular unsoundness is the dog that is perfectly bold, but self-conscious in the ring. This manifests itself when moving and appears to be the brain working on the forelegs. A dog that is a perfectly good mover when relaxed will stiffen its front and even move pin-toed when asked to go up and down the ring. There is absolutely nothing wrong, but "stage-awareness" causes the dog to "ham up" its movement. Another form of this particular mental attitude is that a dog will often throw its legs up and out in front in exaggerated movement, just as an excitable person will throw their arms about. Such a dog, even if it neither pin-toed nor chucks its forelegs about will sometimes copy its owner's movement. Someone with a short stride will have the dog actually keeping in step, again with an entirely false action. Or a person who lopes will cause the dog to do likewise, not because it has to, but because it is putting on an act.

All these things cause unsoundness of movement in the ring and stem entirely from an over-active egotism and not from wrong conformation. The unsoundness is mental not physical, though it causes apparent physical unsoundness - oddly enough the mental attitude only affects the front movement, never the hind.

But now we come to true and awful mental unsoundness and this affects both show-ring and work in the field. Bad temper or sharpness is a terrible thing in a Border, though it seems to be forgivable in the Lakeland. The difference lies in the work. A Border running with the Northumberland hounds, for which they were bred, has to agree with the pack. He must not tackle the stallion hound or pick quarrels. He is supposed to BOLT the fox if he can and only kill it underground if there is no other way. The mounted packs want a HUNT, not a kill underground, though the Border must be brave enough to kill if he really has to. But the Lakeland is a different matter. Here the hunt has usually taken place BEFORE the fox goes to ground, and after a long morning dragging up to the fox and then a long hunt of miles over the fells with everyone on foot, when the fox eventually gets to ground, probably just before dark the terriers go in and kill him.

Hence the difference in the face of the Border and the Lakeland. A Border should not be all scarred up and half his jaw gone, and very seldom is, while the Lakeland is not considered to be a good dog UNLESS he is marked-up all over his face, with teeth knocked out and some of his face missing. So while barely controlled aggression is a virtue in a Lakeland it is a mental unsoundness in a Border, who should be extremely peaceable both with humans and other dogs until actually faced with his quarry, when as the Police say, he should use only reasonable force to shift the fox, or to protect himself. Any form of bad temper in a Border is a very bad mental unsoundness and should be absolutely taboo. Never should we encourage it by setting up our dogs, one against the other as is the common practice of the more gassy terriers in the ring. A sound minded Border minds his own business. That is the keynote of the breed which distinguishes it against and to my mind ABOVE all other breeds of terrier.

Mary Roslin-Williams

The Kineton Borders

The "Kineton" prefix will be no more than a name on a pedigree to many of the post-war exhibitors, for owing to increasing ill health Captain Kinny Pawson was not seen in the ring after the immediate post-war shows. "Kineton" was among the first prefixes to be registered in the breed, and the kennel exercised a very strong influence up to the outbreak of war in 1939, when a number of the inmates were put down.

This is not a history of the kennel, but extracts from some of Kinny's letters and reminiscences gathered from his friends. His first Border, he said, was given to him as a boy by one of the keepers. Borders were never sold in those days; a dog might be given away as a great favour, but the breeders never parted with a bitch to outsiders. After this he was never without one. He says: All my breed were workers and killed goodness knows how many foxes. I never really aimed at breeding for show, though I like a good looking dog. Shawdon Gypsy, born in 1923, was a wonderful dog out shooting; she wouldn't retrieve, but I never lost a runner - partridge or pheasant - and she would just hold them with her paws when she caught them until I came up. She was an excellent swimmer, rat hunting along the brook at Kineton she would watch for a rat, swimming under water, dive in and catch it. Her half brother and sister, Kineton Kid (Dixie) and Kineton Kurly, by Gilsand Grip, were a hard-bitten pair. Dixie was put in with the Old Berks one day when the Hunt terriers had failed to dislodge the fox. In ten minutes it was killed and drawn, a feat regarded with mixed feelings by the master as he liked to bolt the fox, give it a field's start, and lay hounds on.

Minx's sister, Kineton Binty (she was a lovely bitch, but very small), bolted a fox when out for a walk when six months old. I didn't put her in, of course, the youngest I ever saw to tackle a fox. She was best bitch at Richmond Show and was run over and killed shortly afterwards. I sold her brother to a man who sent a snapshot of a large rat he was holding that Binty's brother killed at sixteen weeks old.

Many a Sunday afternoon was spent at the Hugh Adamthwaites, near Cirencester. One of the boys would run a ferret through the rabbit burrows in the morning and block the holes. About ten brace of terriers and their owners would muster; often some beagling enthusiasts from the R.A.C. came, and some real good hunting was had, about ten to fifteen brace of rabbits would be accounted for. One day a well known character broke cover, a big black cat that had gone wild and was very vicious, followed at a slow trot by fat and middle-aged Kandy. No one was near enough to intervene; the cat turned, stood his ground; Kandy ambled up and in a few seconds it was all over. A grab and a shake and Kandy laid the corpse down, sniffed at it and trotted back to the wood while the onlookers heaved a sigh of relief. Kandy killed numbers of foxes and never got a mark on her.

One or two drags were tried. Aldershot drag bait was used and the course was one to one and a half miles, about twenty minutes cold, allowing the runners time to get back and see the start. The finish was between posts with a fresh-killed rabbit just beyond. Besides the Borders all the village mongrels were invited. The dogs were walked up the field until one hit off the line; off they went, giving tongue like a pack of hounds. The mongrels gave up after a field or two and none of them ever got over the brook which scattered the Borders a bit, but they all finished in the same field, with four or five bunched in the lead. Kinny always said that Borders were the only terriers he knew which would hunt a drag.

One of the hardest dogs Kinny bred was Kineton Kurry, by Kineton Kid (Dixie) ex Kineton Kirsty. He was a big red dog with a liver nose, and sired a few pups as hard as himself, but no descendants can be traced today. He got to ground in a big badger earth near Longcot and was dug out four days later. The second day a fox without a brush was bolted and Kandy followed it down the field; the fox waited when she got to it and did something I have never seen before, reared up on its hind legs. Kandy did the same; they came to grips and she killed it. Kurry was found wedged under a root with the brush in front of him, his jaw splintered, several teeth gone and gangrene set in. He was taken to the dentist in Faringdon, who said he wished all his patients were so well-behaved! Kurry made a complete recovery.

Pioneer (Dusky) comes in many pedigrees today through her son McNab of Old Hall. She was killed in a kennel fight and her daughter Bunty, also blue, died whelping when quite young.

B.M.L. Eccles

If It Should Be

If it should be that I grow frail and weak,
And pain should keep me from my sleep
Then you must do what must be done.
For this, the last battle can't be won

You'll be sad - I understand,
Don't let your grief, then stay your hand,
For this day, more than all the rest,
Your love and friendship, stand the test.

We've had so many happy years
What is to come can hold no fears.
You'd not want me to suffer so
When the time comes - please let me go.

Take me where my needs they'll tend
Only stay with me until the end,
And hold me firm and speak to me
Until my eyes no longer see.

I know in time you too will see
It is a kindness you do to me
Although my tail, its last has waved
From pain and suffering I've been saved.

Don't grieve that it should be you-
Who has to decide this thing to do.
We've been so close - we two these years.
Don't let your heart hold any tears.

Author Unknown

The "Deerstone" Story

I have been interested in dogs for as long as I can remember, but it was not until my parents moved to a small town on the borders of Lancashire and Yorkshire that I was allowed to have a pedigree Smooth Fox Terrier puppy when I was just over 10 years of age. I named him "Spot" because he had a black spot near the root of his tail. Apart from this he had an all-white body, black head with a white blaze and tan spots over each eye. As I was an only child he became my main interest in life. I used to groom him and chalk him like the dogs I had seen at shows. He was my constant companion on my walks in the neighbouring countryside, but alas he died from the dreaded distemper at about 11 months and I missed him terribly; for quite a long time afterwards I would wake up from a dream in which he was still alive.

However, some time afterwards local Fox Terrier breeders would allow me to exercise their dogs and sometimes I would have one for a whole weekend. What surprises me now on looking back is that one owner went on holiday leaving me to nurse two wire fox terriers suffering from distemper; at least, one was alive on his return! I made an album containing stud cards of famous champions, wire and smooth, local breeders considering mating a bitch would borrow this from me to study pedigrees.

When I was nearly 17 years of age I became employed in the Estate Office of the Gledstone Estate. This Estate was owned by Sir Amos Nelson and his family, one of the sons being Mr. H. P. Nelson who was a keen dog and shooting man. He was the father of Mrs. June Monaghan, well-known to many people in the States and Canada for her "Birkfell" Borders. Her father had Borders before me so June was brought up with the breed.

My next dog was a Cocker Spaniel which I acquired from a fellow worker in the Estate Office; her name was "Queenie" and she was one of the most intelligent and obedient dogs I have ever known. Then about 1930 I bought an English Setter bitch puppy and bred a litter from her in 1931. I then bought a good Irish Setter dog which won a number of prizes for me: he was kept near the Estate Office for me at West Marton (the village where I still live); he had a lovely temperament but he got out of the house one day and was killed at the nearby cross roads. I eventually replaced him by an Irish Setter bitch and she produced some good winners. In May 1933 I got my first Border Terrier puppy and named him Deerstone Gyp, his sire was Hark Forritt, the winner of 3 C.Cs. in 1926 but as he had won two under the same judge he didn't get his title; I understood that his new owner did not show him.

Hark Forritt was bred in Border country by Messrs. Dodd and Carruthers, his breeding being mainly North Tyne Gyp and Tyndale. D. Gyp's dam had Ch. Titlington Tatler, Titlington Jock, Glanton Tatters and Bronton Mick in her pedigree. I was getting married in the summer and moving into my present house and I had bought Gyp as a house pet and working dog. What a grand little fellow he turned out to be, wonderful at ratting and rabbiting. Almost all my Borders have Gyp in their pedigree.

In the meantime I had obtained a good English Setter dog and in the next few years did some good winning with my English and Irish, often showing and winning in variety as well as breed classes.

In 1935 I was at Blackpool Ch. Show watching the English being judged when a conversation began with a lady next to me; when I say "lady" I mean in the true sense. She was Mrs. Lewis Roesler from the States and owned the famous "Merriedip" kennels of Old English Sheepdogs. A few months later I sent her an English Setter dog puppy named Deerstone Diamond and she wrote to tell me how she liked it. This was my first meeting with anyone from the American show scene and since then I have had many more first meetings with Border Terrier owners from the States which have led to close friendships. Two more of my English went to the U.S.A. and one to France. Later I owned two Cocker Spaniels and bred two litters of Wire Fox terriers. When the war was on I hadn't time to give attention to other breeds so I sold them. In the meantime D. Gyp had been run over when out with my father-in-law on our quiet country lane as it was then. In 1942 I bought a Border puppy Winstonhall Teddy Lad from Miss Long; shortly afterwards I became an ardent correspondent with Dr. William Lilico in Scotland, the owner of the great "Bladnoch" strain of Borders, and after waiting a year for a puppy bitch I got Deerstone Mischief from him in 1943. I mated her to Devonside Diversion and she produced Deerstone Defender, a great showman and when the war was over he won 1 C.C. and 1 Reserve C.C. He was a very popular stud dog and his name appears in many pedigrees. During 1943, 1944, 1945 and 1946, I did well in both Border and variety classes with W. Teddy Lad, D. Gypsy, (a granddaughter of D. Gyp), D. Ornesta, D. Mischief and D. Defender. At a show at Skipton Mr. Walter Irving from Musselburgh, Scotland, was showing and later we formed a friendship which lasted until he died. He had been one of the early Border breeders and exhibitors and was a great character.

I sold W. Teddy Lad and D. Gypsy as they weren't quite the type I was aiming for. The first Border show after the war was held at Skipton on 13th July 1946 under the auspices of the Southern Border Terrier Club. This was a great event as it was the first opportunity for Border people to get together. Mr. W. Irving judged the dogs and Mr. P. R. Smith the bitches. I was thrilled to win three firsts and Best Dog with Defender, Mr. W. Hancock's Alvertune Fury (later to become a Champion) was Best Bitch. Practically all the great names in Borders were present and a number of the exhibits later became champions.

On August 16th 1946 the Border T.C. and the Lakeland T.C. held the first post-war show for the breeds with C.Cs. Mr. John Renton was the judge and his C.C. winner in dogs was Mr. Adam Forster's Fire Fighter whilst Dr. Lilico got the bitch C.C. with Bladnoch Spaewife, later to become the first post-war champion in the breed. At the meeting of the Border Club after the show, I was honoured by being placed on the Club's approved list of judges. A short time later I bought Bladnoch Tinker Bell from the doctor and then aquired Bladnoch Brock of Deerstone, they were from the same litter as Spaewife. I did good winning with both of them and in 1947 Tinker Bell produced Ch. D. Driver. In 1946 I had bred D. Dauntless and did an exchange with Mrs. Mulcaster for what became Ch.Portholme Marthe of D. However in 1949 domestic illness prevented me going on breeding and showing so I parted with most of my dogs, except Defender who was a great family favourite. Tinker Bell had previously died.

In 1952 I bought a five months bitch from Miss Garnett-Orme who had earlier helped me in my breeding programme. She became Raisgill Radella of Deerstone and was sired by Ravensdowne Joker (son of Ch. Aldham Joker) a dog that had done some winning up North. Miss Orme had used him because he had some good working blood, also, his dam had Bladnoch blood. "Della" became our house pet and on April 15th, 1955 produced two dog puppies, D. Destiny and D. Docker, sired by Ch.Portholme Manly Boy. He was by D. Dauntless and his dam was by Defender so I was back to my original lines.

The arrival of these two puppies was of great significance for me and I think for the breed. I showed Docker as a puppy and he won well before going to Mrs. Monaghan who made him a Canadian champion. I kept Destiny back until he was 14 months; he was something special and I remember saying to my wife when he was about 8 months, "He is going to be the best I have ever had". His first appearance was at the S.B.T.C. held at the WELKS Ch. show. Whilst waiting outside the ring before my classes I noticed spectators looking at him as I walked him around. Miss Williams of the "Harranby" prefix who had been a pre-war Border breeder and exhibitor said, "He's the best I've ever seen and I wouldn't care if I could breed one half as good". Later it gave me particular pleasure when Destiny sired her first champion. He won his two classes and was 2nd in Open Dog.

A few weeks later Mr. Lewis Renwick wrote in the dog press, "At Ayr we did not have the pleasure of another look at the sensational WELKS winning youngster Deerstone Destiny. Mr. Hall seems to have a good future for this one who was much admired." His pet name was "Gyp" after his ancestor; he was a great showman with a wonderful temperament and apart from when he was on the table I never put a finger on him in the Border ring.

In Groups or variety classes I stacked him like the other terriers and he became well-known to exhibitors of other breeds. He was only shown a few times each year after he became a Ch., but was exhibited for five show seasons, won 12 C.Cs. and ten of the times was Best of Breed. He won C.C. and B.O.B. three years in succession at the S.B.T. Club held in conjunction with WELKS or at Windsor. B.O.B. at Crufts in 1958 and 1960. He would have been a great dog if he hadn't been a great showdog as he had such a lovely temperament which he passed on to his offspring. At 14 years of age if he had a bone in his run he would have let a child take it from his mouth, but he was absolutely fearless of anything; it was a great loss to my family when he died. I have never kept a large kennel and usually bred two or three litters per year.

At one period there were eight adults, six were champions and of the remaining two bitches, one had won 1 C.C. and 3 Res C.Cs.

Although I have not been able to work my dogs myself except to rats and rabbits, I have bred Borders which have been awarded Working Certificates in their new ownership. I saw a book on 'Working Terriers" some time ago at a show and it mentioned a dog by the "incomparable D. Destiny" and in the same section on Borders the author wrote, "I trained dogs from both the Future Fame bloodlines and also dogs from the Deerstone strain and found them incredibly good workers when entered properly and given a chance to prove themselves".

So what has all these years in dogs brought me? First of all the pleasure brought by their affections, their sometimes amusing characteristics and their loyalty and companionship. Then the pleasure of meeting people in friendly competition (well, generally friendly!) and forming lasting friendships in Britain, the States, Holland and Germany.

In 1980 when judging at the WELKS I didn't feel very well after judging. Fortunately Mrs. Garnett of the "Rhosmerholme" Borders, well-known here and in the States was driving us but when I got home the doctor diagnosed a slight heart attack, so it was decided I would cease to breed or show and I sold my young stock.

We have five oldies so it doesn't feel so bad as I am judging a Ch. show in September but had to give backword for one last year. I still have my interest in Club affairs, representing the four Clubs at The Kennel Club, still President of the Northern B.T.C. after 21 years, Vice-President of the Southern Club, (and a former Chairman), on the Committee of the Yorks. L. & C. Club (having been Chairman twice and my wife succeeded Mrs. Fairley as President) on the Committee of the Border Club. So although I am not showing or breeding, which represents the close of an era, I trust that I am still helping to promote the best interests of the Border Terrier and their owners.

Robert Hall

Reprinted by kind permission of Borderline

History of the Southern Border Terrier Club 1930 - 1990

The Southern Border Terrier Club was formed by a dedicated band of enthusiasts in 1930 - the earliest records that the Club has are an old minute book which started in 1948 and the first Year Book produced in 1946. This Year Book was a small booklet containing officials for the year, the breed standard, Club Rules, three short articles, names of the 87 members and twelve Kennel Reviews - the cost three shillings and sixpence (18 pence today).

In 1946 the Club awarded challenge certificates and ran its first Championship Show in that year at Trinity Hall, Gt. Portland Street, London. The entry consisted of 83 dogs, making 207 entries in 16 classes, an effort which compares favourably with present day shows. The famous Scottish all-rounder Mr. Jimmy Garrow judged the dogs and Mr. W. L. Renwick judged the bitches. The winner in dogs was Ch. Vanda Daredevil owned by Mr. N. J. Fielden and bred by Mr. W. Hancock. The bitch winner was Portholme Mab owned and bred by Mrs. S. Mulcaster whose prefix is still well known today.

In 1947 the Club's second Championship show was held at the same venue with Lorna, Countess Howe judging the whole show with an entry of 133 in 16 classes, Best of Breed was Deerstone Defender owned and bred by the late Mr. Robert Hall, the well known breeder and exhibitor who sadly died in 1988.

After this show the Club relinquished its championship show status, for what reason there seems to be no record, but in 1951 made arrangements with the Metropolitan and Essex Championship show to hold the Club show in conjunction with their general Championship show. The Club shows then went to Leeds, London and L.K.A. (which was held at Olympia) before alternating between Windsor and W.E.L.K.S. (then held at Boddington Manor, nr. Cheltenham) from 1955 to 1963. After having no Club Show in 1964 their shows continued with the W.E.L.K.S. show until 1976.

The first independent Open Show was held in 1971 in a field next to the home of Mrs. Felicity Marchant of Hawkesburn fame, this was in Hawkesbury but later moved to Chinnor when it became an annual event. The Club has now added a Limited Show and "Teach In" to its club events.

In 1977 the Club, after a vigorous campaign, was awarded Championship status in its own right and its first show was held at Cheltenham Racecourse. This first Championship Show was judged by Miss Kate Sullivan, now Mrs. Ronnie Irving, and drew an entry of 229. The Club's Golden Jubilee Year - 1980 was the highlight of the Club's history - a parade of 27 champions gathered in the ring, which was unique in the history of the breed. The judge for this Golden Jubilee Show was the well-known and respected breeder and judge Mr. Jim Short who has just recently retired from judging.

Since 1950 the Club has kept a register of Border Terriers who have been awarded Working Certificates signed by a Master of a registered pack of hounds and the Club has always encouraged members to support classes for Borders holding working certificates. It is interesting to note that in 1950 there was a total of 31 certificates registered, by 1960 this number had increased to 166, by 1970 to 236, by 1980 to 305 and up to last year a total of 346 certificates had been issued. These figures now show a gradual decline, in the last five years only eight Borders have been entered in the Register, which sadly must be due to the strong campaign throughout the country against any type of blood sports.

With the increased popularity of the Border Terrier, membership of the Club has increased over the years. Records now show nearly fourteen hundred members (these include joint members) and the Club enjoys the membership of well over a hundred overseas members from all parts of the world, who regularly keep in touch by contributing articles and photographs for the Year Book and visiting Club shows whenever possible.

Looking back through Club records has been a very interesting experience and one realises the hard work and devotion so many members have given to our Club. We are fortunate to have had such people willing to be custodians of the breed and Club. I feel it only right that these members should be recognised - Our Patron Mrs. Joyce Vigne together with her late husband Capt. Henry Vigne (Chairman and President for many years) did so much for the Club during the 1960's and 1970's. Mrs. Kathleen Twist Secretary for many years in the 1950/60's and still having a keen interest in Club affairs. The late Robert Hall was a member for 45 years and was a Vice President. What, to me, is so remarkable is the length of membership of some of our present day officials and committee and still taking a very active part in Club affairs. Our President, Mrs. Sylvia Clarkson, has been a member for thirty-five years, committee member for twenty and editor of the Year Book up to last year. Our Chairman, Mr. Bob Williams, joined the Club in 1951 and has been Chairman since 1973. Major Derek Ide-Smith a strong supporter of the working Border, member for over thirty years, President from 1981-1985 and now an active Vice President. Mrs. Rosemary Atkins - Treasurer for many years and now Vice President who still does much behind the scenes for the Club. Much praise must surely go to Mrs. Madelene Aspinwall for all her hard work and support, a member for over thirty years, Secretary for fourteen years and still a very active committee member organising the annual "Teach In" - I found her a "very hard act to follow". Other officials who must be recognised by their years of work for the Club - John and Pam Creed, Betty Rumsam, Dennis Wiseman (now Vice President) and where would we be without Phil Sharp our very efficient Treasurer for the past ten years and who has kept the Club's books in such good order- plus other names too numerous to mention.

I know club members will appreciate that without such members to organise our affairs the Club would not be so strong and active as it is today.

Congratulations to THE SOUTHERN BORDER TERRIER CLUB on this their Diamond Jubilee Year, may it prosper for the next SIXTY YEARS.

Frances Wagstaff, Hon. Secretary

Do We Really Care?

At a recent teach in, held by the Yorks, Lancs and Cheshire Border Terrier Club, I gave a talk relating to the Standard of the Border Terrier.

I began by asking, "Is it necessary to have a breed standard?" and a show of hands gave 100% confirmation of this. My second question was, "Do we agree with the standard as it is laid down?", and again the reply was 100% agreement with the standard.

I then went on to say, as everyone accepted the standard, then, as responsible breeders and exhibitors we should be adamant that judges should keep to the standard when judging.

I hear the many arguments (and no doubt they are an easy way out for many judges), that one can only judge the dogs in front of them. This is true, but, if the dog is not correct in size, then I would say, have the courage to leave it out of the tickets. I hear others (among them a prominent all round judge) who consider the standard as some kind of flexible guide, not to be over indulged in, and certainly not something to worry too much about.

So I ask then, why have a standard?

The first paragraph of the standard reads: The Border Terrier is essentially a working terrier, and should be able to follow a horse. (I think we should consider this along with size.)

Firstly, let me say, I am quite certain the people who first drew up the standard never expected the dog, many of them at that time around 13" to 14" high, to keep up with a hunting horse. Look at the terrain where the breed originated. I would think the horse mentioned was probably a short legged hill pony. I could give weights and heights of many good examples of the breed, but refrain from this for obvious reasons, as I don't wish to either promote or offend anyone.

The size as laid down is:

Dogs 13 to 15½ lbs. Bitches 11½ to 14 lbs.

How can a dog of that weight have great long legs to follow a hunting horse? Having worked terriers of all kinds, Lakelands, Jack Russells, Borders and many crossbred ones, I consider the above weights are adequate, but here I must mention that dogs are gaining champion status, who on their owner's admission are 4 to 5 lbs over weight. Possibly the reasons why these large dogs are gaining top honours, is as I have previously mentioned, when judges are confronted with a ring full of overweight dogs what must they do?

Many of our present day exhibitors have never worked their dogs otherwise, they would realise that a 20 lb dog would be useless in many earths or rock piles.

Hence my fears for the breed.

Other breeds, which have become transformed by the exhibitor, Fox Terriers (which were originally more like Jack Russells, weight about 14 lb - height about 14"), Cairn Terriers and Sealyham Terriers used respectively in rocks and earths to bolt foxes etc., Dachshunds, used for badger digging, and many more are no longer capable of doing the work for which they were originally intended.

Do we want our breed divided into workers and show specimens?

I would say to members of the various clubs, take care when nominating people to judge.

How many judges have sufficient knowledge of the breed? Are they promoted to judging after having a little success in showing, or perhaps because they are friends with some of the hierarchy on the committee? Perhaps the time is not far distant when exhibitors will ask for a more competent approach. As in other sports, judges would be required to pass an examination before being promoted to honours, not only the physical biology of the dog, but with a knowledge of the origins of the breed and the work for which they were intended. If we are going to consider all of these questions, then I ask again: Do we really care?

Frank Bennett

For the New Breeder - Keeping to Type

I was asked to write an article on developing a strain of Border Terriers. The progeny of an established strain possesses positively that elusive something that distinguishes one kennel from another to any discerning eye - be it an excellence of head, conformation, coat, quality or whatever. Examination of pedigrees reveals an interlaced relationship between all the kennel inmates. This "line breeding" can only breed to success on a sound and typical foundation as the characteristics of the strain are more and more consolidated. Such a method on faulty stock would be disastrous. But line breeding (using relationships very slightly closer than is normal to the human race) is behind most great kennels. Closer inbreeding is for specialists, and is not within this brief.

Any success we ourselves may have sustained was due entirely to the tuition and constant support of the two great kennels at Musselburgh and Duns, who so generously provided our foundation stock from their own carefully bred lines. Had our lifestyle permitted us to continue this breeding in depth over the years, we might by now have been justified to have achieved our own strain in some small way. Each offshoot from a parent strain appears gradually to make its own particular mark.

Having registered emphatically that we were quite ineligible to pontificate on strains, which should be the province of those in the breed who have claim to possess such, I was again pressed to write "something else on breeding"! I can only recount some of our own experiences and conclusions. Perhaps they may be of help - or warning! - to a beginner.

I think we were lucky, after years of acquaintance with Borders in a pet capacity, to be able to start breeding in the late 1950's and to be living in Cumberland. So many of the grand old breeders were still around, and were so helpful. All, when approached, were unstinting in advice and explanations.

Border Terrier shows abounded - Carlisle, Edinburgh (Waverley Market!), Dumfries, Jedburgh, Kelso, Bellingham, and even Dalston where we lived. We sat at the ringside. I made notes of all the dogs I liked and compared their pedigrees. Often these linked. Tracing the pedigrees further back, I found that many of the dogs from different strains had some common ancestry - Ch. Future Fame, Tweedside Red

Kingpin, Ch. Girvanside Cruggleton Don, Ch. Aldham Joker, Callum, etc., etc. Yet over the years the various kennels had evolved some differences in type as they bred on from the same great dogs.

In those days people did not seem to flit hither and thither to use the current winning dog. They were very proud of their own dogs, and sought to breed mostly from their own stock, or the progeny of dogs they had bred, or buy back a puppy from their own lines. An outcross, to incorporate a required virtue, was only undertaken reluctantly, and hopefully from an outside dog with some of the kennel's own breeding in his pedigree. Any progeny with the required acquisition that might be kept were bred back to the parent strain in order to consolidate back the home type.

Sometimes two kennels with similar aims worked together, producing between them a definite type from a compatible team of stud dogs.

I watched the judging intently (always a passion of mine), and tried to follow and learn from the placings. Why had that beautifully headed bitch I had drooled over been placed below the plain exhibit and the one with a scruffy coat? "A terrier cannot walk on its head," growled the man beside me. "Yes," said the other side, "they are great *terriers,* but if you have not the head, you have not got a *Border.*" There was much to learn. But I set my heart on that head!

Times have changed. Motorways have opened up the North to the South. People travel more to use the stud dog of their choice. This seems to have levelled to some extent the more marked differences in type. The great surge of Dandyhow following Ch. Shady Knight's brilliant winnings made a great mark, followed by Ch. Step Ahead, and now by Ch. Brannigan of Brumberhill, names behind many of the best exhibits currently in the show ring.

Type and conformation remain as vital as ever. My advice to any beginner is to choose with great care what will be the foundation of your kennel. Visit as many shows as possible, and also the kennels of the dogs you have liked. There you will see related dogs, and also check up on temperament. However beautiful a dog may be, he is useless to you if this is faulty, and it is criminal to land unsuspecting purchasers of your future progeny with unsound stock.

Be prepared to wait for the puppy of your choice. Do not expect to be offered at once the pick of the litter which the breeder may wish to retain. Second best, if sound and true to type, is gold dust. If she does not make top honours herself, her progeny bred correctly will be of great value, and set you on your way.

When you in turn wish to breed, take advice from the breeder of your bitch as to a suitable stud dog. He/she will know what lines will fit. Do not undo years of careful breeding by flying off to the nearest dog - or even the current top winning but totally unrelated stud dog. You will only end up with a kennel of unpredictable breeding quality, even in the very unlikely event that you land a "fluke". You will have lost the one bit of elusive gold that attracted you to your originally much desired Border type.

Possibly a great friend has a dog he is very proud of. You will hurt his feelings if you don't use him. He has said how much he would like a puppy out of your bitch. This is a sad hazard of breeding and is not always understood. You must stand fast.

My other advice is not to build up your kennel too quickly. Enjoy your first bitch, showing and breeding. Keep the irresistible puppy when it arrives, and show her if she fulfils promise - but do not quickly acquire a pack of similar ages. God forbid you want to start a puppy factory! And what are you going to do with a host of old pensioners later on - and no room for a young hopeful to enjoy and take round the shows? Space your breeding, and don't fall into this trap.

I think this is where I came in - so I can only wish you joy in your breeding. I know how indebted I was for all the kindness and help I received from so many. One must give honour where honour is due. Your own strain is not built in the twinkling of an eye.

Felicity Marchant

Flint—A Working Terrier

I find Border Terriers the most appealing of all the terrier breeds, but as I watch the dogs in the show ring I often wonder how many of these game terriers are actually capable of going to ground, bolting and killing foxes.

My husband has worked terriers for some years now, Jack Russells, Lakelands and latterly a Border Terrier.

It was I that persuaded my husband that we should purchase a Border. To me there is just something special in the way that they look, the Border Terrier outline is unmistakable for any other terrier.

We purchased a Border Terrier dog "Todgrove Tip Top" (Flint) from Ron Hillcoat, whom we chose because of his excellent record of breeding working Borders and maintaining the breed standard. Flint's father is Ch. John Boy of Todgrove, working cert. no. 135, his mother Todgrove Token, working cert.no. 139, and Flint's great grandfather is Ch. Cuileann Dodger, working cert. no. 117.

It was at the beginning of the 1988 hunting season that I approached the Terrierman of the Southdown and Eridge Hunt about qualifying Flint for his working certificate. As he already knew Flint was a game terrier he didn't mind taking him. After all, the Terrierman of a Hunt needs to know that his terriers are genuine, game and consistent. He told me how, in the past, someone asked him to gain working certificates for their Borders but he had to send the dogs back with no certificates as they didn't want to know anything about working, apparently the owner was most surprised, perhaps the working aspect had been bred out of the dogs - I don't know.

I was thrilled when Rodney Benstead, M.F.H. agreed with the Terrierman that Flint was worthy of his working certificate. It's one thing when you yourself know that your terrier works but it is a great feeling to know that he has been acknowledged by the Master of the Foxhounds and by the Terrierman.

I must add that although Flint's purpose primarily is as a working terrier, in the summer whilst his coat is in peak condition he does his round of the local shows. In the winter Flint is left with a full coat and resembles nothing less than a loo brush, but this all adds to his protection when working.

Many people I speak to assume that because Flint is a working Border Terrier he must be an aggressive dog. He is in general good with other dogs, but if he is provoked he will fight back - who wouldn't? Indoors I couldn't wish for a better dog. I have two sons, James who is two years old, and Peter aged six months - I can say that I trust Flint 100% with my sons. I have never seen such a dog play so carefully and have so much fun!

The Border Terrier - what other terrier offers such a beautiful temperament, is an excellent worker and a stunning show dog.

God Bless the Border Terrier, but let's not forget what they were originally bred for!

J. A. Martin

Why Did You Choose That Affix?

Affixes have always fascinated me and how and why people chose them. Getting this article together has been so interesting and I do thank everyone who has helped me in this task.

Affixes seem to fall into three categories in general, those who use their own or family's names, those that use the place where they live and those that have a little history to them.

Gerry and Geraldine Baker's JASLOU comes from half the names of their children, Jason and Louise.

Pauline Bamford produced PADEVISOR by using the first letter of all the family, Pauline, Donald, Victoria, Sarah and Richard with the vowels A.E.I.O. between. When explaining this to her son Richard, he was told that the vowels were put between all the first letters of the names except U and he wanted to know why he had been left out!

Sam and Heather Mitchell's KELGRAM is the first part of their two son's names.

PADMAC, Laura Brown devised this from her father's name, Peter Arthur Desmond MacCarthy.

Sue Holleron's affix SUPRA is a combination of her christian and surname before she was married. It has the Latin meaning of "above the rest".

LYNDHAY, Tony Tomlinson's father had greyhounds and these were named after the family and friends so Tony chose to do the same after his granddaughters, Lyndsey and Hayley.

At the first Crufts Show after the war George Robson was showing his dogs and wanted a prefix. He went to the Kennel Club stand and asked how to go about it. The gentleman there asked him what he called his dogs and when he said Digger and Bracken, he was there and then allowed to have DIGBRACK.

Chris and Pam Dyer send from Canada, their JANSIM is from the names of the family's first two Alsatians, Jan and Simba.

BREHILL, Francis Wagstaff writes it is an abbreviation of Bredonhill which dominates the landscape in the Vale of Evesham, and was the happy playground of her misspent youth and where she has exercised her Borders for the past forty years.

Major Ide-Smith chose BARBINS, the name of his house which he will be leaving after twenty-nine years but will bring back many happy memories of the time there and the Borders.

Henry Vigne's BROOKEND came from a name on the estate where his house, Pease Hall, was located and mentioned in the Doomsday Book.

Mrs. Twist took the name HALLBOURNE from the place where they lived when they first had Borders many years ago.

Eunice and Dennis Wiseman have LLANISHEN, the name of the village where they lived.

In 1954 the Sullivans built a house and called it DANDYHOW, so Bertha Sullivan decided it would make a good affix.

When Sylvia Clarkson moved to the Chiltern Hills, she borrowed an enormous tome from the local library on the history of the area and found the land they live on had belonged hundreds of years ago to a monastery called Spinguralls, the local people shortened it to SPRIGNELLS, so she felt this would do well. Incidentally, she paid £2 to have it for life over thirty years ago.

Ruth Curgenven's grandfather was one of the last private residents of Alfoxton House, Halford, Somerset where her father managed the estate and had his first Border, Nimble, there. Her father always believed the house should have been named ALFOXDEN, hence her affix. The house is now a hotel. Wordsworth wrote a lot of his poetry whilst living there with his sister, Dorothy, in 1797. Coleridge lived close by at Nether Stowey.

Betty Rumsam's WILDERSCOT, although not her first choice, was the name of the house in Ilfracombe, North Devon, where her grandparents lived. It was a lovely old house and derived its name from a small stream called the Wilder which ran through the garden. Her grandfather owned and ran the *llfracombe Chronicle.* It was a good choice of name as the two middle letters are her initials, the last syllable conjures up Border connections and the explanation of the first syllable "wild" is left to one's imagination.

Mr. and Mrs. Avastu's PAXTON is a fairly new affix. Paxton's Tower is a folly nearby, where they often went with the local hunt. The letter granting them their choice arrived from the Kennel Club on 1st April.

Kate and John Walton chose ENTERLAW as a local medieval map shows the names of all the fields and pastureland where they have always exercised their Borders. Enterlaw is one of the names which appears on the map several times and it is across those several fields that some of the best chases have taken place.

Peter and Maureen Thompson used THORALDBY as it was the place where they lived in Cleveland when they applied to the Kennel Club.

ROCKFERRY, Liverpool, is where H.M.S. *Conway* was moved when Peter Sarll was a R.N.R. Cadet. This is why Sally chose the name. The ship later broke up on being towed back from the Menai Straits where it had been stationed during the war. The school was then established on the Marquis of Anglesey's estate. Of Conway, Worcester and Pangbourne, only Pangbourne still exists.

The Regans decided on DIGMOOR as they were always digging out their Border bitch. One day with the help of the Fell and Moorland after digging for three hours they found her with a dog fox that she had killed but couldn't drag out. They felt Digmoor a very appropriate name.

EIGNWYE (pronounced Eynwye) owned by Bob and Betty Williams. In medieval times the East and West gates to the city of Hereford were called Eign. As they lived east of the city in Eign Road and close to the River Wye, they thought the two names linked together would make a unique prefix for their kennel.

Dr. Rhind tried to get an affix named after an uninhabited Scottish Island, but found even those names had been taken up. She remembered how happy the first G.S.D. she had worked in obedience had been and felt TOILICHTE, the gaelic for happy, certainly applied to her Borders as well.

TYRIAN is descriptive of the colour purple. The dye was originally believed to have been extracted from a snail. Carol and Steve Dean chose it because the University of London adopted Tyrian purple as its colours. Colours are awarded to sportsmen and women who represent the University at the highest level. Thus in the same way Oxbridge students gain their "blue", a London student gains his "purple". Steve was awarded a Rowing Purple for his services as coxwain to the University's first eight. The rowing club uses purple as its colour and call their second eight "Tyrian". After graduation he was part of the coaching team and Carol often went with him and understood that this really was the best club, so what better name than the colours of the best University for dogs bred in the purple.

The McIntyre's KAILYARD came about as a result of a lifelong hobby of collecting old books. Coming from Ayrshire and Galloway it was natural to collect works of the area's better known authors. S. R. Crockett who lived and wrote in the latter half of the 19th century, also Stevenson and Barrie who wrote about country life in Scotland, but were accused of over-romanticising it. They were nicknamed the Kailyard school of authors. Kailyard means the small vegetable garden of a Scot's country cottage.

ASHBRAE is Arthur and Elaine Cuthbertson's affix, after the first six selections were rejected by the Kennel Club. Being landscape contractors and planting many hundreds of trees each year they chose the mountain ash as this was one of the most popular. They changed mountain for brae which is the Scottish name for a hillside and came up with Ashbrae.

Rather like the Cuthbertsons, FARMWAY was my last choice. Living where cherry trees grow in profusion, cherry something seemed a good idea. So originally I was disappointed to get a name that I just wrote down because we live on a farm. However, over the years it has served me well and I wouldn't change it.

It has been very interesting that what comes out strongly in all the contributions is that like myself we are all proud to have our own particular affix.

Madelene Aspinwall

Fox Days

GEORDIE was my first Border. He was seven weeks old when we met in Berwickshire, and before we were half way home to Cambridgeshire he had turned me into a Border devotee for life. He matured into an exceptionally independent but wise and obedient dog. He was four when the phone call came. A fox's earth was about to be gassed, but one cub could be saved if I wanted it. It was an offer I couldn't refuse, but what would Geordie do? Looking on the bright side, he was not a fighter and had long since learned to leave most other animals alone. But on the gloomy side, even he had his weaknesses; keeping him on the lead was the only safe way of walking through sheep country, and if he scented deer he underwent an instant personality change and could not be called back. And a fox was the quarry he had been specially bred for!

When the quarry arrived it was in a cardboard box, tiny, terrified and whimpering. What a little pipsqueak, someone said, and he became Pip from then on. I installed him in the spare room and planned to keep the door firmly shut until I felt sure of Geordie's reactions. He was intensely interested and spent hours with his nose glued to the door, his tail high and body tense in an attitude that wasn't easy to read.

I spent most of the first day in with Pip and as he gradually lost his fear of me he began to explore. I will never forget the moment he discovered the presence of a dog so close to him on the other side of the door. He froze in a low crouch for several seconds, and then exploded in the first frenzy of foxy ecstasy that I had ever seen, grinning, whimpering, dancing about with wild lashings of his tail, scrabbling to get out. He reacted to my later visits with a milder version of the same greeting, but it was clear as time passed how lonely and desperate he was for the company of closer kin. On the third day I decided to risk it.

Geordie was still glued to the spot in the same ambiguous stance he had been in ever since Pip arrived, so I stood very near him and attempted to open the door slowly. Small hope of that! Pip shot out like a bullet and hurled himself at the dog's face, leaping, lashing, rolling, making the rafters ring with shrieks of delight.

Geordie remained as rigid as a statue, absolutely unmoved by this frenzy, until I began to fear the worst. But I need not have worried, he was simply in shock. Gradually his ears turned back, his tail began to wag, he stooped to sniff. Soon he and this wild kittenlike creature were playing together, and the foundations of an enchanting relationship had been successfully laid.

Their understanding of each other was impressive, for although the signals used by dogs and foxes are similar they are not identical. The only time a fox's brush might approach the upright position, for instance, is at the moment of attack against another fox, and yet Pip never seemed to misunderstand Geordie's frequently upright tail. When the dog stood over his food, lips wrinkled threateningly, Pip kept away even though foxes do not snarl. Many of Pip's friendly facial expressions included a wide gape which revealed all his teeth, but Geordie never mistook this for a sign of attack.

On the other hand there are some behaviours which occur in rather rudimentary form in dogs - rearing and bodyslamming for instance - which form a prominent part of the foxy repertoire. I'd expected Geordie to show these more frequently in a relationship with a fox, but he didn't. During play-fights Pip often reared up, no doubt expecting Geordie to rear up too so that they could push with forepaws against each other's chest in the classic vulpine waltz; but this never happened and Pip always ended up with his paws on the dog's back. Nor did Geordie ever show a sideways body slam. This was a frequent element of the fox's play and was almost an art form the way he did it, lightning quick and very elegant.

Pip was as fast as a blur in everything he did. When he was mature enough to face the world with Geordie I made a long lead for him from a spare washing line, naively intending to take him for 'walks'. What actually happened was that he took me for gallops. But his wild delight in these outings was infectious, and the opportunity to watch the two of them going about their business as a pair was fascinating. Between them they choose which routes to take, they followed scents together, dug in unison, pounced in long grass. Pip interspersed these serious activities with much exuberant sprinting about, and a couple of hours toiling behind him in wellies left me with barely enough breath to plod home.

At 3 months playing tag with Geordie (bottom) and digging with him (top left). At 6 months - body slams in competition for a tennis ball, and at 9 months performs a springier version in a mock fight.

An unfit human was clearly a serious hindrance to him and when he was six months old I took the plunge and let him off. Our outings were then as fascinating as before except that Pip was never ready to go home when I was, and would stand watch as we turned back, eventually jumping in through an open window hours later. Out of obedience and politeness Geordie always turned for home with me, but it was easy to see what he would have preferred. There were no busy roads, chicken coops, deer farms or sheep for miles; I let him go.

Then followed six months of canine-vulpine bliss; my only regret was that I couldn't follow or watch in the dark. Pip was entirely free by this time and had made his day bed under a bramble near the house. In the late evening he would come in through the window, greet Geordie and then me, have a quick snack and with a glance at the dog jump out the window. Geordie would be at the door by this time, waiting for him on the other side. They would trot off together in businesslike fashion the fox leading; then nothing more until I was woken in the early hours by a single bark at the door from Geordie, filthy, hungry, tired and very happy. Pip would already be inside, eating ravenously.

When he was a year old our farmer-landlord decided a fox was a danger to local children (!) and either he, or we, would have to go. We got permission to release him on a neighbouring estate where foxhunting was banned, and for several nights I walked him on the lead in their wood, with Geordie, and fed him there before bringing them home by car. The night I let him off he chose to go deeper into wood, and a crestfallen dog had to return to the car with me. Next night when I called he rushed out to greet us with the old rapture, and took the offered food. As the nights passed he came less regularly, and after a week the food remained untouched.

Pip had gone from our lives. Whether he managed to establish a territory there or was forced to move on by a resident fox I will never know. Geordie would stand for long periods staring, sniffing and listening intently into the wood. Perhaps he knew.

Priscilla Barrett

Gone to Ground?

There's a club which can help save your terrier

Anyone owning terriers who live like normal dogs, exercising free in the countryside or even suburban districts, knows the ever-present hazard of them going to ground. They don't have to be working terriers for this to be a risk. The instinct is there and the local moggy or a rabbit only has to flash across the line of vision or the scent range and the dog follows in hot pursuit, continuing the pursuit underground if possible.

If one is lucky, they may come out within an hour or two, responding to the human voice. Sometimes they are so enthralled in what they are doing that they won't come out for days. Sometimes they just cannot come out, earth having fallen in behind them, or another dog is blocking them in or they have dropped down to a place they cannot get up from. They can get wedged in by roots, immovable objects or just get themselves stuck trying to go in further and further until they are wedged like the cork in the bottle.

It is desperate if they go to ground and cannot or will not come out after a reasonable time. Help is needed in the form of experienced terrier men and other terriers, to locate the missing dogs, and manpower to help excavate them as quickly as possible.

Foster Service

For a modest annual subscription to the Fell and Moorland Working Terrier Club, the owner of any terrier, whether a 'working' terrier or not, of any breed, can rest assured that willing helpers with the right equipment will come to help rescue the terrier in such an eventuality.

The club was founded in Cumbria by working terrier enthusiasts in 1967 when one of its aims was, and still is, to rescue trapped terriers. Another aim is to try to provide a foster service if required, which is also worth remembering.

Obviously the club is still primarily concerned with the legal activity of working terriers to their natural quarry. It does not encourage or condone the working of terriers in any illegal or unofficial manner.

However, they have now widened their operation to rescue any trapped terrier, and indeed will rescue any breed of dog owned by a member which is trapped underground. One rescue successfully completed involved two King Charles Spaniels who chased a rabbit into the stone workings of an old railway embankment! Two rescues have involved Yorkshire Terriers.

Sometimes mechanical diggers have to be called in to rescue terriers. Hiring these and their drivers, and transporting same, can run into a huge sum of money.

A Sealyham-cross bitch, Jenny, was successfully rescued in the New Year 1993, on her eighth day underground. She could be seen through a crack three inches wide, which a mechanical digger unearthed, after three days of work with two diggers shifting an enormous rock-face. Food and water were slid into Jenny via a ten foot long by three inch plastic tube. A bigger digger was called in to shift a slab of rock twenty foot by fifteen foot, of unknown thickness. Helpers had to keep the small fissure clear of sand and small stones meanwhile.

The total cost of this huge operation to rescue one small dog was £1,143.27, plus a great deal of willing help from terrier folk and quarrymen, and the drivers who nobly turned out during their Christmas holidays.

Another rescue requiring quarrymen to dynamite a terrier free, little by little, ran up a bill of £900.

A job involving a digger necessitated removing forestry trees (with permission) digging a shaft forty foot deep, twenty foot wide and one hundred foot long, and then brave men being lowered into the earth in the bucket of the machine to dig in with spades to get to the terriers, who were found to be stuck on a ledge.

These men are truly brave - another rescue was concluded by tractor headlights with four men, roped together, lined up head to toe, travelling into a greensand excavation to the depth of twenty-five foot to dig out the terrier who was stuck fast. If greensand shifts, any person *or* dog is liable to suffocation. The dog was brought out at midnight.

Another aspect of the value of this membership fee is that the Association takes legal advice should the terrier go to ground in a badger sett, which one is now not allowed to disturb by law. The club representative will clear this with police and a solicitor so that the rescue of the terrier can begin.

£3 well spent

The club now has twenty-three areas, each with its own area representative who is a responsible and experienced working terrierman. He it is who will organise assistance should a terrier become fast. If this necessitates hiring a machine to dig it out quickly, or quarrymen to blast rock, the cost will be borne by the club.

There will be no shortage of volunteers to help, sometimes there will be twenty or thirty people involved.

Surely an annual subscription of £3 is money well spent for the owner of any terrier as insurance that help will be on hand should it get into difficulties underground. In the event of knowing the area, but not the exact hole into which the terrier vanished, help will be on hand to try to locate the terrier through listening and with the aid of other terriers.

Working terrier folk may have a tough reputation but they are always upset and concerned to learn of a terrier 'fast' and will move heaven and earth, day and night, to rescue one, taking awful risks themselves.

Surely anyone with a terrier would be well advised to join, just in case ...

Anne Roslin-Williams, 1993

Reprinted by kind permission of Dog World

{*Editors note: The annual subscription is now £10. Contact Bill Shorthose on 01505 850 313 for further details.*}

Enjoyable Ratting

Whether we be rich or poor, whether we live in a mansion or a cottage, in the country or the town, there's a little sport we can all enjoy. I am referring to the sport of ratting. The necessary equipment is meagre, and makes no startling demand on the purse. A brace or two of dogs, a brace or two of ferrets, and a light, sharp spade are the only essentials.

The sport can be indulged in with almost any variety of dog. I have known even the dainty Pom to hold its own against a particularly cute and hard Jack Russell type of tyke.

Just before the war I was keen on getting together a pack of Dachshunds for ratting, also a pack of Griffons. At this time well organised ratting clubs or hunts (the latter is the more correct word) were springing up in all parts of the country.

I remember there was one at Sheffield, and others in the Newcastle-on-Tyne district, and that several women, keen on some variety or other of terrier, were running hunts around and about London, and in the southern counties.

For instance, a girl enthusiast of Scottish terriers in the Horsham district, had got in touch with other breeders of this admirable tyke, and was conducting a hunt there, and conducting it well. I attended one of the meets, and the experience was delightful. There was a pack of fifteen well-bred Scotties, half a dozen of the terriers being owned by the organiser of the hunt and the remainder by her friends.

In about six hours we had killed eight or nine rats. Some of the dogs, I remember, were lacking in experience, and, indeed, were mere passengers, but the rest were excellent.

Never shall I forget the way that in which these latter followed an old buck rat for quite a quarter of a mile along a deep, swift, stream. Of course, the quarry, for the most part, was swimming beneath the water yet the dogs contrived to catch the scent from time to time. Eventually the rat was caught and killed when trying to get to ground in a hole in the bank.

Since the end of the war, I do not know that any of these great wee Hunts have been started again, and if such really be the case, it is deplorable. In each case an Honorary Secretary was elected. His or her duties were to procure a little "country" to hunt over (invariably an easy matter), to arrange meets and the means of getting to the meeting places, to keep a record of each hunt and as far as possible, some record of the individual achievements of the pack, and to enrol as members those within so many miles radius of the headquarters. who kept one or more of the particular variety of dog in which the hunt was interested.

There was a small subscription and entrance fee. From 3s.6d. to 5s (17.5p - 25p). it sufficed as a general rule, for expenses were trivial. A "huntsman" was elected to take charge of the pack, a "first whip" to carry and work the ferrets, a "second whip" to help generally, and other "whips" to carry the lunch and the tools. Then there were rules. Dogs of a quarrelsome disposition, for instance, were to be kept on a lead until accustomed to the others, and until they could be relied upon not to fight.

There was to be no shouting, no talking when the ferrets were working, no criticism of the "huntsman" and his methods during the Hunt, no bookmakers and betting. no bringing of crossbred dogs, or dogs of any variety save that specified by the hunt.

Particular stress was laid on the last, for an enjoyable hunt was not the only object of the hunts. There was, also, the aim of bringing together those interested in the variety of dog used under pleasant conditions.

One of the North Country Hunts, whose "fancy" was Border Terriers, a breed of great endurance and courage, and excellent for work, rang the curtain down on the end of each season with a little dinner and the awarding of prizes to the owners of the dogs that had performed best.

The members of the hunt were all miners and about twenty strong. On hunting days the men were most particular to wear caps adorned with a rat's head mounted as a brooch. Their enthusiasm was extraordinary, and their pack wonderful.

Amazing were the prices they would pay to secure a dog of exceptional promise. Comfort in their homes was a very small matter in comparison with breeding a puppy that would eventually kill rats as quickly as he could get them between his teeth.

Occasionally the men held interesting trials. I saw only a portion of one. Rats were being released in a rough meadow and after a start of a few minutes, one by one, the dogs were being put on the trail. A big crowd was present with bookmakers and heavy betting was going on. Most of the rats got clean away, for there was no desire to kill. The dogs were judged in accordance with the skill they showed in following the scent. The judges took their duties very seriously, while the owners of the competing dogs regarded the trial with that importance which we associate with the Derby and the Boat Race.

The men were wise in encouraging the terriers to make the most of their noses. For after all enjoyable ratting does not consist in the number of rats killed, but in the hunting of the rodents, and by this I mean, in the working of the dogs. For this reason the best sport is always obtained in a district where rats are scarce, rather than plentiful, and have their burrows so situated that they can get out of them and away without being snapped up as they bolt. Often in a thick hedge a rat will give a run of half an hour or so, provided the dogs have good noses and have been trained to use them.

On the other hand, if the tykes hunt only with their eyes, the rat is seldom long in escaping them altogether. I have come across terriers of every variety that would not make the slightest attempt to work with their noses. On losing sight of a rat the little idiots would rush madly about for a few minutes, and then as far as they were concerned all was at an end. The quarry could not be seen, so their interest in him had tumbled to pieces, like the castle in the air.

To be possessed of good ratting terriers it is very important that you should begin to train the dogs at the earliest possible age, to rely more on their noses than their eyes, and to hunt slowly and with perseverance. This, as a rule, can only be achieved at the expense of much patience and time. I say as a rule, for now and again you meet with a puppy blessed with so much intelligence that without the least bit of encouragement and straight away he works with the skill and cunning of the old, experienced hand.

Need I say it is a very great treat to be the owner of such a dog!

How still he stands as the ferrets are playing their part, with most serious and anxious expression, and how quietly, even stealthily, he will change his position as sounds from inside the burrow reach his keen ears and tell him that it will be to his advantage and the rat's disadvantage to do so! Then how quick he is to catch the scent of a rat that bolts somewhere or other out of sight! You yourself may not hear a sound, but like a flash suddenly the dog darts away, and then you see him, weasel like, working his way along the hedgerow, now as quickly as he can get through the brambles and branches, now very slowly as the scent rises and falls.

Presently, perhaps, you hear a faint, distant squeal, and not many moments later the doggie returns and lays a dead rat at your feet and resumes his vigil, or he may not return, and on you yourself moving on, you find him patiently watching a hole in which the rodent has taken refuge. He knew you would be along presently to look for him, so he has waited to let you know the exact whereabouts of the quarry, and, incidentally, to try and prevent it from getting away further, should it make the attempt.

It is in the company of a dog of this class that puppies should have their first serious lessons, and a dog of equal excellence that should be secured to lead a pack.

Under all circumstances he is stolid and reliable, and in time it dawns upon his companions what a lot of fun they are losing by not following his example. Then by degrees they drift into his ways and you have a pack of ratters of which you may with justice feel proud.

Before concluding, I may add that a dog of any intelligence can be taught not to try to harm ferrets in a few days. Let him see you handling and fondling them, and putting them on the ground and picking them up, and he understands. He understands that you care about them, and that you want him to regard them as friends, and since he cares about you, he is only too glad to do anything that will make you and him closer pals.

J G Bristow Noble

From Dog World Annual 1924

Sam - Where are you?

It was the day before Christmas. The halls had been suitably decked, the presents wrapped, including one for Sam's first Christmas. There was time for a walk, so, after overcoming the intitial reluctance that is the average Border's way of indicating self-reliance, off we toddled.

Taking a detour after the end of our normal short circuit we were soon exploring territory new to Sam, who was only seven months old. Along the top of the old quarries, we came to the densely planted conifers of a Forestry Commission woodland, soft needles underfoot, dank moisture in the perfectly still air, the light just starting to fade. Sam trotted patiently by my side, occasionally dawdling to examine a particularly fascinating twig, once or twice actually getting ahead of me. I was lost in thoughts of the Christmas to come, enjoying our walk, pleased that at home we were, for once, ahead of the Christmas game.

Every thirty seconds or so I turned round to check that Sam was behind me. There he was, pottering along. We walked on. I turned again. This time, he was nowhere. I called. Nothing. I peered into the gloom beneath the dark branches. Nothing. I called again. Unbidden, that stuff about a dog being for life, not just for Christmas, sprang to mind. Here was I with - or, to be strictly accurate, without - a dog that wasn't even going to be for Christmas, let alone for life.

For half an hour I ran around like a chicken with its head cut off, calling frantically. Part of me knew that this was utterly futile. Even in full view, just half a room away, Sam could be stone deaf to a straightforward summons. What chance was there of luring him away from whatever had distracted him! Still, I stumbled through the woods in ever increasing circles, calling, whistling, shouting. By now I was convinced that he was trapped underground, mauled by one of the plentiful badgers but, being a Border, unwilling to give any indication that he was in intense pain. I panicked, and ran the two miles home.

I explained to my wife what had happened, and ripped open Sam's Christmas present. A squeaky toy, whose label boasted hours of endless fun. Sam and I knew from many pleasant past experiences that in his case "endless" usually amounted to no more than thirty seconds. I also knew that its squeak was the one thing guaranteed to bring him running. Rachel and I jumped in the car and drove as close as we could to where I'd last seen him, then out we jumped, calling again, me squeaking his toy confidently.

Nothing!

We fanned out. I squeaked. We came to a lonely cottage. I screwed up my courage and knocked at the door, but they hadn't seen anything resembling a Border. I squeaked. Still nothing. By now it was properly dark, and even a familiar pinewood becomes an entirely different and much more forbidding place in the dark. Back and forth we walked, calling and squeaking, squeaking and calling. That he had not answered by now was final proof that I was unfit to own a dog. He was dead, underground and unfindable, because I was too cocky to keep him on a lead and too dumb to train him to come when called. I began to anticipate the worst Christmas in my life. Four hours on, I was no more than ten metres from where I had first lost Sam and was on the verge of tears.

Naturally, that was the moment he chose to saunter into view, tail wagging, moderately pleased to see me, and could he please destroy the toy now. Of course I was tempted to shout, but I didn't. I just hugged him and asked, rather foolishly, where he had been.

He's pulled the same trick many times now, and that's still the question I really want answered. Where does he go when he vanishes, wraith-like? What is he doing? And how come he inevitably turns up a few paces from where he vanishes, and yet is completely unfindable in the meantime?

He did it on a visit to find his roots, in a pinewood near Hexham. He's done it on a beach with no cover to speak of. He evaporates on familiar territory and fades from view on walks that neither of us know. He once absented himself during a personal guided tour round a stately home and park, delaying dinner and inconveniencing an entire house-party, though they were too polite to say so.

I'm resigned to these vanishing acts now. The only pattern to emerge is that he reappears near where he disappears. Whether that means he stays in the area, I have no idea. I do know that if I stay put and stay calm, he will return when he is ready to. At least, he always has so far. I have no idea what he does on these escapades, and I also have no idea what prompts his vanishings. It isn't anything as simple as foxes, badgers, or even rabbits, for many's the time I've smelled fox strongly on the air and Sam hasn't turned a hair.

We moved, almost a year ago, to the proper countryside. Now he vanishes from home, stays out an hour or two, and then reappears. He has even learned to bark for admittance, no mean feat for a Border. He is usually muddy, often tired, and I still have no idea where he goes. A neighbour once said she'd seen him three or four fields away, chasing deer. Another said not to worry, he'd never catch them. I do worry that he might take to chasing the sheep roundabouts, although I think his early training with a ewe and lamb has given him a healthy respect for sheep.

There are times when it is a blasted nuisance to hang about waiting for the dog to return. There are times when I fear he has been shot by an angry shepherd. And there are times when his total indifference to my concern borders on ingratitude. But when I hear of Borders staying out overnight, or for days at a time, I thank my stars that Sam has not, so far, pulled that particular stunt. Six Christmases on, I don't think I could survive a night not knowing where he was.

Dr. Jeremy Cherfas

What a Dog's Life . .

I am Bramble, a Border Terrier, and was thirteen on the 15th August 1992. I came to live with Susan when I was a year old, and she lived at Teddington near London. We didn't have a private garden but a communal one around the flats. Being on the ground floor I could see quite a lot of what went on all around.

A very short time after my arrival I showed how intelligent I am. Susan was going out for the day, sailing, and left me with a young neighbour, who took me into Bushey Park for "walkies". It was a very large park with lots of trees, bushes and deer, and when the friend let me off the lead I naturally scooted off to see what I could find.

After some time, apparently, we lost each other, and she thought she had better go home and see whether I turned up. I think she must have been very relieved that I was so clever, as I had to cross a very busy road (on a corner), along two streets, to the station, where there is a path on the side of the Southern Railway. This path has two gates, and of course, I had to wait for someone to come to open the first one, but I got home safely.

Soon after this time Susan decided to come back to Yorkshire and the wide open spaces, and we had a few weeks with Margaret (Susan's aunt) until we found a house of our own. Margaret was in an upstairs flat which meant, during the daytime, when Susan was at work, I didn't get so many walks as I would have liked.

However we soon found one at Boston Spa with a back garden which is private and Susan really worked hard getting lots of trees, bushes and flowers on what had been a bare patch. Lovely smells and sunny and shady parts.

Kittie lives next door to us and I do realise how lucky I am to have Susan who cares for me so well, grooms me regularly (which I am not too keen on) and does everything she can to make my life enjoyable. Kittie is a very good friend of mine, she makes me so welcome in her bungalow, with a bean bag on the hearth, so inviting. I am not keen on being in the car for long . I don't seem to be able to do like many other dogs, settle down to sleep to pass the journey on.The fact is I'm too nosey and must see what is going on around, consequently I tend to stand up most of the way, which gets tiring after a while. When we stop for Susan to go shopping, or whatever, I do settle down and sleep.

I've fathered two youngsters, one lives in Boston Spa and I see that one often - but the other one went on a farm and we never meet.

I am not able to go quite such long walks as I get older (and stiffer) but still do quite well, and, we often go into the Dales for a few days, seeing lots of sheep which I am kept well away from. From time to time Susan goes on holiday over seas and I have to go to kennels. I suppose they are really quite nice kennels, with lots of different dogs (and cats) but it's nice to come back home of course. I have over the years, realized how different human beings regard we dogs, some making a fuss of us and some just putting up with us. Susan, Kittie and Margaret, for instance, seem to understand my funny little ways.

I must admit I don't care for being alone very much, I love company, and am very affectionate, liking to be near people, but I do not like being cuddled - after all I'm not a lap dog, I'm a Border Terrier and proud of it!

If I'm left alone too long I tend to find ways to show my disapproval, like emptying the waste paper basket and chewing up the papers, or, if I can get into the bedrooms I will ruffle up the pillows, etc. I can make a lovely bundle of the hearth rug. One particular day I managed to open the door of the cupboard where my food is kept, and spilt a lot of biscuits over the kitchen floor - a trick which didn't please Susan at all.

Talking of not liking to be alone - until the last year or so I was never allowed to go upstairs to sleep at night. Try as I would to sneak up and hide by the bedside I was always found and sent downstairs (although I hardly ever slept on my bean bag during the night) but now I'm encouraged to sleep in Susan's room at night - strange when you think that as I've got older and stiffer it is much more difficult for me to climb the stairs. But then again, I suppose I am queer because if Susan is upstairs during the daytime for long I have to go and see what she is doing!

I have certain things which really do upset me - I cannot bear the wind, thunder, fireworks, lawn mower and vacuum, and bees and bluebottles making queer noises. Coughs also puzzle me.

Fact is - I LIKE routine and absolutely hate upheavals, and when Susan is getting luggage, etc. ready in the hall I am always at a loss to know whether I am going with her or to the kennels.

According to Susan and her friends I bark if anyone comes to the door when Susan is in, but not if she is out. Obviously I bark to let her know there is someone there!

Bramble's full name is Rubicon Bramblepatch by Wilderscot Persimmon ex Wilderscot Wicked Lady.

He was born in 1979 and lives with his owner Miss Susan Dinsdale in Yorkshire.

The story was written by her aunt, the late Mrs. Margaret Scott when she was 84 years old. She died in 1992 shortly after typing this story on her own typewriter. Bramble is a registered PAT dog and makes weekly visits to the Cheshire Home at Spofforth, North Yorkshire.

"Nick"

- my 'hearing aid' and personal assistant with a difference!

The longer I have my hearing dog, Nick, and the more contact I have with the Training Centre through speaking at meetings, the more I realise the importance of matching dog with owner. I am not so much thinking about breeds, sizes and owners' preferences, but more about the training of the deaf person. Recipients have an infinitely greater variety of complexity of physical and emotional make-up than the dogs. The one common denominator of deafness is not even a constant, any more than the fact that all dogs have four legs can be taken to suggest that therefore all dogs are the same! There is an infinite variety of degrees and types of deafness. My experience has brought me to believe that a deaf person who, through use of hearing aids, can hear some sounds, may experience greater difficulty in working with a trained hearing dog than a person with no hearing at all. I use the term "working with" rather than "the dog works for" because recipient and dog work together - the recipient reciprocating the dog's work. Continuity of practice is vitally important. Working after placement is not far removed from training and "practice makes perfect".

To the person who can hear some sounds (not to be confused with understanding speech) having a hearing dog can present problems of self discipline. A deaf person is often so pleased to have heard something normally, when most of his life is spent in a meaningless jumble of sound, that it is difficult not to react when a sound is heard. A dog is intelligent and will 'read' a person's body language, expression and reaction.

When I take my hearing aids off at night and then do not hear anything, except perhaps a very loud bang, I still do not think that I cannot hear noises! (Of course I do still hear my tinnitus noises so I am never 'noise free'). Because I hear a lot of noise when my aids are on, and they are as much a part of me as spectacles or dentures may be, I still do not really believe that I cannot hear when I take them off. For me, of course, this is the time when I really rely on my dog totally. It is therefore very important that he works at night.

A deafened person so often has a loss of confidence, and confidence in ones self and in the hearing dog is what it is all about - confidence to recognise the 'sometimes hearing' and 'sometimes not' factor, and to accept this rather than let it lead to increased confusion, is extremely difficult. It is confusing living in a world of sometimes hearing and sometimes not. It is difficult to learn to rely on the dog at all times, whether hearing or not hearing sounds.

However, the assistance Nick gives me is truly versatile. He beats flashing lights and vibrating pads hands down, or rather paws down. He comes in one complete lovable bundle of Border Terrier on four feet. My lifestyle does not run to any set pattern at all. I have retired early and travel the country a great deal in my motorcaravan, exploring our beautiful islands and visiting friends. I have no set routine at all. Sometimes Nick and I will be on campsites, or even parked up in some quiet corner. Sometimes we will be visiting friends and sleeping in strange houses.

I expect a lot of Nick to work in all these different surroundings, but he does. I don't have a telephone or doorbell in the van, but I do have all the other sounds. Nick tells me when people call and knock the van door. He gives me such a great feeling of security. I know he will alert me if there are intruders about or if there is any 'funny business' going on outside. It can be a frightening world if you are alone, and deaf.

Nick has made all the difference in the world to my sanity. No longer do I worry about the sounds I may be missing. I know for sure that I will not oversleep. He gives me confidence and stops me worrying! He is an amazing talking point! People are always asking me about him - so very often deaf people are ignored. We have become a partnership. He is my assistant and my companion. In return he gets lots of love, affection and 'walkies'. We are no longer 'My dog and I'. We are 'Us'.

John V. Roberts

Reproduced by kind permission of the editor of the Newsletter of Hearing Dogs For the Deaf

Rearing Orphan Puppies

Disaster struck at 3 a.m. one October morning - my bitch stopped breathing during a Caesarian operation, and could not be revived. Her three puppies lay there gasping intermittently. An overwhelming determination came over me that these puppies would survive, so home they came in my pocket, armed only with hope and absolutely no knowledge of what should be done.

Warmth was the first priority so the three whelps, weighing six, eight and eight ounces, were wrapped in a miniature electric blanket that is designed to give warmth to arthritic joints, but which proved indispensable with its adjustable thermostat and furry washable cover. Feeding was impossible for the first few hours as the effect of the anaesthetic made the puppies very comatose. When they woke up I gave them 1 ml each of colostrum which I had milked from their mother, not a very pleasant thing to have to do but essential. I collected 15 ml of this thick yellowish substance, and I fed it to the puppies every two hours using a 2 ml syringe and dropping it onto their tongues as they sucked. After each feed I used soft toilet tissue to imitate the action of the bitch's tongue so that they would empty bladder and bowels.

As the puppies seemed to be surviving their first day, there was no choice but to make plans to rear them. Should I attempt to find a foster mother, or should I opt for hand-rearing? The chances of finding a suitable foster mother within practicable distance seemed remote, and anyway I did not feel I could entrust anybody with my precious pups, so my decision was made, and I set about finding out how to rear the pups myself.

The good news was that there is a book on hand-rearing puppies, the bad news was that it would take 28 days to be delivered. I searched through all the year books for any help I could find but no-one had written in detail. I would have to learn by trial and hopefully not too many errors.

My first task was to locate feeding bottles and milk substitute. Having found proper feeding bottles for small animals, my problems were not over. I never did solve the problems of making suitable sized holes in the teats. Even the largest darning needle did not make a hole through which the pups could suck. Eventually the local carpenter drilled a hole with his smallest bit to provide the best but not a perfect solution. I had been recommended to use a milk substitute which is advertised as the "closest approximation to bitches' milk", but could not obtain it locally, so used what I could buy. The product I used is made for orphan puppies but I found it caused considerable discomfort to my pups as it recommends quantities far in excess of what they could cope with. Their stomachs became very swollen and they cried like babies with colic. Once I'd changed their brand of milk they were different puppies, but I regretted I had "lost" a fortnight when their weights almost stood still.

For the first week I fed the puppies every two hours day and night, and as it took approximately thirty minutes to feed them, there was not much time between feeds to fit in anything such as sleeping! They slept on their electric blanket in a box by the Rayburn. I fixed a thermometer inside their box and made sure they were kept at 70 deg.F. During the second week I fed them every three hours, increasing the amounts. They did not stop sucking when they were full, so it was difficult to know how much to give them.

At the end of the second week one puppy seemed in distress, crying and not wanting to feed. The Vet gave her various drugs, including one to relax the abdomen which was taut, and a pain killer. She seemed better but a second pup behaved in the same way the next day. Drugs gave a temporary respite from the crying, so I consulted a second Vet who recommended a dose of liquid paraffin followed by a change of food. This proved to be the turning point. In order to control the amount of milk being taken, I abandoned the bottle and teat and fed them from a syringe, using my finger in their mouths. Then as they sucked I gradually dropped milk onto my finger or into the corner of their mouths. I found the microwave invaluable to warm the milk, and I'm almost sure the pups would wake up when the oven "pinged". I got through dozens of rolls of Andrex, plus Baby wipes which I cut down to size. I cannot imagine how people cope with larger numbers of larger breeds.

During the third week I fed the pups every three hours, but by the end of that week one puppy was having trouble breathing. Whether she had a lung infection or had taken milk into her lung I am not sure, but she failed to respond to treatment. The two remaining puppies, one dog and one bitch continued to take increasing volumes of milk. They were slow in taking to solid food compared with a normal litter, but eventually that glorious day arrived when they had their last feed from the syringe, and all meals were taken from an ash-tray, later replaced with a soap dish and finally my usual puppy dishes. Those who have weaned puppies will know how they get covered with Weetabix or Farex or whatever. I hope you appreciate what a valuable job the mother does in cleaning up the brood. I had to practically bath the puppies after each meal!

The puppies are seven weeks old as I write. They eat four normal puppy type meals per day (I dropped the 3 a.m. feed when they wanted to play rather than eat!). They are small for their age, but are doing all the usual things that seven-week-old puppies do. Many questions remain to be answered - how will they behave with the other dogs? When will they catch up in size? Will they breed? Will they be a credit to their breed? One is reminded of the Austrian couple who tried for many years to have a child. They did eventually produce a small sickly child whom they managed to rear. The child's name was Adolph, and I'll leave you to figure out his surname.

Would I recommend you to try and hand-rear puppies? If there is no choice, then yes, of course you must. But if you can find a suitable foster mother, then this is probably the best solution for the puppies as well as for the general welfare of the household. If you need any advice based on my experience but far from expertise, please don't hesitate to ask. Tel: 01686 412 351

Marie Sharp

Diabetes Mellitus

Those of you who were present at the Border Terrier Event in Exeter, will remember that I asked if anyone could give me any first hand information on coping with a Border Terrier with Diabetes Mellitus, as my ten-year-old dog Rocky had recently been diagnosed as suffering from this condition. The complete silence that followed my request soon made me realise that Diabetes is not a common complaint in our Borders, and it was suggested that a few words about the condition might be of interest.

Diabetes Mellitus is a disease of the pancreas, where insufficient insulin is produced to regulate the blood glucose level. Insulin enables the body cells to take up glucose from the blood stream, and when the levels of insulin are low, the glucose levels build up in the blood stream and secondary changes occur in the dog's metabolism. In Rocky's case, the first signs were that he was drinking a lot and urinating frequently, particularly during the night. He spent three days at our Veterinary Clinic, during which time the level of insulin he would require was worked out.

The procedure each day is to collect a urine sample (can be fun) test the glucose and ketone levels, then give the appropriate injection of insulin, along with a quarter of his food, the rest of his food is given eight hours later. The food has to be the same quantity and content all the time and definitely NO titbits. This procedure is repeated every day whilst trying to keep the exercise routine the same.

Unfortunately, Rocky did not stabilise and was back at the Veterinary Clinic for nearly three weeks. When he eventually came home we had to make sure he did no exercise whatsoever for the first week, which was quite difficult, as we have two other very energetic Borders.

Over the next couple of months Rocky had many ups and downs and suffered a number of hypoglycaemic attacks which are caused by low blood sugar levels, the signs of which are drowsiness, weakness and unsteadiness. When this happens, glucose, honey or even a piece of Mars bar needs to be given by mouth straight away - I always carry glucose tablets when we are out, just to be on the safe side.

Thankfully things have improved and Rocky is back to his old self in many ways although he does get tired and his exercise has to be limited. This is the biggest change that his illness has caused as our daily routine of long walks has come to an end, and weekends away and even walking holidays have had to be put on hold. We do get out all together sometimes, as we have purchased a second-hand pram in which Rocky rides quite happily, although our walks tend to take twice as long as we are frequently stopped and asked about our "baby".

Some diabetic dogs carry on life as before, others are even more restricted than Rocky. It is a condition which is quite demanding on owners, as one must stick to the time schedule for injections/food, exercise, etc., but on the plus side it means we have our dog with us for, hopefully, quite some time to come and if, like us, you are lucky enough to have a caring and supportive Veterinary Surgeon who is always there when you need him (or her), then I am sure it is worth the effort.

P.S. Two months have passed since writing the above and Rocky has continued to be fairly stable although we still get the odd scare when he goes hypoglycaemic, however, our Vet decided he was strong enough to do a bit more so we have joined the PAT Dog organisation and visit a local nursing home each week. The residents make quite a fuss of us and Rocky really seems to enjoy himself.

The PAT Dog visiting scheme was described in detail by Mrs. C. Mottershaw of Colchester in the 1990 Year Book, but in case anyone is in any doubt of the objectives, the name says it all "Pets As Therapy". Volunteers and their dogs visit homes, hospitals, hospices, etc. and bring a little tail wagging pleasure to elderly people, many of whom miss their pets.

Janet Gibson

I Much Prefer the Quality, Added to the Ability

The working terrier along with the Greyhound have been the only two types of active dogs that I have been involved with. I have on various occasions taken an interest in both greyhound coursing, and also greyhound racing on licensed tracks.

As far as hounds were concerned, both types were pure bred greyhounds, and not the lurcher type variety, of which we see so much at a good many of the hunt and working terrier shows.

It has always been a policy of mine to go and see the very best of the coursing hounds, running at the cream of venues, that are arranged under strict rules of conduct, by the National Coursing Club.

Strict rules are also applicable to the racing greyhounds. I have never been tempted to direct my attentions to lamping at nights with lurchers, although some very good friends of mine do partake with the long dogs, and enjoy the sport immensely.

The working terrier on the other hand, has been a joint interest, with the widely known "Jack Russell terrier", which is a terrier that varies in type and size to a tremendous degree. But it nevertheless gave me my first introduction into the world of terriers and foxes. The pure bred Border Terrier, that we are all familiar with today, I had at a later date.

Although I haven't had Russells for some time now I still have the greatest respect for their ability, and my opinion of them as workers can only be of the highest praise indeed.

My fullest admiration goes undiminished, and anyone who simply wants a pack of terriers just for work, can hardly go wrong if some of their kennel space accommodates them. Another important factor, of course, is that even in 1996 Russell prices have remained realistic.

There is no doubt that in the coming years this terrier will improve its stature in the show ring, but the standard that is now laid down to ensure its future will have to be strictly adhered to, if it is to make this progress.

Friends and colleagues who don't give a hoot for the show ring, will no doubt carry on in the time honoured way that has proved successful to so many terriermen, for so long now, and that is by mating good working terriers to good working terriers.

It was Phil Drabble (of *One Man and His Dog* fame) a noted Staffordshire naturalist, who in his own words, said to me on one occasion of the Jack Russell, that he wasn't too keen on them, even though unregistered at the time, and considered them to be such big, little men.

I know that Phil much preferred non-show dogs and he did say in his book, *Of Pedigree Unknown*: "To those who like their dogs for the companionship they bring, and care little for the fictitious values long pedigrees sometimes bestow."

He considered that selective breeding, for the show ring alone, was at the expense of the natural working abilities of the said dog, and that all would be forgiven, for two reasons, firstly their glamorous looks, and secondly, the high prices that are demanded. That was his opinion at the time, and just like the die-hard Russell fanatics, who only see Russells as workers, that's their opinion also, and there isn't a lot wrong with either viewpoint.

But surely it will take them (the now formed Russell clubs) a long, long time to establish a consistency, that has been enjoyed by such kennels as *Dandyhow, Deerstone* and *Daletyne* and other such noted Border Terrier kennels, who have long since had established breeding backgrounds, i.e. a pedigree, and with this background, at least you will have a very good knowledge of what to expect when new litters are arriving.

You have got to have standards to begin with, and with this in mind, it gives us all a basis from which to improve upon. We must have something to aim for if we are going to achieve success in both fields.

And to have good working Border Terriers, that can justify themselves in the hunting field, and also in the show ring, gives pure satisfaction, and is a hard won reward for their owners' endeavours, regardless of the many pitfalls that arise.

The Border Terrier has given me a great deal of pleasurable companionship, with its dual purpose, for a number of years now, but I must admit that I have always tended to lean towards the working aspect.

Long days out in the fields and woods, can reap its own special rewards, and the knowledge gained of the terrier can be deemed as priceless. Plus of course the cost of showing and transportation can be a significant amount of money, too much for me on past occasions, when I had looked at priorities realistically.

On many, many occasions, I have put the terriers in the motor, and have gone off in pursuance of the fox the day before a show, and have returned later in the evenings with either tired or knocked up terriers. The consequences of this, of course, was to miss the show the following day, with the cost of entrance fees that I really could not afford, all thrown away.

The satisfaction, however, that will live with me for evermore, is to have witnessed and owned Borders that have had the opportunity to pit themselves against an articulate and clever adversary. The raw courage of both terrier and fox has to be seen to be fully appreciated.

One often sees prints or photographs of fox and terrier facing one another, but no amount of drawings can conjure up the real drama of these confrontations.

The courage displayed on these occasions also needs to be a standard, a standard of "work" if you like, but it is very much required on the hunting field. It is the time when the chips are down, and the Border has to put all his natural abilities together to succeed. (And not all of them make the grade.)

They need brains, fitness, courage, controlled aggression and the physical will and the necessary substance to get on with the job, especially perhaps if they have spent several hours below ground, as could be the case, facing a stubborn fox, who has been handing out the stick.

It is also a certain fact that he will be restricted for space, no room down there for comfortable manoeuvres, and often there are underlying tree roots getting in the way, these the terrier will tear at in sheer frustration, just to be able to move on ... just think about the conditions for a moment? Dark, hot, airless, dry throated, tired, thirsty and facing an animal, the fox in this particular case, that can and often will hand out some painful reminders that it is not going to give away its territory very lightly. The terrier is also at an environmental disadvantage at times, and he must be brainy and experienced as well as being capable enough to handle these situations in his own way, at the time.

It becomes very, very hot beneath ground, especially with all the bumping and thumping that is going on as both opponents cut and thrust in order to seek an advantage, or an escape hole. The terrier will no doubt get very, very dry in the mouth from continual barking at the fox, his eyes possibly filled with soil, limbs that will ache, till they are nearly at a standstill, and the constant clanging of the spades that will be striking on hard soil and stone above his head, as help gets ever nearer towards him, certainly adds to the occasion.

It can also happen at various times, that when you finally break through, the loose earth could collapse on top of the terrier, but believe me, they still persist with their honest endeavours, encouraged no doubt by your voice, as you coax him on quietly.

Beginners please note - that on the point of soil collapsing, and you put your hand in to scoop the loose soil from off the terrier's back, make sure that you are *above* the dog, colours can confuse, and at times like these, your hand will only smell familiar to the dog.

To get back to the job, a remarkable thing concerning the terrier lies in the fact that however tired, or injured he may be, he will suddenly discover an extra surge of enthusiasm when you are getting up to him. And he will double up in his efforts once you are by his side. All in all, he is a remarkable terrier.

Abilities can vary from dog to dog, and it is all down to the owner to understand his own terriers, he alone can and must decide if terriers can work together, or not, if they are too hard for certain times, or not, or if he is capable of bolting a fox , or not.

I have often overheard people around the earth say, it's simple, the easy answer, is to bolt the fox. Well, let me put that theory in its place, to bolt the fox is the *easy question,* and not the *easy answer.*

In a quiet artificial drain, it is possible he will bolt without a great deal of fuss being made. But if he has been hard run, and manages to find a big earth, he is more likely to stop there until the end, rather than face the open once again.

I have seen a fair number of champions made up, I have also seen a number that haven't been as well rewarded as they might have been, but certainly I would dearly have wished to own a good many of them.

They will stand there looking quite insignificant at times, bored perhaps by the whole goings on, but give them a natural choice and they become different animals. Standards, as well as natural instincts, are the making of the Border Terrier, and it is nice to have the best of both worlds.

You can bet that, when they get off their beds in the morning, all of the aches and pains that belonged to yesterday will soon be forgotten, and they will be throwing their tails about in hopeful anticipation that today is going to be the day.

One final thought on the Border Terrier is for the show exhibitors, who have never experienced the working side of the breed, to give a little thought as to what his requirements are.

You may agree with the working aspect, or you may disagree. But you can't disagree with the fact that you have chosen an active working breed, and not a breed for which acclaimed abilities have long since been confined to the bin, and discarded for ever.

The standard laid down is quite sufficient, it only has to be observed to be appreciated.

It is the varying interpretation of it that sometimes lets us down.

E. Bannister

Working Dogs

A letter on the showing/working certificate issue comes from Bryn Chittenden whose family has worked and shown the breed for many years and who is terrier man for the Essex Farmers and Union Hunt.

"There have been various discussions about the Border Terrier going in the direction of other terrier breeds - i.e. two types - work or show. Unlike the views expressed in Mr. Bruce Wallace's letter of 22nd November, I believe that keeping the working classes in KC shows will help to prevent this happening to the breed.

"There have always been different types in Borders, but not necessarily work or show type, just variations based around one standard. I don't think that there is anyone who can look at a Border and say that it is either a show or working type, provided that it is of the correct size.

"There are too many Borders being placed at shows who would never get down a hole and do what they had been bred to do. It's the judges' job to recognise this and stick to the Standard when making their decisions, whatever the class.

"It seems to me that, whether you work or show your terriers, there is a certain amount of jealousy towards the other aspect. For example, some people who are only involved in working their terriers, whether they be Borders or otherwise, will have you believe that if you've got a quality KC registered Border it can't work - and at least by having the working certificate class it helps to combine the two.

"Then there are those who think that working certificate classes are for Borders of poor quality. This isn't true either; it's a class for Border Terriers which have been lucky enough to have had the chance to prove their working ability and earn their certificate accordingly.

"After all, its understandable that not everybody would let their terrier work, even if they had the opportunity to do so. So why shouldn't the few who do have something to show for it, and not be penalised because of the minority with certificates that are not genuine.

"In that connection, if Mr. Wallace knows of someone who has received certificates that are not genuine, he should name the people and dogs concerned and inform the issuing clubs - otherwise can we assume that they are fictitious characters?"

"Certificates shouldn't be issued for the odd occasion a dog goes underground while out walking, whether witnessed or not. It would also be interesting to know what Mr. Wallace's terriers had actually killed.

"There are also some people involved in the breed who are against hunting and working with terriers. Well, like it or not, Borders are still being worked throughout the country. If those concerned cannot accept the Border for what it is, "essentially a working terrier", perhaps they should consider another breed, preferably one that's already split into two types, instead of trying to change a breed that has been reasonably unspoilt for many years.

"I think that people from both showing and working backgrounds should try to understand and appreciate the other's interests and share their knowledge. This would be much more beneficial to the breed."

"This seems to me to be one of the most balanced responses I have had to this debate and I can only reiterate what Mr. Chittenden says: "... people from both showing and working backgrounds should try and appreciate the other's interests and share their knowledge."

What a sensible approach and a most conciliatory one on which to end the year.

W. Ronald Irving

Working Border Terriers

I have always been with dogs all my life. As a child my father was a very keen shooting man. We had black Labradors. I very soon started having Cocker Spaniels which I bred successfully mainly using Treetops and of Ware breeding.

I have always hunted from a very early age and while I was at Stowe School I had several greyhounds and used to go coursing.

I worked on a farm, Greythwaite Hall, near Newby Bridge and used to go out with the fell packs. Johnny Richardson had just come back from the war and hunted the Blencathra. Then I went with the Coniston, the Ullswater, the Bewcastle who had good Border Terriers, and also the Liddesdale and of course the Border Hunt with the Robson family.

When I farmed in Devon, Major Knight-Bruce was Master of the Silverton and I think he had some of the first Border Terriers with Working Certificates in the Southern Border Terrier Club.

If I start telling you of all the Border Terriers I have worked it would take up the whole of a Year Book. I had good Borders from Miss Jackie Eccles, Mrs. Simpson, Jack Cobby, Huntsman of the South and West Wilts and several others. However the start of my best dogs came from Miss Hester Orme's "Raisgill" Kennel. The first one I had from her was Raisgill Rosealba who I called Tweedie. She was by Tartar Boy (Hambledon Hunt W.C.) out of Raisgill Ramberline (W.C. Liddesdale Hunt). This bitch ran with the Liddesdale and was an outstanding worker as was Tartar Boy. Both are pictured in *Border Tales*.This breeding all goes back to Mrs. Twist's Hallbourne, Ch Aldham Joker and Ch Barb Wire.

Tweedie was tiny yet she would face the biggest fox and was as brave as a lion. She never got badly marked - she was lightning quick. I've bolted a fox through a flooded drain that other terriers wouldn't face. She swam under the water to get to the fox. I eventually had all this litter. My best of all was Raisgill Raffles, litter brother to Raisgill Rosealba. This dog I called Pickle and I had him from John Booth of Thrussington.

I took him otter hunting in Devon and I lent him to Charles Parker who was Whipper-In to the Hawstone Otterhounds. To my mind and to many, many others Charles was and is the greatest naturalist and expert on all quarry. He was at that time with the Heythrop as Capt. Ronnie Wallace's right hand man, terrierman, etc.

Charles worked him (Pickle) with the Heythrop and Captain Wallace signed his Working Certificate No. 189. Charles said he was very, very hard and had to be careful where he used him! He was a leggy dog and very, very powerful. He would kill and draw a fox back to you. Charles Parker used him to all legal quarry at that time, 1963-64. When I went to collect him Percy Durno the Kennel Hunstman said he was the grandest terrier he had seen. Ronnie Wallace also spoke very highly of him.

Brian Plummer in his book *The Fell Terrier* said: "he was the gamest terrier to draw breath."

Prior to 1963, I had used my terriers with the Whaddon Chase Hunt together with the terriermen Bill and Richard Stone. Then Richard Cooper became Joint Master of the Bicester and Warden Hill Hunt and asked me to organise earth stopping terrier work, etc. I did this until 1968, when I went back with the Whaddon Chase until my wife and I took the Red Lion at Evenley near Brackley in 1971 where we stayed for fifteen years. I used to go out with both hunts as often as possible, and still do now that the two packs have become the Bicester with Whaddon Chase. Both my Border Terriers have Working Certificates. Nettleby Spearmint (Minty) No. 360 and Brockfox Minnie the Minx (Moss) No. 377. Moss, who was lent to me by Miss Barnett, is a terrific worker. If I had been able to work her as much as I did thirty years ago - she could have easily been as outstanding as my old dogs. Unfortunately these days it is extremely difficult and the rules and regulations are serious. If I hadn't been the terrierman myself once it would be impossible to work my terriers.

To go back to Pickle. Once, in the snow, from Astrop House we were hunting on foot. Pickle was running with the hounds and they found a fox and got completely away from us. We eventually heard them marking to ground a long way away. By the time we got to them some time later Pickle had got the fox out which was lying dead next to him. He and all the hounds were lying down completely exhausted. Some people say hounds could mistake a Border for a fox because of his colour. I do not believe this. I have seen Pickle buried under hounds when they have killed and he would tug at the dead fox with the hounds. Another time I did not want to use him and left him in the Land Rover. When Albert Buckle blew to ground I walked the other terriers to where I could hear him. Unknown to me the boy I had left in the Land Rover had opened the window and Pickle jumped out! I met Albert Buckle coming back with the hounds, Pickle and the dead fox. He said to me: "You're too late boy the job's been done by Pickle."

My other outstanding Border dog was Huntlaw Grip. He had the loveliest deep voice you could hear at any depth - his big advantage was you could call him back and he would always leave the fox. I had some lovely Border Terriers from John Booth, one in particular Thrussington Midge. She was like Tweedie - tiny, but worked like a demon.

I would like to say as so many of the old breeders said a long time ago. Don't let them get too big.

I've had so many good working terriers of all breeds. Sir Jocelyn Lucas gave me an Ilmer Sealyham bitch. She was a fantastic worker but was so jealous - and would fight anything. Sinbad was a J.R. who Plummer said had the straightest legs of any terrier. He was by Sandy, a Bicester Hunt dog of Brian Pheasey's, but he was very hard and would also fight. Lakelands are the same and to a lesser degree Border x Lakeland. A good cross was the Border x Sealyham, and I wish I had developed this more as my breed.

Some terriermen don't like Borders as they say they are slow to enter. I think more Border Terriers have been ruined by sheer stupidity. I say never enter a terrier - let the terrier enter itself. Let them listen to other terriers working and let them take their time. I have seen people literally shove a terrier in a hole and put their boot behind it. I have had Border Terriers given to me because they wouldn't work. One when she was two and a half suddenly started to worry a dead fox I had dug out - after that she never looked back.

Of all the terriers I have had, I love the Border Terrier the best of all. They have such a lovely temperament. My two now sleep on a bed and yet go nearly mad when out hunting.

If Borders can keep the standard like Brockfox Minnie the Minx, and can breed from such as her and her stock the future of the breed is in safe hands.

John Morgan

Essentially a Working Terrier

Borders were for many years kept for their ability to work and little else. In more recent times the Border has become much more of a pet and show dog with few doing the job they were created to do. This is not another article moaning on about the fact that too few work the breed or that too many are ruining it. Those of us that take work seriously have our bloodlines that we have tried and tested in the field and we are happy with them.

No, what this article is about is RESPONSIBILITY, from breeders and owners of Borders to ensure a long and safe life for this plucky breed.

The problem lies with the fact that breeders are not warning new Border owners of the dangers of letting their terrier wander unsupervised in the countryside. Even a terrier bred from show stock will start hunting rabbits if it sees them often enough. Once hunting rabbits, the Border will soon discover the delights of holes, this is where the trouble starts. Terriers left to roam in the countryside are at great risk, sooner or later they chase a rabbit into a hole and start digging after it, rabbit holes are tight, most pet Borders are a little round, the two don't mix. There is a real risk the terrier will push on and get stuck, if it's in a dead end there's a danger that the air will run out before the terrier is located. In sandy soil the terrier digs on, and in doing so leaves debris behind it which mounts up, again blocking off air. Some terriers push on so tight that they constrict their own chests and are not able to draw breath.

The dangers really mount if two terriers are allowed liberty together, they get each other hyped up and not only do they dig on rabbits but, with confidence gained by having a companion, they are likely to seek out bigger game. Fox earths pose similar problems to rabbit warrens as usually they are simply slightly enlarged warrens in the first place, but to cause more problems the Border who leads the way will now have a mobile gin-trap of a mouth in front of him and his companion pushing and often biting him from behind.

A hard terrier, working alone, will on occasion take severe punishment from his quarry, but as it's his choosing, his scrap so to speak, it won't really bother him. But put a half-hearted worker in the same situation but forced into the confrontation by another terrier blocking his retreat and you'll have quickly produced a terrier in severe shock. Unless located quickly and given prompt veterinary treatment such a terrier will die.

Badger setts are large roomy affairs with good ventilation, suffocation is rare in these places except when a dog digs on after a badger in sandy soil or very, very rarely, when during a battle, bedding is pressed into the entrance to a chamber. The problem here though is that a pair of terriers can often work side by side in a big sett, this really gets them hyped into a frenzy. Frenzied Borders fight like hell, the trouble is, so does the badger, and he's bigger and better at it than they are. If you are lucky they'll realise they're beaten and crawl out. More often than not though the braver of the two gets killed and only one slinks home to have its wounds tended to.

Pet terriers are much more likely to get into serious trouble than experienced working terriers. The problems being that they are often unaccompanied by their owners, they are inexperienced, and if it's discovered that they are gone to ground, the owners are also inexperienced.

It is important that should your terrier or terriers show an interest in hunting that you only exercise them under supervision. Learn what earths and setts look like and avoid them, remembering to check your walk route regularly for new ones being opened up. Get a locator collar and box and use it - yes they are expensive but not half as expensive as a new Border! Join the Fell & Moorland Working Terrier Club, for less than a fiver a year they can have expert rescuers on call to help you dig out your pet. Providing you are a paid-up member they will cover costs of any machinery such as JCBs needed to get the dog out, thankfully in most cases the manual digging device (spade) will do.

In the past couple of months I have been involved in searches for two lost Borders, both pets. The first was never found, the other suffocated in straw bales after its owners left it four days before trying to get help. It only took us twenty minutes to find the body. Borders are worth more than this! Owners, it's time to take the responsibility of owning an "essentially working terrier" seriously. Breeders, it's up to you too, to advise new Border owners on terrier nature. Next time you sell a pup to a country home, make sure the garden is fully fenced and that the owners are aware of terriers going to ground. Advise on locator collars and the Fell & Moorland.

For those who have a terrier stuck, don't call the RSPCA, they're invariably a hindrance more than a help, they despise working terriers and that includes your pet. Don't call the fire-brigade, they have better things to do. Call the Fell & Moorland WTC. If you are sure it's not a badger sett and you can hear or feel the position of the terrier, dig it out. Get the landowner's permission if you haven't already done so. If it's in a badger sett the F & M WTC will contact the relevant authorities and get a licence to permit digging into the sett for your dog. If you're not sure what type of hole you're dealing with contact your local F & M WTC area representative for advice.

For more information on the Fell & Moorland rescue services, contact Bill Shorthose on 01505 850 313.

Perhaps I should finish by quoting area representative Mark Jarvis, " We get more call outs for pet Borders than for any others".

Please keep your Borders safe!

Lisa Jenkins

The D'rekly Lad

or

The Life of a Cornish Border Terrier

My name is Olly and this is my story as relayed to you by my mistress.

Life changed for me on 1st January 1996. Up until then I had been living on a rare breeds farm with my parents, my grandmother, and my remaining brother. (My other brother and sisters having already gone to new homes.) That was the day that my new mistress and master took me home to live with them and their cat Mimi.

Since then I've had lots of fun and games in my new home. First of all I've got myself a lady friend - Mimi the cat! She's a lovely nine-year-old tortoiseshell cat but unfortunately she doesn't seem to appreciate any of my attentions and she disappears whenever she thinks that I'm around - I really can't think why as I'm such a handsome young lad - even if I do say so myself! At first my 'mistress' seemed to have the most to do with me - 'the master' only ever really taking me for walks. Apparently (dare I say it!), he is more a cat person really. A two week holiday in Ireland in the summer of that year managed to change that to a greater degree - because I charmed him with my best Border know-how and showed him what I'm really made of. Now we're really great friends.

When 'the master' is away on business my 'mistress' takes me to work with her. She works at an elder care hospital and everybody (well, nearly everybody! just in case you thought I was exaggerating a little bit) seems to like seeing me. The really good bit (as far as I'm concerned - but don't tell you know who!) is that I seem to come by a lot of titbits - I really can't think why - they just seem to keep coming my way!(ho ho!). Apparently I am also able to brighten someone's day while I'm there too.

As well as being an enthusiastic enjoyer of life - (well what else would you expect from any self respecting Border Terrier - I hear you ask!) - my 'mistress' says that I have what she calls some embarrassing habits. (Huh!) Although what she really means by that I really don't know!

I know how to make my 'owners' (other Borders will know exactly what I mean) feel guilty if they have to leave me - to guard the car for instance - even for a short while, by the amount of pitiful noise that I can make. Don't they know that there is a whole great big new world out there to explore as far as I'm concerned and sitting in the car isn't at all adventurous (and anyway I'm not a guard dog- but don't say that too loudly to you know who).

Whenever I get taken to the seaside - which I really enjoy by the way (and who doesn't?) - I can really get up to mischief. Last year when my mistress went to the beach with her relatives, I got a little bored with all that sunbathing and started my own amusement - digging the biggest possible hole I could manage, in the shortest possible time, in the sand. Unfortunately, in the process, I was spraying sand all over her relatives, but because of my inate charms I managed to get away with the offence on that occasion!

Apparently my worst misdemeanour to date was when they were staying in a hotel and I was allowed to share the room with them. It appears, according to you know who, that I nearly got them thrown out because of my bad behaviour. As if I would do such a thing! I think she was exaggerating a bit because I was only doing my doggy bit and anyway the hotel owners thought I was cute - so we were allowed to stay. (The hotel have even allowed us back, more than once! So there.)

As well as regular activities, such as ringcraft classes, lovely long walks and the odd trip out to the Isles of Scilly, via helicopter - no less; my owners organise some lovely holidays for me. One of the latest was a lovely castle in Ireland with his relatives that included four little girls who were to become my adoring fans for the week - Oh what it is to be so popular! It seemed that the fan club were in almost constant attendance and, along with all the other stimulation around, it was enough to leave this little Border exhausted and in need of a second week's holiday to recover from the first! But it's amazing how an open peat fire and a comfy sofa made for the perfect evening's relaxation.

1998 saw a trip to Scotland for two weeks and what a fun time that was! There was a large black cat hanging around...(apparently I am not allowed to say any more about that!)

One of the highlights was walking from Glen Etive through to Glen Coe on a less than clement weather day (for humans that is). It was a great walk through ideal Border terrain, several people thought that I wouldn't make it as I am so small. They obviously hadn't met up with my kind before.

All in all I enjoy owning my mistress and master, although they don't always appreciate my attempts at interior design eg arranging the rugs whenever I have my five minutes of keep fit. I think they are getting used to what they call my funny habits but no doubt I'll keep springing a few surprises - as life isn't at all bad when you are a Cornish Border Terrier you know!

Now, where's my favourite squeaky toy? (And another tale to tell. Or is it tail?)

Lesley Pallett

Thirty years of Information

Changes in the Year Book since 1971

It is thirty years since I bought my first Border Terrier and in 1972 I joined the SBTC. Turning out the bookshelves recently I discovered the Year Books from that year to the present day. I am sure there are others who have this run or perhaps more, and so they have a mine of interesting reading and information to say nothing of the evocative photographs.

In the past thirty years much has happened in the dog world, especially in Borders, some of it starting from Audrey Dallison's famous remark 'that untrimmed terriers could never hope to compete with trimmed terriers in a group!' Shortly after that a Border confounded her predictions. It started people noticing Borders. Now few TV advertisements or indeed plays, featuring dogs, do not have a Border somewhere in the cast!

Looking through the Year Books for the years 1972 to 2000 is to realise how much the Border world has altered. From 1972 to 1980 the shiny white covered books were stapled together and the 1972 issue was sold at 75p post free and compiled on behalf of the Club by the President, Mrs. E. F. Twist.

The Chairman, Bob Williams, had as his Vice Chairman, that lovely man Capt. D'O Vigne. He and his wife were the first people to welcome me when I attended my first SBTC show. Madelene Aspinwall was Secretary. Famous names on the committee in 1972 included Robert Hall (Deerstone), Felicity Marchant (Hawkesburn), Mrs. Sullivan (Dandyhow) and Miss Sybil Churchill (Campanologia) among many.

The standard given for the breed includes the old Points Scale and on page nine this instruction. 'Exhibitors and judges should be reminded that it is not in keeping with the sporting tradition of the breed to have the coat trimmed, or have the head or tail supported by the handler in the ring. Borders should be shown on a loose lead.'

The Report for the Year, concerned compiling "a Judges List that will command the respect of the Kennel Club". Subscriptions were 75p single and £1 joint. The SBTC Ch show was held in conjunction with WELKS and Mr. R. Clements judged. His dog CC and BOB, Chevinor Rasamat, went on to the last six in the Terrier Group.

There were 15 pages of advertisements, £2 per page was the charge, the advertisers kennel names read like a roll of honour. By 1975 the book was thicker and the price increased to £1.25 including postage. The frontispiece, an historic picture of Mr. Andrew Irving the judge, and Capt. D'O Vigne at Chinnor. This issue contains some interesting articles, especially an illustrated story headed 'Our Gundog'. Ch. Hobbykirk Destiny is shown retrieving as cleanly as any retriever! - (see page 48)

There are 33 pages of kennel advertisements including two each from New Zealand and USA, one from Canada and two from Bermuda. In the latter Llanishen Rebet bought from Mr. & Mrs. Wiseman's kennel is shown with a Winner's Trophy and there is a photograph of Gil and Mary Walker's Ch.Workmore Waggoner who went to the States and became top Border over there.

The1975/76 issue contains a great article by Mary Roslin Williams, ARW wrote for various issues.

In the 1977/78 Year Book there is a photograph of Capt. and Mrs. d'O Vigne who had celebrated their Golden Wedding. It was the first year I was listed as a member; when I joined in 1972 there was quite a muddle in the treasurer's department and although I paid up each year I was not listed as a member. It was not until 1977 that the correction was made! I often wonder how many more the muddle affected.

1977 was H.M. The Queen's Silver Jubilee year and this was celebrated at the Club Ch show held for the first time at Cheltenham Racecourse and the judge was Miss Kate Sullivan better known to modern exhibitors as Mrs. Ronnie Irving. There is a lovely picture of Kate receiving a bouquet and another with Mrs. Clarkson and Ch. Sprignell Selina and Mr. J. B. Baxter with Beenaben Brock, the CC winners.

The 1977/78 Year Book records that the Presidency was taken over by Capt D'O Vigne. The Vice Chairman was Major D. Ide-Smith.

Over the years a number of dedicated Border folk had helped with the compiling of the Year Book. In 1978/9 Felicity Marchant and Janet Melly had taken on the task. Although the book was much thicker the price remained the same. There were good articles especially one by Paul Davey M.R.C.V S. Two pages feature the details of Borders with Working Certificates and a four page article by Walter Gardner on breeding a type for work and show.

The first of the ring bindings 1981/2 is edited by Janet Melly who gathered some grand articles including one from Felicity Marchant and another from ARW and a most amusing 'pictorial essay' of Dennis Wiseman judging at Three Counties. Advertisements ran to 32 pages. It was the 'Year of the Diver', ARW campaigning Ch Mansergh Pearl Diver won BOB at the SBTC Ch show under Bob Williams. It was my proudest year as one I bred, Westacres Wild Iris, owned by the huntsman of the North Shropshire, was one of eight new holders of SBTC Working certificates. The 1982/3 book records the death of the much loved Capt D'O Vigne a sad loss to the Border world and SBTC in particular. Madelene Aspinwall retired as Secretary but remained as assistant to the new incumbent, Frances Wagstaff.

The Year Book by now was a thick publication and cost £2.50. Robert Hall contributed an article on "The judge's angle on the breed", amusing but thought provoking. Mr A. P. Willis of Ryswick affix wrote on Working Terriers, indeed in all these earlier books working is very much to the fore in the text. There are some wonderful photographs of Borders ratting on the river. The advertisements are from well established kennels no new names cropping up.

In the 1983/4 book there is an amusing article by Dorothy Miller, 'You ought'a get an otter, or aren't standards wonderful,' and another of Paul Davey's useful veterinary offerings, this one on skin care, while 'Colour inheritance' is covered in an interesting offering by Diane Swales.

By 1985 a few new names were appearing and there was an expanding list of club items for sale. Border Terrier Welfare had its first report by the co-ordinator Mrs. Wiltshire. Mrs. Twist carried on the discussion on colours and Felicity Marchant had a four page article on mating procedures.

The Year Book faithfully chronicled the successes of the two annual non-competitive gatherings of Border folk, the Lane End Teach In and Joyce Patterson's popular Border Event at Exeter.

The 1986 Teach In had both Mary Roslin Williams and Ted Hutchinson as speakers, much was learned that day and there is a photograph of the speakers above an article on soundness by Mary. The 1986 Year Book foreshadows the shape of things to come, it includes a photograph of the Best in Show at Driffield, one Ch. Brannigan of Brumberhill. There is also a splendid photograph of a svelte Bill Gillott who ran in the London Marathon for Border Welfare, presenting his cheque to Gwen Baldwin and Ann Wiltshire! Sylvia Clarkson was now President and Mrs. d'O Vigne was Patron.

In the 1987/8 issue the new judges lists were printed, together with an 'Honours List'. There was some confusion at the time over this and several people resigned their membership, not agreeing with how the matter was handled. There was also a change in committee when the Club's vet Paul Davey, Gil Walker and Dennis Wiseman stood down after many years service.

The advertisements picture some notable kennels such as the Todgroves with Ch Cuileann Dodger and his descendants on display, an object lesson in breeding to type. There were a number of new advertisers. Last picture in the book heralds the dawn of a new age in the breed. There is Ted and Brannigan after winning Reserve Best in Show at Crufts. From then on Borders became the 'In' dog, and succeeding year books mirror the change in the breed.

The white covered Year Book for 1988/89 is square bound with a green spine and gives the breed standard as revised by the Kennel Club in 1986, gone is the Points Scale. Due to health reasons Mrs. Sylvia Clarkson had retired as Editor and her place was taken by Betty Rumsam and Val Read. Gwen Baldwin was busy with Kennel Reviews and also Border Welfare which, with the rising popularity of Borders leading to a lot more breeding, was becoming more and more necessary.

There were 63 pages of kennel advertisements. The report contained the sad news of the deaths of three stalwarts of the breed, Robert Hall, Nancy Turrell and Dora Abraham. A large number of interesting articles and this Year Book includes the winners at all shows offering CCs, Working Certificate Holders, pedigrees of new champions and CC winners, Junior Warrants, Breeders Diplomas and exports, it also noted CC judges for the coming year and a list of members willing to help others with advice on the breed. In a few years the Year Book had radically altered to meet a new demand.

The first of the now familiar yellow square bound Year Books appeared in the SBTC Jubilee Year 1990, it was from then on to be a very professional publication, and although the previous format was followed, articles were fewer but the overseas reports had increased. There were 74 pages of advertisements, the cost now £8 a page. Membership was greatly increased and 27 pages were given over to their names and addresses, three pages were overseas members.

The hunting side of the breed had not been forgotten, there is a compelling article on the "Liddesdale Foxhounds Then and Now" by Leslie Gosling, and possibly the first article about a Border as a PAT dog. Steve Dean had taken over from Paul Davey as the SBTC vet and he contributed a useful article on False Pregnancy.

Since the introduction of the smart and solid yellow covers, the Year Book does not alter much.

Notes on changes in committee, records of the sad demise of many of the older breeders and exhibitors, the appearance of new members and kennels. The 1993/4 records that Mr. R. A. (Bob) Williams had taken over from Mrs. Clarkson as President and Madelene Aspinwall was now Chairman. A new Constitution and Rules was published, this to receive Kennel Club approval.

In 1995/6 the first of the colour pages was introduced and these have lent tone to each issue since. Last year's book featured an excellent picture of Vice President, Sylvia Clarkson, and the Chairman, Madelene Aspinwall.

With still good articles and a full spread of all Border affairs over the year, plus the kennel advertisements, although reduced last year to 58 pages there is something in the Southern Border Terrier Club's Year Book for anyone interested in the breed.

So much is this production valued that back numbers have become collectors items. Next stop, Antiques Roadshow!

Peggy Grayson

Indispensable

It is frequently said: "How did we manage to rear puppies without Vetbed" and this set me thinking of other items essential to the smooth running of my kennels. Along with Vetbed I would include "puppy panels" of various heights to make indoor and outdoor playpens, and of course newspaper. So far I haven't waylaid people on their way to the paperbank, but the idea is there for an emergency. My newsagent has always been kind enough to let me have his "returns".

Still on the theme of puppy rearing, I have discovered in the last couple of years that the frozen free-flow beef mince produced by several supermarkets is ideal for puppies, being easy to measure out, needs no scraping or cutting up, just needs a few hours to defrost - everything that saves time is a boon.

My latest acquisition is a garden vacuum, and an odd look or two was passed between the shop assistants when I asked for this in the middle of winter! It has proved invaluable for sucking up the shavings which I have always used as a carpet for the dogs in their inside kennels. Years of sweeping out with a broom has left my back with a twinge whenever I assume the brushing position, repetitive strain injury, I expect. My garden vac does the job in half the time, although it does sound like a jet aircraft taking off, and it cannot cope with anything bigger than shavings, which you might guess would be found in a kennel overnight.

Talking of shavings, that is another modern improvement. I used to collect shavings from a builder, not a very reliable source, and often contaminated with hard wood shavings and wood treated with preservative. Nowadays, at considerably greater expense one can buy compressed bales of softwood shavings, made for the horsey people, but ideal for kennels.

An item of considerable capital expenditure which has repaid me handsomely is the carpet shampoo machine. Having dogs living in the house inevitably means hair and mud trodden into the carpets, and I am always horrified to see the colour of the water that comes out of this machine after use. With puppies in the house, the shampoo machine comes into its own, but have you ever thought of using it outside in the kennels? With detergent in the tank, it gives the floors a good clean once a month or so, and with disinfectant, without the suction switched on, it can be used to spray the walls without making them too wet. I would not be without my Jeyes

Fluid, a smell that does not appeal to everyone, but preferable to the fragrances of many canine disinfectants today. I find it invaluable for removing the green algae which thrives on the concrete outside runs.

Now to an even older product I use every year - lime (slaked lime, calcium hydroxide). This is an incredibly cheap alternative to white emulsion paint, and each year the kennel interiors get a coating, and does it cover a multitude of colours! It is a chore to mix the very fine powder, (beware those with breathing problems), but the creamy paint can be slapped on with abandon, and it dries to a brilliant white finish that doesn't rub off. I suspect that over the years the paint layers will chip off, but judging by the white-washed cottages one used to see in the countryside, I won't be around to see this happen.

Along with the yearly limewash goes the creosote to treat the wooden kennels, only the outside ones as the odour is over-powering, and the bitumastic black paint for the metal gates, both products that probably have more modern and expensive equivalents.

Cages used to be called "terrier boxes", and if one has ever seen a terrier who has recently been doing the job for which he is designed, one would know how it is necessary to have a solid sided box. So a wooden box, with thick newspaper is essential, not just for a working terrier, but for any dog who delights in mud. Cages nowadays are de rigeur, not only for travelling but for shows, so that one can take a team of dogs on one's own. Many people find cages essential for a peaceful life at home when dogs do not agree with each other, but Border Terriers are supposed to be sociable creatures, aren't they? Even my dogs are sometimes caged in the house, for instance when they are wet and muddy, or to keep them safe.

Finally, one last desirable for any kennel is a multi-talented "kennel helper" who can turn their hand to brick-laying, carpentry, welding, electrical installations, to get the kennels built, then be able to drive you to shows, feed the puppies when required, cook the dinner if one is unavoidably detained by a group win (one hopes!). This kennel person should not be able to count more than six, so that it is not noticed when the kennel numbers get high. Such a person is truly indispensable.

Marie Sharp

Memories from Hexham

The Border Terrier 2000 Millennium Event

How can I possibly distil the Hexham Event into words? There were Border Terriers and Border Terrier owners in all directions smiling broadly. It was something to behold.

On Friday, the Committee all met at the racecourse, with various kind helpers to prepare the venue. From the moment we arrived at the racecourse, it was apparent that an exciting event was about to unfold.

Up in the Memorabilia Room, the sight and scents of old documents, books and paintings, and all manner of goodies filled the senses and we met Jena Tuck and her wonderful family team, complete with Anne Roslin-Williams busy sorting and mounting the various items they had received from all parts of the country.

What an artistic eye the Tuck family must have because, not only was the content fascinating and wide ranging, but it was also exhibited with a real flair to produce a very inviting display. Oh, to have had time to sit and study!

Outside, Bill Gillott and his squad were busy fixing signs and putting equipment in place ready for the big day. When the security guard arrived on Friday evening, it was a happy but tired team who retired to their accommodation.

Many of us had brought our Borders up with us, so it was up especially early the next morning to exercise them. We variously met at the band stand in the middle of Hexham Abbey Park and speculated as to the nature of the day before us. After a hasty breakfast, on to the racecourse and off to our respective posts, ready to meet the public. I had the pleasure of staffing the reception desk with Susan Shorthose, and the enthusiasm for the event from organisers and visitors alike was matchless. Whether people had travelled from near or far, they showed that Border Terriers were close to their hearts. How amazing that this small breed engenders such huge support and affection.

The Souvenir Programme was indeed a magnificent production and we have to thank the wonderful Bob Hand and Janice Johnson for its sheer style and innovation. Get one if you can. Not only did it have the necessary details of dogs participating in the event, but also additional articles and the history and stories behind the Millennium Calendar pictures and all in full colour.

There was a busy agenda for the day, starting with Terrier Racing. Excited cheers proved that the event was causing much pleasure both for the Borders and their owners who sported jaunty green rosettes to identify the winners. The dogs taking part were very keen to race again and again. There were no dust-ups at all and the dogs were good-natured throughout.

At noon, the racing ceased and we adjourned to the lecture room for a marvellous talk by Mr David Jones from the Mid-Wales region, who spoke about his experience hunting with terriers and in particular with Borders. When asked what was the greatest fault in a terrier, he confirmed that it was for them to be too hard. Aggression is not something we ever wish to see in our Borders.

Mr Jones led a rousing rendition of the Terrier Song in his wonderful and mellifluous Welsh tones to complete the seminar. Frances Wagstaff tells me that everyone was singing too, Frances included!

Outside again, and the sound of the hunting horn in the distance heralded the arrival of the Hounds. What a sight they were with the Huntsman in pink and the Hounds covering the ground with their fluent and economical movement.

Border Terriers looked on, some perhaps a little bemused, but very soon the Hounds were mingling with the Borders and their owners. This is what Border Terriers were all about. This was something for each and every Border Terrier owner to take home.

It was time to remember that if there had been no hunting there might have been no Border Terrier. What will become of the Hounds if hunting is banned? Surely nobody present could have failed to be moved as we all realised the jeopardy these fine and noble creatures and our country way of life stand in. As the Huntsman gathered the Hounds in, I truly feared for their future.

On to the beautifully manicured lawns of the Parade Ring came Mrs Ruth-Ann Naun from America to judge the Allcomers Match. An experienced Border Terrier judge she found her winners in Mr. & Mrs. Hollingsbee's Gaytime Girl of Otterwood for Best in Match with Mr. Wren and Ms Langdon's Dandyhow Sir Toby in reserve. I think all the competitors as well as the eventual victors appreciated Mrs. Naun's judging.

After the Match there was a showing of Trak Fryer's wonderful video compilation. Trak Fryer and husband Dave spent hours preparing both the video and also the superb computer generated Champions display, which was on view throughout the Event. The CD is excellent!

After the video it was time for the Parade of Champions. This started with a lone Northumbrian Piper in full regalia to herald the Parade. Our Piper, Susan, said to me that at first she thought there were few people about because it was getting late in the day and the sun was starting to set but as she started to pipe they seemed to come from everywhere and she was very moved by the whole experience. Border Terriers had truly come home.

I particularly remarked that the last time I commented on a Parade of Champions was at Cheltenham in 1990 and it was wonderful that so many of the dogs albeit no longer with us themselves were represented in their progeny. How splendid indeed it was to see the veterans like Ch Dandyhow April Fool and our own Ch Syrosa Reasonable Doubt of Risdene enjoying themselves so much and clearly happy to be on show again. They paraded as enthusiastically as the youngsters and were simply delightful.

We were also pleased to have Ch Dandyhow Cleopatra, the bitch CC winning record holder, who was on top form fresh from her triumph at the Birmingham National Show where she topped the veterans from all breeds to qualify for the prestigious Pedigree Veteran Stakes Final.

Of course all these grand dogs were Champions and really it is unfair to single out any of them but I certainly had a lump in my throat at seeing them all grouped together and when we gathered on the steps of the racecourse Parade Ring for a final photograph I cannot think that there was anybody who was not impressed by the quality of the Border Terriers on show which even included a Luxembourg and German Champion from Holland.

As the mists began to fall over the racecourse after a lovely day we made ready for the evening Gala Dinner. Border Terrier people are hungry people and the caterers reported that all the food they had prepared for the weekend was already sold out on the Saturday! Similarly with the dinner there was almost a stampede for the buffet tables and everybody tucked in to an excellent meal with gusto. I think even the caterers were surprised by the appetites.

During the meal our Piper made a welcome reappearance and we also had a wonderful local band who played folk songs and appropriate music all through. Maestro Auctioneer Gordon "Tag" Knight then took to centre stage and began the auction of five special items, which it was felt were too significant to go into the silent auction, which had been held during the day with much success and fun had by all, I might add. This was the first time I had seen Tag in action and he is definitely a master of his art.

After the auction the floor was cleared and the next band began to play. Almost immediately the small dance floor was full to the brim with exuberant Border Terrier owners from near and far. The sight of Bill Shorthose in his kilt jiving professionally with Susan was certainly worth watching.

I was also delighted to see Arthur and Elaine Cuthbertson take to the floor, what hidden talents! Rhythmic and light on their feet, I understand they have won medals and were soon busy ensuring everyone joined in. I should just add that we must thank the Event Chairman, Ronnie Irving, and Anne Roslin-Williams who jointly sponsored the wine during the evening, which was a very kind and generous gesture. What good friends to Border Terriers and Border Terrier people.

After midnight the dancing ceased and we all gathered to sing Auld Lang Syne in the best tradition. I think we all wanted to meet again very soon and how lovely it had been to see old acquaintances and real Border Terrier supporters such as Mrs. Bertha Sullivan, Mr. & Mrs. Jim Short, Mrs. Eva Heslop and Mrs. Molly Nicholl to name but a few!

Next morning with the mist still shrouding the racecourse the Committee gathered again to make preparations for the day ahead. Despite any sore heads that may have been left over from the night before the number of visitors were not diminished and we were soon overwhelmed with people ready for the fun.

The day started with either a bus ride to the Heydon Kennels to visit the Hounds and then off to the Carter Bar to see the Border, or a wonderful demonstration by the Agility and Working Trial teams with their clever Border Terriers.

Behind my reception desk I was disappointed that I could not see all of the display but one of the features about the whole Event was that it was all being videod and relayed to screens, which were in place throughout the racecourse building.

I confess that at one point the laughter from outside was too much for me and I left my post to see a beaming Border Terrier astride the A frame far above its owner's head. Grinning, he stayed up there despite her best endeavours to call him down. Eventually his concentration returned and off he went to finish the round.

It turned out that this Border was usually very successful but he had been racing the day before and had already made one exit from the arena to re-visit the racing track and had obviously decided that from the top of the A-frame he had the best view to spy the racing again. Both Betty Orrin and Janet Strawbridge are to be hugely congratulated on the talent and experience of their teams. Everybody I spoke to was impressed with the level of concentration and ability of these Borders.

At about 1.00 pm. the walkers and visitors to the kennels began to return and all of them reported that it had been a great success. During the morning the mist had lifted and while the racecourse was bathed in sunshine the walkers confirmed that they had had wonderful views from the Carter Bar across to Edinburgh as the Committee had hoped.

In the afternoon the finale of the Event was of course the CC and the Reserve CC Winners Match. This wound up to a great crescendo and it was with much delight that the well known Mrs. Madelene Aspinwall, the judge, handed the winner's rosette to Mrs. Marian Reeves and her Baywillow Sunspice with the reserve slot going to Steve Dean handling Ch Barsetta Burning Mists for Mrs. Barbara Richards.

As we stood there, we remarked on the huge number of photographers clustered round these two dogs; it resembled Best in Show at Crufts! Finally the Committee gathered on the steps to be photographed. What a very happy and proud set of people who had all worked so hard under the auspices of Chairman, Ronnie Irving, and Event Organiser, Jim Stewart, to bring the event together. As Secretary I can only tell you that I was almost bursting with pride at having been a part of this wonderful event and experienced much fun working with these gifted and dedicated people. How can one top that?

Finally we tidied up and I think the weekend's events were exemplified for me by a lovely Finnish lady who told me that she had brought the ashes of her very first Border Terrier to be scattered on the Carter Bar. How appropriate for that little Border Terrier to be laid to rest where her forebears originated.

I will never forget Hexham 2000. For many years to come we will reminisce about the marvellous event and the comradeship it engendered. Some of the Committee dined together to celebrate the event that evening and at 11.00 p.m. we all went with our Borders out in to the park for one last walk together to the Band Stand.

As we gathered there in pitch darkness the Band Stand suddenly sprung to light and my abiding memory will be the faces on the Border Terriers and their owners as Bill Shorthose blew one final cry on the Hunting Horn. What an appropriate and fitting end to a truly splendid and remarkable occasion.

Sally Leslie